Travelling Scot – a collection of political and historical essays – reflects the patterns of Scots voyaging, economic, philosophic and literary, from the Middle Ages to the present. The varied features of Scots people's personal and political journeys are covered in revealing detail – inventiveness overseas against internal apathy and political disconnectedness; trail-blazing, receptiveness to strangers and new ideas contrasted with drink and despair. This absorbing collection has been written by a lifelong socialist, who has also been fascinated by writers and thinkers of the centre and right, such as Buchan, Elliot and Carlyle. Whether on Scotland and the Atlantic, the grandeurs and miseries of political life, and exactly how, in the unstable world of turbo-charged capitalism, the country can develop a lasting economic order, these essays of sixteen years, several specially written, show the mind of one Travelling Scot operating at full throttle.

Since 1979 Chris Harvie has occupied the Chair of British and Irish Studies at the University of Tübingen in Baden-Württemberg. Never in any political sense an emigrant from his own land, he has continued to interpret Scotland to Europe and *vice-versa*. *Scotland and Nationalism* (1977) and *No Gods and Precious Few Heroes, Twentieth-Century Scotland* (1981) are both in their third editions, and *Fool's Gold: the Story of North Sea Oil* was the basis of an acclaimed television series *Wasted Windfall* in 1994.

Travelling Scot
Scotus Viator

essays on the history, politics
and future of the Scots

CHRISTOPHER HARVIE

Argyll
publishing

First Published 1999
Argyll Publishing
Glendaruel
Argyll PA22 3AE
Scotland

**British Library Cataloguing-in-Publication Data.
A catalogue record for this book is available from
the British Library.**

ISBN 1 874640 99 8

Cover illustration
Permission National Galleries of Scotland
Detail from William Gillies *The Peebles Train*

Typeset & Origination
Cordfall Ltd, Glasgow

Printing
Bell & Bain Ltd, Glasgow

in memory of James Boyack,
Robert Campbell and Allan Macartney,
and for Hamish Henderson

'O, come all ye at hame wi' freedom
Never heed what the hoodies croak for doom
In your hoose a' the bairns o' Adam
Can find breid, barley-bree an' painted room.'

ACKNOWLEDGEMENTS

The provenance of the articles reprinted here is acknowledged in their introductory paragraphs. I would like to thank the editors of the various periodicals concerned for their permission to reproduce. Thanks also to Ken Cargill, John Milne and Douglas MacLeod at the BBC; Brian Groom and Trevor Royle at *Scotland on Sunday*; Win Bogaards, Tony Judt, Karen Hewitt and Boris Proskurnin for arranging trips I drew on for 'Timberlands'; Dai Smith, Frank Donnelly, Gary Geddes, Ian Wood, John Brown, David Daniell, the late Baroness Elliot, Bill Knox, Cairns Craig, Alex Salmond, Mike Russell for information, hospitality and conviviality; and Tony Peake, my agent and Derek Rodger for making publication such a smooth process. My own family – Virginia and Alison in Germany, London and Wales, my parents in Melrose, Jane and John George in Edinburgh, Aunt Jessie in Motherwell – have been endlessly generous. Whether an essay about the Harvies as history is an adequate recompense I don't know.

CONTENTS

PREFACE

Who would have thought it, and not me, not me. . .
It was a long road back to this undeclared Republic.
I came by the by-ways, empty of milestones,
On the roads of old drovers, by disused workings.

By this long circuitous road we all come, like the tramps in Douglas Dunn's great poem 'On the Destitution of Scotland'. Though the verse does not say so, one thinks instinctively that its heroes have come back across the Border, into the *terrain vague* of our country, the land of inner tinkerdom, 'raddled by a destitute polity', soured by ancient soot, its fields abandoned to rusting supermarket trolleys and 'the Clyde returning to its nature'. The author of this book is one of these heroes. He is the most articulate and irrepressible of the twentieth century wanderers, in uninterrupted motion around the globe, yet never forgetting the fractured and desolate landscape of the lives behind his own.

Nearly all outside observers have either failed to perceive that landscape, or misjudged it. This isn't their fault. It was a unique domain of ghosts, a society which surrendered its state and hence the integrity that had previously been defended for half a millennium. The payoff for that loss was colossal: co-option into the greatest empire of modern times, an economic ascendancy far beyond the modest aspirations of 1707, a place among the lords of human kind. The philistines were over-rewarded, and for many generations. One of Scotland's leading modern historians, Christopher Harvie has never avoided the chronicles of Union and Empire, or pretended that Scotland was just another colonised or suppressed nation.

But neither has he (unlike many others) ignored the underside and the enduring costs of that route into modernity. In *No Gods and Precious Few Heroes*, his history of twentieth century Scotland, he traced its decline and fall, and the pitiable attempts at propping it up from the 1920s through to the '90s. 'Devolution' is merely the last of these. As (in Dunn's phrase) a true 'archivist of Red desires', Harvie has followed, worked in and described the disintegration of Union Scotland in a uniquely imaginative and stimulating way. There is more to be learned from the jokes and salutary asides in this book than from most sober narratives.

The Wandering Scot is also, as he puts it, the 'surrogate Jew' (p.201). He brings the world with him back into the *shtetl* and indulges the rest of us with one dizzying comparison after another, as we squat round a provisional campfire in this nocturne of modernity, rediscovering our dead and hoping for a better permanent lodgement beneath some upturned boats (rumoured to be up ahead). The Scots travelled because they had to, like the Irish. They both benefited and suffered from it, in much the same way. The intellectuals, especially, were forced into a kind of extruded or outward-bound mould. Many of them have become over-accustomed to this, to the point of concluding that such dependent interaction may be in the nature of the Scots. Do they really need an independent nation at all?

'Yes!' replies this author, in a dazzling number of ways and with an inexhaustible-seeming profusion of reasons. He has himself made the journey, there and back. The essays here recount one episode after another of his travels. Obsessed since boyhood by trains and trams, he knows travelling is about neither getting there nor merely enjoying transition: it's about learning, comparing, understanding other people's jokes, and deciphering the secret shabby encampments to which, in the end, one must return. It is there, in the blue-red darkening dusk, that the truth smacks you in the face. As he says with typically discordant humour, the result of the September 11th referendum in 1997 was 'like shipwreck in the mid-Atlantic, where past life flashed before you' (p.222). He suddenly recalled having been Robin Cook's referee for his first job – 'tutor-organiser for the WEA, since you ask' – and 'the Hellish winter of 1979'. Such truths will flash before the reader too, a hundred times, as he travels through these chapters (and the route isn't fixed, by the way, in fact a personal itinerary is preferable).

'Sing me your songs in the speech of timber and horse' cries Douglas Dunn's narrator, from the midden of warm faces and frozen backs somewhere in the Debateable Land. I think he means songs like the ones here, the new images of a country recovering from half-life and outcast silence, and joining Europe and the world at last.

Tom Nairn
Kilmore, Ireland 1999

INTRODUCTION

When the Scottish Parliament convenes, in June of this year, I won't be among the members of a body which for about thirty years, I've been promoting. A variation on William McIlvanney's 'Cowardly Lion'? Maybe. But the qualities needed of an MSP and a researcher are different. The latter requires memory, system and something which – files and books, databases and past articles – can only be described as learning. Faced with the prospect of change, I realised where my real utility lay. In 1982, when we were mentally on the canvas, Cairns Craig pointed out the unhistorical nature of the Scots' attitude to their predicament; something which, before then and since, it has been my business to try to remedy. The message was, stick to what you can do.

I did my first article for the Scottish press in 1962, at the age of eighteen. It was on Scotland's first railway, between Tranent and Cockenzie – the only time I'm going to mention an otherwise obsessive theme. Since then like all historians I've worked on three levels: the research article, the book and journalism, but this early venture contained much of a continuing mixture. The newspaper or periodical article business was undertaken partly to make money and get to interesting places, and partly, because it snowballed, to process research findings and travel experiences for public consumption. If to the academic was added the politician and what the Germans call the *publizist*, then I think that in most of my arguments – on Europe, on transport, on Scotland – I was more often right than wrong.

I have coralled these essays into four thematic fields: Scotland's place in the international industrial order; careers and ideas from the history of 'unionist' Scotland; my own experience of Scottish politics from the 1970s to the 1990s; and finally speculations about a possible 'Commonwealth of Scotland' which will offer its people work, decency, dignity and an international role worthy of their past and their potential.

The Scottish historian has to be simultaneously revisionist and remembrancer. There's an ever-present need to counter 'what ought to have been', to insist on what was. At the same time, explaining the influence of 'ought' is essential. All nations are part of larger structures and derive some of their values from them. For the Clydeside businessman in 1910 understanding Scotland mattered less than understanding the statistics of the *Glasgow Herald Review of Trade and Industry*, working out who was building a wooden river-steamer on the Amazon and why. Twenty years later, with such industry shrinking, the matter of Scotland was more salient.

So my first essay is an experiment in locating a master-project for my bus-pass days: the development of the Atlantic in the 1880-1960 period. Trying to get a perspective for comparing Scots, Welsh and Irish nationalism, the question of industrialisation became crucial. As a result of this, the visible and tangible presence of the communities left behind cumulatively registered on me through apparently random journeys in regions whose development hinged on the demand for power, physical and political.

If this showed a rapacious, dynamic Atlantic capitalism far removed from anything Adam Smith or Karl Marx had imagined, 'improving' Scotland didn't altogether conform to it – although enough of its sons did. The alternative was a douce European commerce, and the next section is, unashamedly, the Bailie Nicoll Jarvie view of history. When I was about twelve, I saw a marvellous, haunting adaptation of John Buchan's *Huntingtower* on television, with James Hayter as Dickson MacCunn, supposedly Jarvie's great-grandson. Buchan, like Scott, was so much a wizard as to conjure up precisely the *timbre* of twentieth-century Scotland, in the great, new, deserted house by the firth, MacCunn the shrewd old romantic, and the young, tough realist Diehards – an image of hope, but tinged with the minor key of time and death.

Unionist Scotland didn't imply a capitulation to metropolitanism; figures like the lawyers, the journalists, MPs like John Buchan and Walter Elliot, negotiated this debateable land, which engaged Scotland – not always positively – with a wider world. We forget its presence at our peril.

The autobiographical element is always awkward. Scottish newspapers have more columns than the Parthenon, and our opinion mountain is a problem. If the historian is to be in the market-place, he or she has to provide materials, discovered or compiled, to enable others to make their minds up. Ideally, we ought to be 'lost wax', the mould that vanishes when the bronze is poured. But in circumstances where a history has to be re-imagined, where the historian is venturing into an ambiguous landscape, where the features are indistinct if not mirages, the only honest procedure is to say, 'Well, this is my experience. This is the sum of the sources, the limited nature of the secondary enquiry, and my own impressions.' This is Carlyle's strategy in *Sartor Resartus*, Hugh Miller's in *My Schools and Schoolmasters*, or in our own day Andrew O'Hagan's in *The Missing*, perhaps the most sensitive account of post-1960s Scotland.

There again, the position of an emigré academic may be distorting. The battle is happening some distance off. Sides may be taken, but that intimate politics of friendship and enmity, enthusiasm and disgust, is equally remote. Yeats, managing his Dublin theatre, was much more conscious of the reality of philistines and gombeen men, yet Ibsen, living for years in Italy, never shook off the politics of small-town Norway, and gave them universal meaning.

On the other hand, Baden-Württemberg, immediately and obviously to hand, makes concrete the problems – environment, equality, 'luxury and corruption' – which, even in the eighteenth century, the Scottish philosophers concerned themselves. Observing it has been a consistent and on the whole positive education. This is a community marked by 'severitas', as Walter Elliot would have put it: rational, technologically competent, and disciplined by the terrible lesson of 1933-45 into responsible politics. How much my own Scots and Welsh loyalties have contributed to a philosophy which sees the metropolis as more problem than solution, I'm not sure. It's not always pleasurable to see the seriousness of *Die Zeit* advancing on you rather than the fun and games of the British broadsheets, but it is educational. We have prided ourselves in Scotland on a higher standard of journalism, but a comparison with even ten years ago shows the mark of the public relations handout and of a generation which, however streetwise within the media, is less than half-educated outside it. Restaurants, horoscopes, footie, soaps and stars: Elois just wanna have fun. But the Morlock world continues, down in the tunnels.

Self-government is not in itself a solution, but a complex of institutions which enable socio-economic regroupings, the ingestion of best practice, and the formulation of general political goals. As the computer-men would say, this 'default position' is the sort of community idea that, for example, brought Grassic Gibbon and MacDiarmid together in the early 1930s. What I've tried to suggest in the last two essays is that, given the decline of centrally-planned economies and the extreme instability of turbo-charged capitalism, Scotland's international role has to go out from its national predicament. We have to use the resources we have, and close up the diseconomies. But at the end of that (essentially socialist) process, we will have something to sell on the international market.

This is part of a more general *Kulturkampf* – MacDiarmid's word, as well as Bismarck's. Ours has been an American century, warring against a warped and malignant Europe. But the dynamism has worn away. Fifty years of European peace and civic progress contrast with an altogether more febrile American history, the political will of the New Deal or Great Society sapped by the dynamism of capital and the rigging of politics by the well-off. Newt Gingrich and Jesse Helms will ensure there is no place for the dissenting voice, in an intellectual landscape as authoritarian as anything that Europe has so far seen. Our experience, so far, of 'Cool Britannia' doesn't suggest anything more reassuring. But it seems to emphasise the fact that this division – 'Rhenish' versus 'Anglo-American capitalism' – passes straight through Scotland.

The country looked for so long to America, yet has now shifted perceptibly to Europe. But the fissure still lies deep: between the ideal of community and the dynamic of the media; between Patrick Geddes' ecological politics and the allure of consumption; between the intellectual 'severitas' needed to cope with a complex continent and the smooth surfaces of Anglophone cool. There's no question of total solutions. Europe requires much of the flexibility of the USA; but the notion of a benign 'democratic' cultural package out west has gone. We are on our own.

Thomas Mann, in *The Magic Mountain*, remarks on the subjective nature of time: in a hectic, active, varied life, time is always on ration, vanishing. Yet in retrospect it expands, opens out into the complexities of memories and dreams. In a confined, enforced tedium, the minutes and hours seem immense and endless; once the routines are over, they dissolve into nothing – a pretty good working definition of hell. Being well past the middle of the journey, the years start to be numbered, and other teachers, now gone, must be remembered: Allan Macartney, witty, diplomatic colleague at the Open University and as MEP ambassador for what was best in the Scottish tradition; Jimmie Boyack, as architect building his own Corbusier house, and keeping the home rule cause going when we all felt like giving up; Bobby Campbell, musician, engineer, socialist, who remade himself at the *Scotsman* as a wizard of the online newspaper. They leave huge gaps in the lives of their families and friends, but vast legacies.

Chris Harvie

Tübingen, January 1999

SECTION ONE
Reconnaisance

I
Timberlands
(1998)

The Swabians have a verb 'tufteln' which
means playing around with an invention until it
works and a market is created for it.
This essay, the Russian part of which appeared
in *Chapman*, plays around on a geo-political
scale and moves from travel and observation
into ideas about the need to acknowledge past
history in planning the route to the future.

I Conferring

> 'If I'd known it was poets,
> I'd have claimed double-time.'

Voices remembering slaughter, of Jews, of American Indians, of anti-Vietnam students, floated across the St John River as the skipper cut his engines. Seals flopped off rocks; a backwoodsman disturbed in a lonesome cabin took down his jeans and mooned at us. Downstream were the Reversing Falls, where at high tide the Bay of Fundy poured in, and at low tide the river poured out. Above the woodland which masked the city of St John, the Irving Corporation's pulp-mill trailed white smoke across the August sky.

Perm had been last year. Where Permian sandstone comes from. The ascription of another wandering Scot, Roderick Murchison, had branded the place, like luckless Neanderthal. Perm was Yuryatin, where Zhivago found Lara amid the Russian Civil War. Like St John, rail and road bridges crossed a broad river, and woods stretched on and on, but this was where trains six days out from Vladivostok began their last twenty-four hours to Moscow. Perm had a spell as Molotov – after Stalin's charmless, resilient henchman – arms factories mushrooming when production was moved east in 1941. It was a closed city until 1986, by which time a million Permians were living along fifty miles of the Kama – a city stretching say from Greenock to Grangemouth – making guns, aero engines and at the Felix Dzerzhinski Factory what else but chainsaws.

Why Perm, why St John? Charming girls, nearly all called Natasha, whisper translations of papers – Stevenson, Auden, Yeats, John Stuart Mill. Is this Bradbury-Lodge's Venusberg Campus? Interchangeable airports, airport-clone universities, jumbo beds and bimbo delegates? No, not MLA-land, or the opaque *Theorie-provinz* of the German *Anglistentag*. The Russians want seriousness. In 'philosophy and the novel', literature is to be invoked to recreate a civic imagination for the new democracy. In my case it's post-Enlightenment Scottish realism, sordid to magic, and the novel – Scott and Galt, George Douglas Brown, Grassic Gibbon and Alasdair Gray, via the usual Proteans, Adam Smith, Thomas Carlyle, Patrick Geddes.

There are worse routes. 'If a city hasn't been used by a writer not even the inhabitants live there imaginatively,' Alasdair Gray wrote in *Lanark*. I was trying to pack a baggy monster of a concept into an academic suitcase, to intuit an economic world from masses of library information, literary images, impressions derived from my own experience and involvement. Perm was already a palimpsest of Chekhov, Gorki and Pasternak, though since a map of the place wasn't to be had for love or money, its geography – where the station, the university, the river-port were, relative to north and south – had continually to be re-imagined.

In St John the same bunch figured, seen from a different angle: speculating, in hope and fear, on an Atlantic leviathan, industrial and democratic. Seaport conurbations, linked by Kipling's 'monstrous five-deck cities', were still around in my teenage years, then something had happened, occluding the view. The map question became important, because wood-and-tree clichés are right. Timberlands are difficult to read, unlike Wales seen from Aberystwyth beach, or Scotland from the Pentlands. Only as the plane got to cruising height did the splayed-out geography show those scratchy darkened segments of a pale curvature. MacDiarmid's 'gowden lyric' seemed inevitable:

> In the how-dum-deid o' a cauld hairst nicht
> The warld like an eemis stane
> Hangs i' the lift
> An' my eerie memories fa'
> Like a yowdendrift
> Like a yowdendrift, so's I couldnae' see
> The words cut out i' the stane
> Had history's hazelraw, an' the fug o' fame
> No yirdit them.

A drift of facts and impressions seemed, in these two summers, to harden into something more logical – what the eighteenth century Scots *literati* would have called the 'notion' of a conjectural geography. A century ago, at the birth of the 'modern', Patrick Geddes, MacDiarmid's patron, had sorted industry, society and history into his intersections of *polis* and *technic* – a sociological evolution analagous to Murchison's geology. Geddes's strata were blitzed by war, dived sub-oceanic, but had with increasing insistence, surfaced again in localities where I lived or had visited. Beneath the plane, in that landscape of tiny details, generalisations about globalisation and the post-modern meant interrogating shared experiences, pleasures and threats.

II Places

Cityscapes were similar, paleotechnic: scarred by the century's fight with the machines.

> 'Curious little timber houses with steep roofs,
> decorated doors and carved and painted patterns
> round the windows'.

Pasternak on old Perm could have been Pasternak on St John. Later buildings on grid-iron streets of 'saracenic brick', 1880s post-fire stuff, dropped gap-toothed to glittering water and dark, serrated woodland. Maritime evergreens ringed a rifleman in a boy-scout hat, mourning four local heroes of the Boer War; a green Soviet howitzer marked the graves of thousands of wounded who came to Perm to die. Perm was as far from Moscow as St John was from Toronto but war had wrapped itself round both.

Perm had had by Soviet standards the modest wealth of an arsenal-city, up to 1989; the Maritimes were into honest poverty. Sixty percent on welfare. Collectivist Perm had vast public buildings, some of which were still functioning: the circus, the ballet, the Stalin-baroque palace of culture. Flats were much larger than those of Moscow, while in St John small clapboard houses were fitted into the interstices of roads and carparks

The New Russians, cannily handing flats over to sitting tenants, had curbed the worst of hyperinflation for most people and made the tiny salaries of the professionals ($50 a month) count for something. The queues had vanished, though the streets seemed in permanent gridlock. Like huge hedged bets, the old icons persisted. Lenin still fronted the Opera House, shook hands with Gorki at the University. The art gallery was supposed to revert to being the cathedral, but not yet: aggressive abstracts roomed with a wonder-working ikon of Nicholas II. There wasn't a whorl of graffiti to be seen.

Nor was there much graffiti in St John. But there were more

Union Jacks than in Edinburgh. This had been Empire Loyalist country, a 1776 province of refugees from republican America which even embraced Jacobite Catholics: an unimaginable ecumenical Ulster. After 1800 it had become the world's fourth-largest shipbuilding centre, whose softwood clippers were often owned and crewed from the little ports of Cardigan Bay – Abersoch, Porthmadog, Llangranog. A classical mansion, now an Irish club, could have looked out on Cleland or Hamilton; its blackened stonework had come from the Clyde, ballast in their bowels.

The paleotechnic stretched from West Britain to these Atlantic and near-Asiatic remotenesses. The last coaster had left Aberystwyth harbour in 1988, the last freight train came from Shrewsbury in 1993. In my birthplace, Motherwell, dynamite had just knocked over the Ravenscraig steelworks cooling towers, which I'd seen built in 1961, leaving a landscape as scarred as the Welsh Potosi in the Cardigan hills or the ironworks of Cape Breton Island. Timberlands had ridden the rapids of change, military and civil, until they hit 'post-industrialisation' and were left beached.

The West and the market had triumphed after 1990: Fukuyama and Dahrendorf told us we were at the end of the dialectic. Good or bad? Or, as ever, had the privileged battened on an environment, exploited what they could, then pissed off? MacDiarmid's 'wunds wi' warlds to swing' had swept the timberlands into metropolitan history. New Brunswick had produced proconsular Sir George Parkin of the Rhodes Trustees, Bonar Law, Beaverbrook; not far away was Roosevelt. Perm had Diaghilev, whose *Ballets Russes*, for Virginia Woolf, 'changed human nature' in 1911; it wasn't far (by Russian standards) from Boris Yeltsin's base in Ekaterinburg, and the mineshaft down which they'd thrown the Romanov corpses.

III Getting There

Perm: Station Perm Two loomed up in the drizzle of evening, and the sound of 'the Slavic Womens' March'. A posse was waiting on the platform with the one car they could commandeer. Handled like parcels on every stage of the trip from Berlin by Volodya, Sasha, Natasha, *et al*, careful to extract us from the hell of Moscow Sheremetevo airport, we rolled into Perm after a full day on the Baikal Express. The trip took Zhivago months, a French *Train à Grand Vitesse* would cover it in six-and-a-half hours; we trundled at thirty-five miles an hour over the great Russian plain: a mobile commonwealth, with total strangers offering, rather peremptorily – 'Eat please!' – masses of food and drink and not minding at all if you just curled up and fell asleep.

Unending wood and moor and *one* hill, about 200 feet high; collapsing timber-yards and cement works lying around in cosmic untidyness; a mile of disused electric locomotives. From time to time girders echoed above a river and barges, an onion tower, allotments and *dachas*, and long canyons of shabby green trains, where grannies sold beer and rolls out of Claudia Schiffer plastic bags.

St John: On the TV screen in the New Brunswick Museum the old amateur movies flicker. A highlander in full fig blows into mute bagpipes, three Queen Mum ladies caper into a reel on the platform. Behind them, gun-metal coaches and a huge locomotive pouring steam. Union Jacks and a big car: lesser royalty – the Duke of Gloucester? – waving. Behind his back the goblin face of Beaverbrook. Glengarries, homburg hats and dark suits, then a train trailing its smoke across the lakes and low pine-covered hills of Acadia. Forty years ago and a different, steam-powered world.

You get to St John by a small plane to a branch-line airport. They opened a new railroad station in 1982, to replace a Victorian monster demolished to make way for a sports stadium. In 1994 the last train left it, when the Liberal government cut its subsidy.

Of 2000 miles of track in the province in 1930 only 700 are left, bearing a single passenger train six times a week from Montreal to Halifax, Nova Scotia. The Newfie Bullet has gone, and the Prince Edward Island Railway. In Canada, a country fashioned by Scotsmen from rails, since Macdonald, Strathcona and Mount-stephen carried the Canadian Pacific coast to coast in the 1880s, the railway appears to be racing the Confederation to extinction.

Perm was maybe where the Three Sisters moaned about being days away from the the capital. Chekhov lodged for a few weeks in the 1890s, on his way from Moscow to Sakhalin. His house had gone but we conferred in a little theatre built around then by the governor's wife in the Summer Residence, now wedged in by concrete blocks. At Perm the land route crossed the water-route. When the Trans-Siberian got here in 1892, the place was already a great port. Stroganoff of *Boeuf* fame founded it in the 1560s, and went on to use timber from the Ural forest, rafted down the Kama, to smelt local copper ore and purify salt. Diaghilev was born in 1872 in a big pink merchant's house; Gorki, four years older, was a cook on one of the river steamers – proper coasters, not barges – which still bring fruit and vegetables from Astrakan and the tropical south. In 1919 Zhivago saw,

> a ridge of buff-and-cream Tsarist terraces clinging to
> the summit of the hill in tiers, house by house and
> street by street, with a big church in the middle on the
> top, as in a cheap colour print of a desert monastery or
> Mount Athos.

A cliff drops to the Kama and its wharves. Via the Caspian Sea and the Volga-Don canal, you can sail to Rotterdam. If you turn right at Volgograd, you reach Grozny.

IV Trade and Power

St John: Timber Addams Family houses of the sea-captains look out at the Bay of Fundy, and the world's most powerful tides. Freighters, rather than steaming up the St Lawrence, ice-bound for six months of the year, discharge their containers at the port. It takes eight hours. Sailortown, with girls and bars, is as *passé* as steam trains or, for that matter, Canada. Quebec lies between here and Ontario; the natural partner is south, in the forsaken territory of the United States. But marketisation and free trade haven't led to the anonymous rule of distant shareholders.

Everywhere Irving. At the airfield, a corrugated iron hut, vintage 1935, with 'Irving Airways' flaking from it. Irving owns the pulp mill, the shipyard, the forests, the salmon farms, the oil refinery, the newspaper. Irving Corporation is valued at around $8 billion Canadian; about the fifth-largest group in Canada, and still in family hands. The old man died three years ago: his sons live in big villas fronting the St John River, their kids go, unguarded, to local schools. Lady Beaverbrook died not long after Irving, the last of the old Calvinist's collection of women, and seemingly the last of the old transatlantic order which had produced the unknown prime minister Bonar Law. The Irvings are secretive where Beaverbrook was imperiously and scandalously public. This is a one-party province – with derisory opposition to the Liberals – but a one-family economy.

Perm: World Literature is an uneasy partner of New Russia. In the first my host Boris Proskurnin is trying to get the western canon up and firing, yet the life of the imagination which kept the Russian *literati* going in bad times is now threatened by expenditure cuts and the collapse of subsidised literature. Not much sign of austerity at dinner with the 'New Russians': Yuri Pinyagin, professor of English language at the university and his banker friend Dmitri – 'another old Comsomol man'. They seemed rather like Gordon Brown and Tony Blair learning capitalism while keeping in touch with 'this great movement of ours' – not completely for sentiment's sake. The bank has computers and armed guards and Dmitri is on his mobile phone to the regional government: 'Party isn't important here. What we feel is our remoteness from Moscow. We have to go there all the time. Weeks out of our lives.'

Banker and professor haven't so much as a Lada between them, and depend on the crammed buses and trams. At the universities law and economics are the big growth areas, and after them English. Perm is fortunate; because it was a closed city, outside partnerships matter more. Big money isn't in education, even less so in manufacturing, but in import-export.

'How many New Russians succeed?'

'About one in three. You need connections; if you haven't got them, and you're up against the Mafia, you haven't much chance.'

The Mafia is real, so are the drunks wanting to try things on in the streets. The 'New Russians' may – they think – get some kind of civic society going, and something in the easy familiarity and hospitality of people on the train, in the university, or in tiny methodically-run flats is encouraging. For Perm, town-twinning – an international *Blind Date* – had brought assistance from Oxford, and the reason that I was there was that Karen Hewitt from Kellogg College and Boris Proskurnin had managed to get practical academic collaboration, part of a 'know-how' operation which showed a shrewd British initiative.

Two years later, I hear that Dmitri's bank has folded. Perm's economic salvation might come faster through a second Cold War and lots of orders for guns.

St John: Gary Geddes, poet and professor, is researching his Orcadian ancestry. He doesn't know about his kinsman Patrick. He was a working-class kid from Vancouver and the protégé of the anarchist George Woodcock, Orwell's friend. Just as Orwell both needed and hated the Empire, Geddes needs Canada, not in any enveloping patriotic way, but as a frame for individual radicalism.

He fears it moving from Commonwealth to dissolution. Unlike the USA, postwar Canada was a sort of social democracy. Now it has a middle class and a Confederation at risk, with the political bookstalls in Toronto radiating *Endzeitstimmung*. The dismantling of welfare makes provinces aim at a commercial quasi-nationalism (of the sort pioneered by Alberta with its oil or by Quebec), or invoke communitarian solidarity of the Etzioni sort. But without a common identity, what defence is there against the capitalist dynamo to the south?

There are winners and losers in this – and Canada has writers in spades. At the very least writing articulates protest, offers therapy to prevent the ultimate slump into alcoholism or despair. At dinner in a fortress-like hotel in St John, listening to David Adams Richards talking about his own novels, I might have been hearing James Kelman or William McIlvanney on Glasgow, or Christopher Meredith on South Wales, with their need to keep on imagining the local place, however pessimistically. Adams Richards' Miramichi – once one of the shipbuilding rivers – is poor man's country, its folk coping with a fitful 'modernisation' which episodically comes, exploits, goes, leaving the inhabitants like the Highlanders after kelp collapsed, or the Clydesiders after the shipyards closed. And in a far harsher land. A paperback on New Brunswick said Adams Richards' novels sold over 300,000 in the old Soviet Union. For Gary Geddes the Westerner, the adoptive Ontarian, travelling the Maritimes has a precariousness as much social as scenic – like avoiding in Scotland that hellish challenge: 'You looking at me, pal?

> Today even the fog
> is unemployed in St John's, tanked up
> down the coast, or getting a proper head on
> for the next assault. I hadn't noticed
> the path peter out until my foot settled
> on a horizontal ladder of pegged logs
> stretching over a narrow fissure in the rock.

A hundred feet below the sullen Atlantic
emits unfestive gutterals
and sharpens its teeth on granite.
Out here the elements are in cahoots.
Speech is a wound. The quaint harbour
and pastel houses might never have occurred
A misplaced foot or word, and I'm a goner.

V Culture

St John: Switching on the telly in the early morning discloses St John's own Donald Sutherland, all sharp teeth and sneers, as the fascist boss in Bertolucci's *1900*. Is this a discreet Sutherland festival, offering films that aren't perforated by ads every five minutes? *1900* looked marvellous, but seemed to be where the grand Marxist drive of Visconti in *Senso* and *The Leopard* slithered into transnational marketing – stars, fashion, daft sex and art-deco frocks. Residual Marxism was still around – the money-fascists opposed by monumental Guttuso workers. But the more insidious national seduction – that 'we are someone again' which Fellini captures in *Amarcord* when the Rimini folk row out on a cellophane sea to greet a Mussolini liner – had vanished.

The triumph of surfaces means a rightist victory of sorts, over a sixties Marxism whose supine juveniles let history take them wherever. Like in Raymond Chandler, money was keeping the girls in couture clothes, hotels, big cars, all of this bankrolled by the big corporations *as sovereign states*, flanked by ex-lefties. Gary Geddes remembered Barbara Amiel – 'Conrad Black's moll', now one of our manic Sunday preachers – as a Toronto radical. The Edinburgh University Labour Club's far-left press officer is now the *New Statesman's* post-socialist expert John Lloyd. The scarlet editor of the *Red Paper on Scotland* is Iron Chancellor Brown.

Perm: Market and communism were running in uneasy tandem;

the big state industries slashing their labour forces, or simply not paying them, desperately searching for markets – for guns or whatever. The map was changing: the railway direction East-West was now overlaid by a North-South trajectory. Chechnya was at one end of a chain, and the New Russians supplying the Permians with food and electronic gadgetry flown in from the United Arab Emirates were at the other. Somewhere south and east of here, centred on the Caspian, was a non-Atlantic economy where guns and oil met a bulging Islamic population. In 1919 the Tory geographer Halford MacKinder, MP for a Clydeside constituency and thus up against Lenin's Scottish allies, saw South-Asiatic Russia as the 'heartland', the key to world power. Now it was a Jurassic Park dinosaur of unimaginable violence waiting for its slug of DNA.

Gradually the various matrices began to come together – though this was after more departure lounges, more glimpses of miniscule forests 30,000 feet below. Renan said that nations sought above all their own history – in 1880 when the railway was on hand to pull baggy particularisms together. Patrick Geddes said: look beyond nationality, at technology and living-space; the unity brought by one sort of transport can be menaced by another. In 1997 the railway, the novel, the national army have given way to the internet, satellite TV, and the airliner. But the result isn't some post-modern cultural pluralism. Before parties and legislators have quite grasped what has been going on, groups and individuals ranging from speculators to psychopaths have used force and money and a short time-scale to re-establish an exploitative disorder recognised from the past.

Democratic hopes, vividly alive in 1989-90, have made room for fascism, if we define fascism in the classic Marxian sense as the post-national defence of great wealth by authoritarian means, manipulating the nation as last resource for the afflicted. Russia is ruled by Orwell's 'gangsters and shiny-bottomed bureaucrats'. Canada is more subtly being disarticulated by sectionalism, ethnic nationalism and the naked corporate power of America. Perhaps it's easier to appreciate this from West Britain: a society exalted and then destroyed by paleotechnic capitalism, which was – for a brief but still crucial moment – the moulder of the world settlement now splitting asunder.

VI Leaving

Perm: I appear on Perm Three television – a change from endless game shows, American crime movies, and Vladimir Zhirnovsky thumping people in the Duma. The television landscape is as dire as the USA; there are now hardly any Russian films; the bookshops of the 'last reading nation' have gone. What would anyone make of Scottish common-sense philosophy, the Adam Smith of 'sympathy' rather than the absolute of self-interest peddled by the toxic economists parachuted in by the West? Did talking about benign nationality help as the walls of the nation crumbled apart?

In the ex-cathedral art gallery a realist painting – school of Repin, sometime in the 1880s – shows a conscript being dragged on to a train by guards while his mother and other peasants form a distraught chorus. Western airports, dull and undemanding places, are literal *utopias*, noplaces whose transnational style makes them interchangeable. In Russia they retain that alarming railway-like quality, proscenia for *biznesmeni*, drunks, high-price whores and nationalist strongmen. In Shermetyevo the line between mass and market showed up knife-edged. The dim departure hall was clogged with huddled masses clutching huge suitcases, filing with geological slowness past Sharon and Tracy doing their nails in customs. The hours to the Berlin departure ticked into minutes.

Periodically, though, girls in floppy hats and beige coats would swan through the barriers, greeting or leaving men who spoke Mercedes and bodyguards. Karen Hewitt had told me the magic formula was Persist, so I swooped on the nearest Sharon and shouted that I had to get through or I would miss my plane.

'Nyet!'

Persist!

'The Berlin flight is leaving in twenty minutes. I'll miss it!'

'Moment.'

Then a small official popped round a counter, stamped everything in sight and motioned me through, case unexamined and notionally packed with guns, dope, freeze-dried plutonium and what have you.

St John: Halifax airport had troupes of Japanese bound for Prince Edward Island to see the places associated with *Anne of Green Gables*. Along with the Brontës and the Loch Ness Monster, LM Montgomery had joined (or evicted?) the tea ceremony and the films of Mizoguchi from the Japanese pantheon. In world-as-website/airport/McDonald's, with unlimited access to more of the same, such weird pilgrims at least upset the routines of metropolitanism. Otherwise, reportage, from the centre or crisis areas, was always the same. Demonstrators had better talk helpful English; otherwise red flesh would burst out of roadside corpses in vain; and refugees trudge pointlessly along raw colonnades of telephone poles. What clutch of beards and scowls was in charge of Afghanistan? Who was murdering whom in Rwanda?

Perm: Province must be victim or menace to get noticed. A Belgian pervert or Gloucester mass-murderer is box-office; the crepitation of greater horrors vanishes from sight. In 1990-93 the West invested $2.5 billion in Russia, while Russian 'wild capitalists' smuggled $40 billion abroad. Business visitors to Moscow observed an order dissolving from Plan to Clan, but there was far more interest in New Russians strutting it in Mayfair or the Cote d'Azur than in citizenship in remote towns, however huge. Was it possible to outdo the corruption of Brezhnev? The homicidal violence of Stalin? After Grozny, yes.

VII 'Who is in Charge of the Rattling Train?'

St John: At Saint Andrews the white bulk of the Algonquin Hotel – far removed from Manhattan, Thurber, Parker and Ross – stared over the golf links to the Maine shore. This was the Canadian Pacific's eastern terminus. Union Jacks still fluttered where Sir William Van Horne's carriage splashed over the causeway from the station to his offshore island with its huge *art nouveau* mansion. The Greenock Church of Scotland stood for over sixty years before the rails were laid, replicating in birdseye maple the classical severities of John Galt's seaport: that centre of 'the West' where civic virtue did battle with 'luxury and corruption' and lost. Now this was the holiday town for Boston, 250 miles south; Toronto was six hundred miles away, Canada almost a mirage.

To the south Campobello, FD Roosevelt's holiday island, was just visible. For a few weeks annually, in 1941-45, the world revolved around here. A phone-call or telex message produced some action in the arsenals of Perm. Beaverbrook, hyperactive, touted Russia as the earthly paradise, praising Stalin and passing the ammunition, via the Murmansk supply convoys assembling on the Clyde. But even then the geography of American politics was tilting south-west: Kennedy, thirty-three years ago, was the last north-eastern president. New Brunswick's glory days had gone with his father Joseph's bootlegging motorboats.

In 1996 booze was more difficult to get in Canada than in Perm, where vodka bottles, the glass Madonnas of the hopeless, glittered in the windows of tiny tin stalls. A thousand miles away from St Andrews, over the forests, Fordism, as much as the railroads, was in eclipse: Detroit a ruined, ungovernable city. Fordism was what Russia had thought it was getting – in 1990 as in 1917 – but the reality was a marketism that only the wealthy or ruthless could ride out. At St Andrews, the Canadian Pacific had been long abandoned, but with it, too, had gone a federal dream, that New Deal of work, equality and entitlement. Out on the end of an event, in the malls and car parks, the atmosphere was unthreatening; hard times were being met by resigned-looking couples with quiet, overweight children, in a country where fat means poor.

'Who is in charge of the rattling train?' Beaverbrook used to ask,

> The axles scream and the couplings strain
> And the pace is hot and the points are near
> And sleep has deadened the driver's ear
> And the signals flash through the night in vain
> For death is in charge of the rattling train.

Perhaps he was echoing Carlyle in 'Hudson's Statue', the old Manichean cursing a railway capitalism which deracinated. After the plane took off from Toronto the curvature was again perceptible, beyond the white-grey streakiness of the Canadian shield: a literal globalisation, which prompted the notion that impressions and histories were fitting together as a thesis, however awkwardly.

VIII Making Maps

Alasdair Gray, at the end of *Lanark*, in which a disaggregated post-industrial Scotland is only just saved from complete destruction, rephrases MacDiarmid's *Eemis Stane* in one of his Implags:

> I started making maps when I was small
> showing place, resources, where the enemy
> and where love lay. I did not know
> time adds to land. Events drift continually down
> effacing landmarks, raising the level, like snow.
> I have grown up. My maps are out of date.
> The land lies over me now.
> I cannot move. It is time to go.

MacDiarmid wrote about history in 1925, when the magisterial positivist sequence of human improvement – the force which had pushed railways through Siberia, sent steamers to the Maritimes, bypassed Niagara, had jammed its gears on the Western Front. Lenin was his scientific man, the Carlyleian hero who would restore consciousness to this process. And now this grand, ungeographical mission had stopped, too. In the post-modern mosaic we had replicated the turmoil of Carlyle's 'society without whereabouts'.

Gray wrote *Lanark* after a writer's block of several years was dislodged by the Scottish referendum catastrophe of 1979, and its remarkable impact in 1981 was as much political as literary. He seemed to have been prompted by the Canadian writer Denis Lee, from whom he'd borrowed what became the slogan of the Scots literati in the 1980s:

WORK AS IF YOU WERE LIVING
IN THE EARLY DAYS OF A BETTER NATION.

Lee wrote a lengthy article in the new Scots magazine *Cencrastus* at the end of 1980, having been a Canada Council fellow in Edinburgh. A decade earlier he likewise had been blocked, but this had been broken by a sense of the possibility of an independent Canadian culture, in part a reaction to the tyranny of the United States in Vietnam. The guiding spirit here had been the Canadian philosopher George Grant, proconsul Parkin's grandson. As technology-preoccupied as Geddes or Mumford, Grant became in the 1960s for Gary Geddes and the Canadian Vietnam generation the 'central singer' of their literature. Grant's position was that, in contrast to the dynamic liberalism of the United States, the Canadian tradition derived in part from the Loyalists who had retreated to New Brunswick in the 1780s. It was concerned with limitations instead of opportunities, with conservation rather than exploitation: unchecked technology would lead as surely to disaster as Beaverbrook's clattering train. A Scots intellectual historian could recognise the same sort of project that had concerned Adam Ferguson in his *Essay on the History of Civil Society* in 1767, after him Carlyle in 'Characteristics', then Patrick Geddes.

Where was Canadian literature, *vis-a-vis* Scotland? What right, anyway, had I to talk about it? Margaret Atwood, Lee's predecessor as a Canada Council fellow, had interviewed me back in 1979 in Edinburgh. She was baffled by Scottish politics and wouldn't have been made any the wiser by me, devolution being flat on the deck and most of us morose and giggly. Yet it had mattered, because Gray's mapmaking – something acquired in its turn from Patrick Geddes, became a metaphor for what my generation was up to: a move away from the post-modern condition – and from a *British* political initiative which had played itself out – to a process of, as MacDiarmid had put it, 'seeing Scotland whole, and in relation to the infinite.'

Lanark's frontispiece was a great panorama of central Scotland, from Kintyre to the North Sea rigs. Behind the globe's curvature towered a reinterpreted version of Hobbes's 'multiple man', in whose body the men of power – bureaucrats, troops, judges – confronted the masses. We were, at the time, being told that postmodernism had melted the canon and ripped up the track. Lodge and Bradbury were touring scholarly micro-communities in an airborne network, like spaceships: Woolf Voyager, Moonbase Austen, Satellite Heaney: each with its life-support system of theory – not World but Interstellar Literature. (An earthbound parallel being the Bryson-Theroux Company's hilarity special to Quirksville Heritage Site . . .) Yet Gray, filed by the English *literati* under post-modernism, was concerned, as much as Hobbes had been, with 'the matter, forme and power of a commonwealth ecclesiastical and civil'. He was the 'central singer' of Scotland in the 1980s, and his concerns were the classic modernist ones of force and reason.

Soviet literature ironically fitted into this. What was supposed to be canonic social realism became a clutch of arbitrary specialisms chopped up by party diktat. It went postmodernist *just like that*. Solzhenitzyn, old canoneer, got on to the train at Vladivostok to preach to his countrymen, station by station, about the evils of market society. Did he ever reach Moscow? No-one was bothered.

IX Looking for Our Saviour

We had a couple of hours free in Perm and the two Natashas (whom, being bad at patronymics, I surnamed Hogg and Grassic Gibbon after their research) took me in search of Our Saviour. This was an Orthodox chapel being restored on the fringes of the Dzerzinski works, built by a nativist architect roughly contemporary with Rennie Mackintosh. It was either a very tiny chapel, or huge child's toy, with exaggeratedly battered sides, a new copper onion-dome, and at the back a mural of Christ Pantocrator gazing at a breeze-block wall. The whole area of scruffy urban forest seemed to have been ripped up for drains. 'How can we reach Our Saviour?' asked Natasha Hogg. We couldn't. Instead we tagged on at the end of a huge wedding irrupting from the Dzerzinski Palace of Culture, fine-looking, bold-featured bride in white, groom in tuxedo, all sorts and conditions of relatives.

New Russians? 'No' said Natasha Gibbon, 'Everyone does this sort of thing.' Not altogether approvingly – both girls were going through a religious, celibate phase. Their fathers were Communist officials whom, I got the impression, hadn't done too badly out of the change. But their views were a sort of liberal idealism, seeking what remained of civil society in Russian tradition. Whether the Orthodox Church was there, I tended to doubt. Yet there were various ways, not all of them immoral, for girls with good English to get very rich, very fast, and they didn't seem at all keen on them; they had chosen their roles out of Turgenev or Chekhov. New Russian was quite different from Great Russian.

On the Perm-to-Moscow train a young engineer, Nikita, was Nearly-New Russian. He was mad about hang-gliding. He couldn't do it in Moscow. He wanted to go to the Alps. He had lost his job in the space programme, but had made a bit of money, buying and selling. The landscape – forest, moor, forest – loped alongside, unrelentingly horizontal. Would he end up like Auden's Icarus, ditching in the sea while others got on with living, or – having caught the panorama bug from his satellites – would he clear the treetops and see where the eemis stane had got to?

What age were we living in? Holy Russia? Post-modernity? Or that monkish world of the Web, with its geeks and bozos, its scrolls of obsession. I stumbled ineptly into the last: doing a project for the Scottish National Party, I keyed in *millenium* and roused the whole gibbering dark age. Was it any different, down there in Silicon Valley, smug under its smog, from forty years ago, when Bertie Ohls, the good cop, told Marlowe all about modern capitalism:

> 'There ain't no clean way to make a hundred million bucks,' Ohls said. 'Maybe the head man thinks his hands are clean but somewhere along the line guys get pushed to the wall, nice little businesses get the ground cut from under them and had to sell out for nickels, decent people lost their jobs. Stocks got rigged on the market, proxies got bought up like a pennyweight of old gold, and the five per centers and the big law firms got paid hundred million grand fees for beating some law that the people wanted but the rich guys didn't, on account of it cut into their profits. Big money is big power and big power gets used wrong. Maybe it's the best we can get but it isn't my Ivory Soap deal.'
> 'You sound like a Red.' I said, just to needle him.
> 'I wouldn't know,' he said contemptuously, 'I aint been investigated yet.'

Maybe, if its leaking reactors didn't blow us up, Russia would look like post-New Deal California. Add the technology and you had that other leftie dystopia of 1953, Pohl and Kornbluth's *The Space Merchants*: a polluted world-order run by multinationals and their advertising-agency *avvocato*, proles doped with Coffiest, and the Conservationists on the run to Venus.

Weird tourism – trekking in the Antarctic – was the payoff for

Pohl and Kornbluth's admen. As today, where the travel pages of the posh papers are a Kim's Game of succulent moments, and supermodels descend on Romanian coal-mines. Had academia become a Bradbury-Lodge novel where the lucky nerd would articulate whatever discourse was *in*, and get a bedful of Pamela Anderson Ph.D? Then the auld dialectician got his teeth out of the tumbler, and muttered the great formula, 'It is no coincidence that . . .'

From journeys which had started off roughly in the same seemingly random way, connections began to spin themselves. 'Did you meet anyone you knew?' my grandmother used to ask, when I'd come back from somewhere like Norway or Austria. There was the vagueness of old age in this, but also the feeling that in such places you were quite likely to come across someone from Huntly. Buchan folk got around a lot, not least in Russia. I'd been invited to Russia because Boris had read my book on political fiction when trying to reform the Perm curriculum; to Canada as the indirect result of setting up a Welsh Studies Centre in Tübingen. And that had stemmed in its turn from having a house near Aberystwyth, which I'd once called, thinking about the great library, the Alexandria of the Welsh. Alexandria also had its lighthouse, and this metaphorical, explicatory function still kept a few of us in circulation. Which was why, I suppose, I found myself flying westward again scarcely six months later, on the eve of the British election.

X Stored History

'He used to be a Marxist, now he's a neo-liberal,' said the girl on the cruise boat as we chugged out to the Statue of Liberty. For Tony Judt, thus made over, New York was the place to be. He had organised a conference on 'Remembering World War II'; I was shipped over. A doddle, I thought, chairing someone else's paper. Then the someone else dropped out, and I drafted, 'Was there a British patriotism?' – taking the period from the war to the Wilson government. The trend will be evident from the foregoing: an amalgam of Dunkirk spirit, the two-party system, Bevanite collectivism, cultural social-overhead capital (BBC, Arts Council, Open University) locked us into this for a couple of decades. Churchill's funeral, in 1965, was the moment at which this crumbled into 'heritage'. But that didn't obscure the fact that Churchillianism – and the man was Anglo-American – had been real, on the left as well as on the right. My presence in New York wasn't irrelevant to Timberlands because I and my contemporaries had become, as it were, the 'stored history' of the British element of the story.

Later I was on the lower east side of Manhattan, at the Maritime Museum. New York gave me a chance to get a bearing on paleotechnic origins – the moment when the Scots and the Americans almost simultaneously invented the steamboat – Symington's *Charlotte Dundas* on the Forth and Clyde Canal in 1802, Robert Fulton's *Clermont* on the Hudson six years later. From one particular angle, two old four-masters, the boardwalk, the brownstone houses and fish market could just be what the sailor would have seen as he rolled down the gangway for a week of drink and girls. But behind them soared the glass cliffs of Wall Street, reflecting crazy minarets of the 1920s. The library of the Museum was up a wooden stair, dusty, friendly and archaic. Every book I'd want about Fulton, Symington and the early steamboats was there. A block up was the Seaman's Church, with its own memorial museum. The Charles Addams edition of maritime history: models of the *Titanic, Morro Castle, Andrea Doria*.

> 'O hear us when we cry to thee
> For those in peril on the sea.'

In the bus for Central Park, neighbourhoods swung in and out of chronological focus – urban *shtetls* scarcely changed since the 1880s, New Deal libraries, hippie stores from the 1960s. I ended up, that evening, with the winners – the seriously rich who were bankrolling this show: providing the limos which swept us – on salaries of $5000 a month (Germany) to $120 a month (Yugoslavia) from airport to hotel, banging up Fritz Stern against Hans Mommsen. A liberal opponent of Tujman of Croatia had been rescued by Harvard. A Boston editor spent his vacations at his farmhouse near Huntingdon. Huntingdon, England. This was the American hour and it functioned – at least for the moment – on dollar patronage and low transport costs coupled with virtual communications. The great linkages of 1905, it seemed, were back in place, but income gradients were so alarmingly steep that democratic communication, understanding how the non-privileged ran their societies, was a matter of total chance.

More than it had been in 1905? I'd like to get the precise figures, but my hunch would be that a Clydeside worker and his family were, in real terms, no more than three times better off than an African peasant. Now the difference in per capita income was about twentyfold: a comparison infrequently made. A public critique, itself a function of capitalist Empire, had then been easy to wire into: lots of cheap, articulate, grab-your-lapels books – Shaw and Wells and Whitman and Upton Sinclair and Jack London, and, and, and – the international socialist movement, the Wobblies, even the churches. The liners weren't like Jumbo jets, super-efficient, with tiny crews: thousands of sailors and stewards and engineers and musicians had been constantly shuttling back and forth on the boats: keeping tradition and the machine in unending friction.

The interpreters had gone, while some sort of *Raubergesellschaft* remained, its artificers strung across the northern hemisphere, dropping into hotels, lounges, art galleries, conference centres, watching CNN or Sky or (while never admitting to it) Interporn: 'adult' videos where young men either drove around, or went in and out of women like pistons. Timberlands had been a frontier society, where the essence was survival: so Tolstoi and Ibsen and Scott and Margaret Atwood told us. Now it seemed to have mutated into Kubrick's *2001*, closer to a space odyssey than to the careful little craftsmen in their Old European social market.

What Marx got wrong were the capitalists. At these latitudes they weren't rational maximisers, Trier *burgers*, but something more baroque, madder, more interesting and dangerous. If contemporaries like James Buchan were going on about money as 'frozen desire', then New York, this phallic cluster, was their *Kultstätte*: a controlling, religious complex which had bought in talent and memory from everywhere else, depriving others of consciousness. Whether it had gained any itself was another matter, but it was necessarily dynamic, or it ended in that Woody Allen line: 'A relationship is like a shark. It's got to keep on going forward. What we have is a dead shark.'

XI Entropy

It is no coincidence that . . . by now assertive grand designs were ordering the post-modern Kim's Game into a who-whom business. The linkage seemed to be energy – timberlands were chopped and burned. Writing *Fool's Gold* about North Sea oil, I had to start from the fact that carbon – coal and oil – was the stored energy of crushed, decomposed swamps and jungles. Paleotechnology had liberated it, scarring the landscape indelibly: the rise of Britain as a world power had been bought with it. The Caledonian forest had been laid waste to get charcoal for iron, timber for ships; copper had been gouged out of Anglesey for their sheathing, lead for shot, tin for provisions. Above all heat for cities and workshops. This northern exploitation was different from Braudel's Mediterranean, where the corresponding trade had been in snow and ice for the cellars and storerooms of the rulers and merchants of an urban, easeful civilisation.

Marx and Engels' *Communist Manifesto* was promptly falsified by the railway, which allowed capitalism to body-swerve the doom that pair had predicted for it; a decade later Marx co-opted Darwin to give scientific materialism its metaphors. But there was another, less confident, scientific paradigm, which became relevant as the railway drove energy-production steeply upwards. About 50 million tonnes in 1845, European coal output had quadrupled by 1875. By then Kelvin and Clerk-Maxwell, housed in the neighbourhood both of the Scots enlightenment and the Clyde engineering industry, were articulating the second law of thermodynamics, that heat was produced by the movement of atoms, and that all energy tended ultimately towards entropy, cooling, death. Like Darwinism, this was a law that ventured out of the natural sciences, and housed itself in the Victorians' world-picture. It projected the sense of the accession of strength, energy, virility, originality, but outside of it a cold, measured annihilation. On one side of that huge liberation, Matthew Arnold imagined his scholar-gipsy as trader breaking out of the Mediterranean:

> To where the Atlantic raves
> Outside the western straits; and unbent sails
> There, where down cloudy cliffs, through sheets of
> foam,
> Shy traffickers, the dark Iberians come;
> And on the beach undid his corded bales.

On the other, Landseer had the polar-bears ripping the last shreds of Franklin's sails, human bones scattered around them; Caspar David Friedrich's ship was smashed by giant angles of ice. Frankenstein and his creation died on one iceberg; the *Titanic* hit another.

In this zone, energy was essential. It required movement, and in return shrank distance. With steam, the ocean stopped being a barrier and became a link. With the railway, water when frozen or in flood could be replaced as a traffic artery. With timber you had heat and enlightenment. With electricity and cables, instantaneous communication. But, as computer-speak would put it, there was no default position. The alternative to movement was entropy. Auden's 'Fall of Rome' starts with a rain-lashed abandoned train, and ends mysterious:

Altogether elsewhere, vast
Herds of reindeer move across
Miles and miles of golden moss,
Silently and very fast.

He had a point. Reindeer apparently move, fast indeed and continually, because in the Arctic summer the midges that live off them can get into their lungs and kill them. Something cognate applies to what the Germans would call the *Raubergesellschaft* of the later human settlements. Auden was still speaking the scientism of grand gestures – Clerk-Maxwell, Huxley, Wells, and behind them Carnegie, JP Morgan, Lord Pirrie and so on. Such people Yeats loathed, looking south to the sanctity and loveliness of Urbino, though not the Irish themselves disagreed. Larry Doyle, the frustrated engineer of Shaw's *John Bull's Other Island*, wanted to put Rosscullen within three hours of London and London within twenty-four hours of New York. By 1998 his great-grandchildren had done so.

Marx had the notion that, once he had settled the score with capitalism, there would be some agreeable utopia where you worked a bit, had a good meal, drank, gardened, philosophised. Essentially Mediterranean. There's a lot about machinery in *Capital* but mainly about factories, not about steamers, railways, or energy. Even Orwell's dystopia in *1984* was founded on capturing areas of cheap human labour. Assume, however, that a predatory technology, and the limited scientific advance necessary to activate it, latches on to clan or trading societies to whom movement is indispensable, from the time of Viking raiders or Scots cattle-drovers on – the people of the Sagas or the Táin – and you get something a lot more aggressive. William Morris realised his arty-crafty Thames Valley in *News from Nowhere* by slaughtering two-thirds of the English population, which sounds a lot more northern. Samuel Smiles used to go on about the rural communities which bred his Northern inventors and engineers, which would fit Emmanuel Todd's notion of clan-like 'political' families. Such people carried through the building of the British railway network as the Irish population starved, drove rails across the plains, annihilating the buffalo on whom the Indians lived, forced the Chinese to accept their opium. Their disciples industrialised Russia in a dozen years at the cost of millions dead.

Movement increases the further north you go; miles travelled by all means are far greater, even in Russia, than in say South America or Africa. Status expresses itself in other ways in the south, in family size, palaces of unnumbered rooms, prowess as lover or patron, dignity of the city: Lampedusa's Sicily in *The Leopard* is entropy made stucco. In the north the fetish is mobility, retinue: the hotel suite, the steam yacht, the private train of the millionaire, even the armoured train of the Bolshevik.

XII Where we came in

Stuck in the middle were the European powers, run by retrospective aristos and timid bourgeois, borrowing from the new dynamism for dynastic purposes – building railways to shift armies – but trying always to keep it in check, and the Marxian opposition under control. After 1900 they were wrenched by the effort into war and breakdown, and divisions which allowed a deformed, predatory version of Marxism its head.

Civil society, gentle, voluntary, honest, was supposed to be the remedy for the ruin that Lenin, Stalin, and Brezhnev caused. Tom Nairn reckoned that Ernest Gellner had got it all wrong: the real civil society, which Gellner had experienced in Scotland, was mechanistic and institutional. Employed against *Raubergesellschaft* after 1989, the gentle, cooperative version had simply fallen to bits. The limitations of civil society, the importance of history and perceived pattern, were things which we were only now beginning to recognise. This brought me back to Wales.

In the early 1980s, when I was spectating on the place from Germany, Wales began to feed into Scottish politics. In 1981 Welsh nationalism ought to have been in a far worse condition than

Scotland, given the appalling outcome of the 1979 referendum. But it had got off the floor through culture and history: the campaign for S4C, the Welsh television channel. When Gwynfor Evans announced that he would fast unto death, he was the sort of person one believed. In Scotland we raised a laugh by announcing that two prominent Gaelic intellectuals had threatened to drink themselves to death if an Assembly wasn't granted. But it was an awkward laugh. By 1983, when that midget Atlanticist Gwyn Alf Williams was leaping about the hills asking when Wales had actually happened, our notions of Scotland were literally mobilised. By 1986 various activists, ex-politicians, academics, had written collective histories, social histories, literary histories, created a Scottish Poetry Library, had reinstalled the canon; two years later several of them turned up drafting *Scotland's Claim of Right*, which started the move to the Scottish Constitutional Convention.

This resulted in a geographical reordering – the old line, articulated by Michael Hechter, had our two countries peripheral to an English core. Now we saw that they had lain along paleotechnic trajectories, absorbing ideologies from the impulse of expansion, as well as from their margins: one trajectory was the arc of Europe's Atlantic coast; the other the emigrant-utopian *magistrale* from the Mid-West to the Urals. The first was salient enough in the ports, mines, railways; the second more complex, not just trade and migration but the geography of expectations: the new-found-land, the workers' state. When in the 1980s Scots and Canadian writers had recognised and *placed* this, the economic compulsion was over, though the train was still racketing along its track. We had, it seemed, taken in some bitter wisdom – ecological and pacifist motives penetrated the autonomy movement of the 1980s, explicit in Wales and underlying the Campaign for a Scottish Parliament – but the new thing was that this hadn't affected the core at all. England's consciousness was indifferent.

XIII On the steps, glass in hand

This article was aimed at the travel pages and then, draft after draft, modulated into something different: a perspective of sorts, like the sun that, rising over the pines, chased our train across the plains towards Moscow. Journalism doesn't sit easily with history, and the travel journalist – 'Gulliver visited Brobdignag as the guest of Aero-Brobdignag' – is a gamekeeper on a well-fenced post-modern demesne. Introduce history, and the angle of vision changes: new unwelcome constellations appear. The cruise boats which bring the international rich up the Kama to Perm were the ones that used to carry Russians to cheap holidays. Now they were symbols as alien and ruthless as Strelnikov's armoured train had been to Zhivago in 1919.

In 1981, when Atwood and Lee were over in Scotland, Cairns Craig was complaining in his essay 'The Body in the Kitbag' about the expulsion of history from the Scottish novel:

> . . . felt history, history people are aware of living through, has disappeared and even the silent drift of progress is no longer discernible because there is no longer any visual or distinguishable point from which the speed of the current can be measured.

In 1981 I'd put the history of twentieth-century Scotland in place myself, but now found myself in regions which since then had become precipitately ahistorical. From that smooth, fast river of capitalism, Russia, Canada, Wales and Scotland might seem illusions in a post-modern world of hermetic *micropoli*. But so too did England, the envied centre in Craig's world. Watching the crowds bawling and shrieking as the coffin of the Princess of Wales was borne through the centre of London, this wave of emotion seemed utterly ahistorical: a discovered identity which was part media-created, part the grimmer sort of fairytale, Auden-style:

Lest we should see what we are
Lost in a haunted wood
Children afraid of the dark
Who have never been happy or good.

Five days later we voted for our parliament, for our own history, and as I believe for our future.

Wood vanishes. At Kingston-on-Spey there was until a century ago one of Scotlands biggest shipyards. Nothing discernible is left. An earlier shipyard had upped and left for the Miramichi, and nothing is left there, either. Realising the problems we have with an elusive history puts us ahead of those who were content with something they believed was secure, but now find doesn't answer at all.

Minerals, on burning, release carbon dioxide. For every dollar that we pay for our fuel, we need to pay another two to meet the global costs. This would mean a much less mobile economy – fewer Japanese on Prince Edward Island, fewer glossy girls in BMWs, fewer malls and cars. Yet the sums weren't noticed by the mass of the world's population, whose accession to the market mattered to the West, whose timberlands were their only resource.

Perm. Presbyterians always seek the clinching symbol for their perorations, the come-to-Jesus bits. Where was the Russian image? The place seemed more Chandler than Solzenitzhyn. But, remembering the theatre in the Governor's Summer Residence, there was *Uncle Vanya*. In 1996 the old drunk seemed universal. There was a New York Vanya, an Australian one; Anthony Hopkins was filming Uncle Ieuan in a North Wales mansion, under the mountains seen from Aber beach. And that was just the films. Faced with paralytic establishments, flash, directionless dealing, and desperate persistence we, the Timberlanders, were looking for their human semblance.

In Perm a shadow crouched on the steps of the Governor's house, glass in hand, looking at the wrecked garden, the new asphalt and the concrete blocks beyond. Where did Chekhov's Dr Astrov get these notions from? Ruskin through Tolstoy, I'd guess, filtered through the civics of the good doctor of Taganrog:

> I would consent to cutting wood when people really need it, but why destroy the forests? The Russian forests are groaning under the axe, millions of trees are being destroyed, the homes of animals and birds are being laid waste, the rivers are drying up, and wonderful scenery is disappearing for ever – and all this because people are too lazy and stupid to stoop down and get the fuel from out of the ground. Man is endowed with reason and creative power so that he can increase what has been given him, but up to the present he has been destroying and not creating. I can see your expression, and I know this doesn't seem serious to you, just crankiness, but . . . when I hear the rustle of the young trees I planted with my own hands I realise that the climate, too, is in my hands, and if mankind is still happy in a thousand years' time, I'll have been responsible for it, even though only to a minute extent.

The Wood Demon himself. *Gruß dich*.

SECTION TWO
Old Fathers

2
Veere and After
– the tradition of Scotland in Europe
(1992)

The towns of the Low Countries – Ghent, Antwerp, Haarlem, Utrecht – were where early modern Scots travelled and traded. When *Scotland on Sunday*, celebrating the Europe-fest in Edinburgh at the end of 1992, wanted a piece on the Scots in Europe, this seemed to be where to start. The fest itself, culminating with 25,000 Scots demonstrating for home rule in the Meadows in Edinburgh, redeemed a difficult year.

Suddenly, as the bike turns the corner, the Groote Kerk launches itself into view, riding above the poplars, dwarfing the baroque spire of the Staatshuis. The Groote Kerk is a shell, burned out in 1686. Where the Drummonds and Davidsons are buried in this huge barn, God alone knows. Where they worked remains. The cistern where the Scottish merchants washed their wool stands in the shadow of the church tower. By the quay, these days crammed with motor boats and slick yachts, rear the elegant gables of the two Schotse Huizen. Inside, on a table, a letter from the Convention of Royal Burghs, dated 1692 instructs Scottish merchants to desist from trading with Rotterdam, and channel their trade – 'All sorts of Wool, Wollen and Linen Yarn, all Wollen and Linen Manufactories, Hides and Skins of all Sorts, Playding, Kersies, Scots Cloath, Stockings, Salmond, Tar, all sorts of Barrel Flesh, Pork, Butter,

Leather Dressed and Undressed' – through the Scots Staple. 'Those who neglect this Advertisment may expect exactest Diligence, Real and Personal, to be done against them, that the Law will allow to be done by. . . John Buchan, Agent.'

From 1541 to 1796 Veere in Zeeland was Scotland in Europe. Nowadays perhaps four hundred live within the overgrown fortifications of this Dutch version of Culross. In the seventeenth century the population was 5,000: an ominous symbol for an Edinburgh summit for which the auspices look anything but good?

But the Veere connection lasted for almost 250 years; Ravenscraig steelworks for barely thirty. And the Scots dialogue with Europe is an investment which still has potential. Even Iain Lang, in a confused address at St Andrews, seems to sense the easing of the atmosphere which 'Not English, Scots' usually brings. Behind this lies an historical reality, important if not always straightforward.

The 'Auld Alliance' has lodged in the national memory: a grab-bag of the claret trade, Scots regiments in the Hundred Years' War, Mary Queen of Scots, the Jacobite exiles at Vincennes. But there was probably a denser affinity with Calvinist Holland. The Scots connection didn't stop at Veere. The other John Buchan sent one of his earliest heroes, John Burnet of Barns, to study, like so many other Scots lawyers, doctors and gentry, at the University of Leyden, where he met the great Leibniz, German polymath and forerunner of the Enlightenment. Two hundred years later, Holland became a centre for leading Scottish artists such as DY Cameron, James MacBey and Martin Hardie, while Donald MacKay, Lord Reay, Dutch radical MP and international lawyer, went on to run the London School Board and found the British Academy.

The Dutch experience was replicated along the coast of the North Sea and the Baltic. The names are still there. In Finland Crichton's shipyard at Turku and the Finlayson textile works at Tampere; in the Scots ancestry claimed by Edvard Grieg at Bergen and Immanuel Kant at Königsberg. Throughout eastern Europe in the seventeenth century the Scots pedlar was as frequent a sight as the Scots mercenary – and there might have been as many as 100,000 of the latter – causing some local annoyance:

> Mark you what the proverb says
> Of Scotsmen, rats and lice;
> The whole world over take your ways
> You'll find them still, I guess.

Even today a bargain in German is *zum Schottenpreis*, not derived from ancient Aberdonian jokes but, according to the Grimm brothers' dictionary, from the fact that *Schott* had become the word for travelling dealer – the man whose prices were keenest.

The pedlars and soldiers followed the monks and scholars of the middle ages, although many of the *Schottenkirche* to be found in German towns were in fact founded by Irish monks, and the 'subtle Doctor' Duns Scotus, who lies buried at Cologne, was almost certainly Irish. John Mair and George Buchanan, in the sixteenth century, were as emphatically Scots. The first (whose name anglicises unhelpfully into John Major) was the friend of Erasmus of Rotterdam, and like him tried to get the Papacy to reform itself; Buchanan, Mair's pupil, taught at Coimbra, Bordeaux, Paris and latterly Edinburgh, became the friend of Montaigne and Scaliger, a strong Reformer and the greatest Latinist of his day. His intentions for his *Rerum Scoticarum Historiae*, to purge the national history of 'sum Inglis lyis and Scottis vanite' seem still to the point.

Recently, Prof Alex Broadie of Glasgow has shown how Scots philosophers of this generation had created a 'common sense' tradition well in advance of Hutcheson and Reid in the eighteenth century. They also brought a 'civic ideology' from the Italian city states, and Machiavelli in his patriotic, non-toxic version. Buchanan refined this in his powerful tract against absolute monarchy *De Iure Regni apud Scotos* (1579), influencing Andrew Fletcher, who spent much of his life in Holland, and Adam Ferguson. It was not enough for the *polis* to exist; its purpose was good government, in which the individual found his moral fulfilment. These ideals have marked the Scottish political tradition down the years, via John Galt, James Lorimer (who drafted the first scheme for a European federation in 1884) and Patrick Geddes (of Edinburgh, Palestine, India and Montpellier), to *Scotland's Claim of Right*.

Finding it incredible that the Scots could have generated the Enlightenment, Hugh Trevor-Roper put it down to Jacobite exiles picking up sensible ideas abroad. There *was* a Jacobite cosmopolitanism – witness Sir Thomas Urquhart of Cromarty, with his translations of Rabelais and that idiosyncratic *tour de force* of nationalism and strange learning *The Jewel* – but many strands went into the Scotland of which Thomas Jefferson wrote, that in matters of science 'no place in the world can pretend to a competition with Edinburgh'. But the new learning was conveyed by books, and involved the Scots in the machinery of a print-capitalism based on a London market. In the process of great-power-building which was accelerated by the French Wars of 1793-1815, the writers who could be fitted into a frame of evolving British-ness presented the sharpest profiles: David Hume, Adam Smith, Walter Scott.

Scott was, uneasily, a Jacobite nationalist and patriotic British Tory, whose work was the prototype of countless nationalist outpourings. Not surprisingly, schizophrenia, from Hogg and Stevenson to RD Laing, became one of Scotland's characteristic exports. Our links with Europe are important, but they aren't one-way, or at all consistent. There are points where other force-fields supervene, relationships get tangled, voices garbled. Nowhere more so than in the nineteenth century.

In 1828 Goethe wrote to his Scottish disciple Thomas Carlyle in terms which show how much the great internationalist valued the identity of Scotland:

> One must study and make allowances for the
> peculiarities of each nation, in order to have real
> intercourse with it. The special characteristics of a

> people are like its language and currency. They
> facilitate exchange; indeed they first make exchange
> possible.

A century later the German-Hungarian Marxist Georg Lukacs, in a book which valuably reassessed Scott, and showed his influence on nineteenth century nationalism, refers to him throughout as an 'English novelist'. Industrialisation and imperialism seemed to combine the national histories, and although the Scots made their presence felt as engineers and entrepreneurs throughout Europe – the massive steam locomotives which linked up the continent were pioneered by John Haswell in Vienna, the great ports were crowded with steamers built in or owned from the Clyde – the Scots orientation had changed. As a Polish sea-captain noted, 'He was in the habit of alluding to his Scotch connections, but every great man has done that.' But Joseph Conrad encountered his Scots off the Malay peninsula.

If their own sense of nationality was reoriented, pushed out to new frontiers by Great Britain Limited, Victorian Scots still managed to empathise, far more than the English, with European national groups. The great authority on Russia was Donald Mackenzie Wallace; the great opponent of Russia David Urquhart, kinsman of Urquhart of Cromarty. James Bryce stood up for the Armenians, RW Seton Watson for the Slav subjects of the Habsburgs. English Liberals reacted suspiciously to Gladstone's sympathy for small nationalism, but this was part of a 'European mind', which went through processes which weren't part of English empiricism.

Despite these enthusiasts, and Carlyle's own ambiguous fame among the Germans, Scottish democracy realised itself through the politics of the settler territories – Canada, Australia and New Zealand – and the great age of foreign missions. The move furth of Europe even accelerated as the Scottish economy started to fall apart after World War I, and trade in herring, coal and ships declined. Although some intellectuals, like Edwin Muir, AS Neill and Naomi Mitchison involved themselves in trying to create a rational and progressive society in the Weimar Republic and federal Austria, the land was brighter to the west. Tom Johnston enthused over the Ontario Power Scheme; Pat Dollan over Fiorella La Guardia's New York (whence came the point blocks!), while John Buchan, John Grierson and Norman MacLaren went to Canada, Sandy Mackendrick to California, joining the hundreds of thousands – most of them skilled and adaptive – who left the Tail of the Bank for good from the 1920s to the 1960s.

In Europe what mattered was the soviet experiment – MacDiarmid's image of the perfectability of socialist man. Few left-wingers were more tolerant of Stalin than Scots communists who conceived of him as an amalgam of John Knox, Sir William Beardmore and Willie Gallacher. Many were the souvenirs of trips to Sofia or Kiev you could find in trades council clubs – and also a host of anti-régime jokes which suggested that, overall, a fairly realistic view was taken. But – are haggis, whisky and pipers still flown to Mr Yeltzin in the Kremlin every 25 January?

When did things change? Scotland was notably less enthusiastic about Europe than the rest of Britain in the referendum of 1975. But Europe took a solicitous interest in the referendum of 1979: the *Enarques* of Paris, the *crème de la crème* of the French bureaucratic élite, were packed in the stalls when the reborn nation staggered onstage and fell into their laps. Whatever they made of this, they successfully carried through the regionalisation of France three years later, accelerating a new political movement which finds more space for Scotland than for a querulous, incompetent Westminster. With David Martin Depute-Chair of the European Parliament, Bruce Millan a respected regional commissioner, energetic lobbying by Scottish local authorities, and most recently Scotland Europa under the shrewd and effervescent Prof Grant Baird, the Scottish profile is now disproportionately – perhaps, to Westminster, embarassingly – high.

Was the débàcle of 1979 in fact the Scottish 1968? In the 1980s, as Thatcher blew North Sea oil revenue on shopping her way to the Falklands, Scotland's self-examination again raised European themes. And Europeans have been consistently interested in the country's intellectual recovery – powerfully regional and civic as well as original and adventurous.

Kenneth White's 'Geopoetics' commanded the Sorbonne; the fierce republican prose of Tom Nairn loped alongside that of Jean-François Revel and Hans-Magnus Enzensberger. Sean Connery went the distance against Umberto Eco. Even Scottish football fans, found droll and knowledgeable – *Die Schotten sind immer fair* – where their English equivalents were appalling, got themselves cited as model European citizens.

Regional partnership has been less impressive. Baden-Württemberg and the 'Four Motors' (Catalunya, Rhone-Alpes, Lombardy and Ba-Wü) once beckoned, but the Scottish Office seemingly blew it. The Welsh moved in, with enthusiasm and considerable success. Iain Lang has been strutting his stuff in Bavaria: not promising, given political traditions which are so far apart. North Rhine-Westphalia seems a better option, or Schleswig-Holstein, with its links to Scandinavia and East Europe. If Labour parliamentarians – Smith, Brown, Cook – could show more initiative here, they would do a lot for the profile of the German SPD, whose Länder government is the best prototype we have for a regional Europe – and in these ominous days, needs all the help it can get.

If not? After the euphoria of 1990, the nation-states are again on the march. Just down the road from where I write, in Stuttgart, the Second International decided in 1908 on a general strike against war, one of the schemes of Keir Hardie, Lanarkshire miner, socialist leader and home ruler, friend of Bebel and Jaurès, of the Indian Congress and the South African blacks. In 1914 the nation states loosed war on the continent and broke his heart. Being Scottish Europeans isn't just an interesting option. It's the only chance we've got.

3
The Most Mighty of Goddesses:
the Scots and the Law
(1983)

Scottish nationalism, with hardly
any martyrs in sight, was Europe's
most boring liberation movement.
Yet this fetishisation of law had a grounding
in the highly structured nature of Scottish civil
society, and the regular 'beating of the bounds'
between the Estates of the Realm:
kirk, law, local government and education.

In 1938 three founder-members of Plaid Cymru, led by Saunders Lewis set fire to buildings and materials at a bombing range which was being built on the Lyn peninsula in North Wales. After giving themselves up to the police they were put on trial at Carnarfon where the jury refused to agree on a verdict. Amid vehement Welsh protests, including that of David Lloyd George, the trial was shifted to the Old Bailey, where an English jury found them guilty. The three were sent to prison for nine months.

'Why we burned the Bombing School' (Saunders Lewis's speech from the Carnarfon dock became one of the greatest pieces of twentieth-century pamphleteering) has marked the cause of Welsh nationalism to the present day. Lewis, otherwise a very conservative figure, has maintained that 'careful, considered public violence is often a necessary weapon for national movements.'

While Plaid Cymru, in its radicalism and pacifism, has moved towards other, non-violent, forms of resistance, the threat of sabotage, for instance, remains a factor in Welsh pressure-group politics. Gwynfor Evans's threat of a 'fast unto death' in 1981 against the Home Secretary's attempt to deny Wales a Welsh Language TV channel gained force not only from Evans's integrity but from the evidence of a campaign of arson by extremists directed against second homes in North Wales. If concessions were not made to a peaceful agitation, the unspoken logic ran, something more menacing would take its place.

A broad repertoire of agitational methods, shading from the straightforwardly political to the blatantly violent has always been a feature of nationalist movements. A strictly law-abiding nationalist movement is virtually a contradiction in terms, for the premises on which it is founded implicitly reject the laws under which it has to live.

On the other hand the pervasive actuality rather than the threat of illegality – the Provisional IRA's campaign in Northern Ireland for example – destroys the leadership's freedom of manoeuvre and favours the meeting of force with counterforce. The greatest nationalist leaders have usually kept the repertoire, and themselves, securely in control.

Not so in Scotland. Not only has Scottish nationalism been almost pedantically law-abiding in pursuing its aims, but worsening economic and social conditions have not led to any breakdown of obedience to authority. The SNP's attempt at civil disobedience in 1981 was extinguished by the party's lack of enthusiasm as much as anything else; that summer's riots took place in English inner cities, not in the slums and problem schemes of Glasgow or Dundee. The closure and dismantling of factory after factory – Singer, Chrysler, Corpach, Beardmore – have been met with, at most, muted protest. 'Upper Clyde', that false dawn of workers' control, happened when today's young unemployed were still toddlers. Is there something in the nature of Scottish society and its institutions and values which inhibits protest campaigns and inculcates instead an almost exaggerated respect for the letter of the law?

As I meditated on this, a pattern seemed to emerge. Throughout Scottish history, it seeemed, there ran a deep popular conviction that reform was only attainable through legal action, and that political movements ought to be oriented to achieve this. The belief in legality might break down, when law had become unbelievably arbitrary, but even then the Scots response was more likely to be demented litigation of the 'Plainstanes versus Peebles' sort than rebellion. My thesis is that this legalistic tradition has filtered so far down into our structures of social and political behaviour that the usual nationalist 'mix' of constitutionalism and threat cannot normally be replicated. The public sanction for extra-legal action seems to exist only in circumstances in which a total constitutional breakdown is in prospect.

Legalism is flesh of Scottish flesh, bone of Scottish bone. On the land the gentry had elaborate procedures governing succession and entail whose reform in the eighteenth century was to accelerate the development of agricultural capitalism. But even the farm labourers prized their bargaining power over their employment, and the conventions which sustained it; lawyers alternately aided and arraigned the early trades unionists. Scots housing law was biased towards the rights of property and landlords but judges were often amazed by the skill that working-class tenants displayed when defending their rights in court. In the First World War period the most emphatic victories of the Scottish workers were the imposition of rent control in 1915 and the repayment in 1922 by landlords of excessive rents. Both were victories of organised labour, but victories confirmed in the courts.

Like so much in Scottish history, this behaviour pattern is masked by an overgrowth of romanticism. Highland outlaws, Robert Burns, some nationalist activities and of course the 'Red Clyde' exist to provide an image of romantic rebellion which never goes deeper than that. Burns's lines from 'The Jolly Beggars':

> A fig for those by law protected,
> Liberty's a glorious feast.
> Courts for cowards were erected;
> Churches built to please the priest.

don't personify a Scots attitude to law and church. Bailies and ministers can sing them at Burns suppers simply because the proposition advanced is so implausible and absurd as to be entertaining.

This is true even of religion, supposedly the great emotive force of Scottish history. The novelist Robin Jenkins found only recently, when exploring the Disruption of 1843 as the subject for *The Temptation of George Darroch*, that even in this great and fateful issue legalism was paramount, emotion and conviction fatally lacking.

The role of law as a component of bourgeois civil society is obvious enough, and in Scotland its position has always been a privileged one. That the status of lawyers is higher, and their training both broader and more academic than in the South is a tradition which goes back to the Scottish Enlightenment and the importance of 'civil history', the academic study of law, as a pioneering field of sociological and anthropological studies.

Scots lawyers have been, then and since, commercially involved as estate managers and property agents. In the late nineteenth century it was the great legal partnerships of East Scotland which set up the Scots-American investment trusts to export capital from Edinburgh and Dundee. But above all law has been an integral part of Scots politics.

Between 1746 and 1885 Scotland was ruled by the Lord Advocate, the profession's head, in collaboration with the Home Secretary, a system which reached its climax in the 'Dundas despotism' of 1775-1826. Even when the Secretary for Scotland was restored, it took until 1912 for him to be granted precedence over the Lord Advocate; and as late as 1915, when trouble threatened on the Clyde, Downing Street regarded a strong Lord Advocate as more essential than a competent Secretary.

The history of Scottish radicalism since 1745 – and even before – shows few episodes of rebellion, and many more appeals to law to redress grievances. The Porteous rioters, of 1726, were deeply imbued with a strong consciousness of the letter as well as the spirit of the law. To them the hanging of the guilty town-guard commander was the execution of a due process of law which had been perverted by illegitimate Royal interference. The freeing in 1799 of the Scottish colliers and saltworkers was achieved after an court campaign, although a further attempt, by weavers in 1812 to gain statutory wage-regulation, failed when it reached the length of the Court of Session.

Even more law-centred were the religious issues which obsessed the Victorian middle class. The 'Ten Years' Conflict' 1833-43 between evangelicals, eager to free the Kirk from landlord control and the 'Moderate' establishment was fought out by advocates in the Church and law courts – it was, anyway, largely a contest about their relative competence.

The century would also be closed by a massive religious lawsuit, when the vote of the Free Church to merge with the anti-Establishment United Presbyterians was contested by a minority who demanded the Church's property on the grounds that they adhered to the Church's 1843 programme of 'establishment on the church's terms'. The 'Free Church Case' went to the House of Lords, wbere RB Haldane, MP leading for the new United Free church, baffled everyone with the complexities of Scots religious law.

The Lords found in favour of the minority, which they judged had adhered to the intention of the founders in 1843. This grotesque situation meant further remedial legislation but the trauma of the whole business was such that the new United Free Church soon replaced its campaign against the established Kirk with negotiations to rejoin it. This was not, however, to be the last that was heard of their Lordships' rationale.

The twentieth century left was equally touchy about its legal status. Much of the trouble which erupted on the Clyde during the First World War stemmed from the Munitions Act's interference with the working customs of the skilled tradesmen. When Lord Balfour of Burleigh, inquiring officially into the crisis, interviewed a group of Fairfield's shop stewards in Barlinnie, he found a clutch of very patriotic and very angry Labour aristocrats – 'some of them Church elders, with sons at the front', scunnered at the way management and the munitions controller had broken agreements which they considered had the force of law.

When Labour broke through to take 29 of Scotland's 71 parliamentary seats in 1922 the lawyers were quick to accommodate the new order. In 1924 the first Labour Government's Lord Advocate had to be the Conservative Lord Macmillan but by 1929 several leading figures of the Scottish Bar, including Craigie Aitchison and the present Lord Cameron, had become Labour candidates. This commitment lasted until MacDonald threw over his party in August 1931 to form the National Government, to which most of the advocates transferred their allegiance. Nonetheless by 1936 another advocate, Robert Gibson KC, was Chair of Labour's Scottish executive. In 1947, with the entry of John Wheatley KC, now Lord Wheatley, into Attlee's Government as Solicitor-General and later Lord Advocate, the Catholic tradition in Scottish Labour reconciled itself with Parliament House.

Possibly the most curious legal entanglement, however, was the one which throttled the Scottish Socialist Party, formed in 1932 by the majority of Independent Labour Party members who remained loyal to Labour when the ILP disaffiliated from it. Some SSP members sued the ILP for recovery of halls and property which, they claimed, should pass to the majority. The case dragged on for several years and the Court of Session in 1940 found in favour of the ILP minority, on the grounds that they – Jimmie Maxton and co. – were faithful to the spirit of the drafters of the ILP's 1892 constitution. The parallel with the Free Church case of 1900 was almost complete; but the SSP, whose nationalism and pacifism had led to friction with Transport House, could not afford the legal fees and dissolved itself into the Labour Party.

Where do the roots of Scots legalism lie? The historian EP Thompson has written that the eighteenth century English regarded their law as a national icon, regardless of its class bias: 'If the law is evidently partial and unjust, then it will mask nothing; legitimize nothing, contribute nothing to any class's hegemony.'

The law had still to 'seem to be just'. The Welsh and the Catholic Irish had less cause to agree. Law was remote not only from the Welsh speaking peasant but from the raw new industrial towns, where episodes of violent industrial conflict persisted into the mid-nineteenth century. While, in Jonathan Swift's words, 'the law presumed no Catholic to breathe in Ireland', inculcating an alienation from 'protestant law' which has lasted to the present.

The Scots outdid the English in their enthusiasm. Why? After 1707 law was, certainly, not just a national possession, but – in the absence of a parliament – a critical institution of nationality. Some argued that it was more. Writers of the inter-war Scots Renaissance saw it as a substitute for the emotional element in nationalism; generated by the country's struggle for independence but destroyed by the Reformation. Thereafter, the appeal to defiance and sacrifice could no longer be made. Legalism was part of a Scottish identity frozen by religion's winter, its national heroes buried deep. The 'poor frozen life and shallow banishment' of the modern Scots mocked, in Edwin Muir's words,

> All the kings before
> This land was kingless.
> And all the singers before
> This land was songless,
> This land that with its dead and living,
> Waits the Judgement Day.

In Calvinism, the Reformation had bequeathed a religous ideology both legalistic in its Talmudic attitude to scriptures and deeply preoccupied with church government and social discipline. Over a century later Viscount Stair published his *Institutes of the Law of Scotland*, in 1681, at the beginning of the period which was to see the settlement of the Church of Scotland and the enactment of the Act of Union of 1707, which contained special provision for the law and the church. This process was not completed until the

63

territorial jurisdictions of the great magnates were abolished in 1746; but thereafter the General Assembly of the Kirk and the Faculty of Advocates (whose memberships frequently overlapped) were to act as components of a type of Scottish legislative system.

Law was part of politics, but also had its own politics. Law transacted business between the great institutions and the other Scottish power groups. Court actions were, and are, part of the ritual whereby they beat the bounds of their power, publicly staking out the area of their authority.

Sir Walter Scott, lawyer, politician and novelist, attained his greatness as the 'fictional historian' of this period, and through his writings recreated symbolically the dominance of law, from grotesques like the demented litigant Puir Peter Peebles in *Redgauntlet* to Mr Pleydell the urbane 'writer' of enlightenment Edinburgh, in *Guy Mannering*. Scott's fiction is a record of the establishment of the 'rule of law' in Scotland. In *The Black Dwarf*, set in the aftermath of the Union of 1707, he assembled a representative clutch of malcontents in a Border peel to assent *inter alia* to the proposition that:

> Thae were gude days on the Border when
> there was neither peace nor justice heard of.

In 1825, towards the end of his life, law seemed to him so ingrained into the procedures of the Scottish propertied class that its significance had shifted from the functional to the totemic:

> There is a maxim almost universal in Scotland, which I
> should like much to see controul'd. Every youth of
> every temper and almost every description of character
> is sent either to study as a lawyer, or to a Writer's
> office as an apprentice. The Scottish seem to conceive
> Themis the most powerful of goddesses. . .

Scott, perhaps, already realised the costs of this obsession. He feared that his Whig lawyer contempories such as Francis Jeffrey and Henry Cockburn would destroy the fabric of the conservative Scotland which he revered, of which law was only a part. Something like this, of course, happened. Parliamentary and local government reform, the Disruption of the Church in 1843 and the emasculation of its poor law and education functions gravely weakened the traditional institutions. But law was, at least relatively, strengthened; it became *primus inter pares* among the traditional estates, the arbiter between them.

The problem is that legalism can be carried to extremes. Ritual procedures and conflicts can blunt and distort popular initiatives. John MacCormick tries in 1952 to prove that the Queen is Elizabeth I in Scotland and earns a commendation from Lord Cooper; JS Malloch drags the General Teaching Council through the courts in the late 1960s to deny its powers to compel the registration of teachers. Meanwhile the underlying great causes – of self-government, of educational reform – somehow drop from view. The ghost of Peter Peebles stalks Parliament House.

Perhaps the role of law in Scots politics can be summed up by one overarching concept. In 1886 the great English jurist Professor AV Dicey, anxious to defeat Gladstone's plan for Irish Home Rule, contrasted this seditious scheme with the practice which had determined Westminster's relations to Scotland. Scotland, he wrote, had been governed 'in accordance with Scots ideas': no attempt had been made to impose legislation on the country which did not meet with the approval of Scottish institutions and most Scottish MPs. The principle was probably as old as the Union, but with a fairly practical modification in 1832 when the cement of patronage and corruption was changed to that of party alignment. Liberalism was more or less equally dominant, north and south of the border, for the next fifty years. Thereafter the development of the Scottish Office and its elaborate administrative and consultative structures has supplemented political alignment with the 'imperative coordination' – in Max Weber's phrase – of a smoothly-running bureaucracy, and

Conservative régimes interpreting Scottish preferences in a flexible and on the whole collectivist way.

In all of this law has acted as a kind of self-trimming mechanism, facilitating integration and cooperation. But what if, as today, discontent spreads to all the Scottish institutions and even a great Scots judge, Lord Kilbrandon, denounces the system under which Scotland is governed as one so 'absurd . . . that it hardly bears examination'?

Echoing MacCormick's nationalist agitation – albeit for his own ends – Sir Winston Churchill threatened in 1950, 'I should never adopt the view that Scotland should be forced into the serfdom of socialism as the result of a vote in the House of Commons.' The political situation has been reversed, but the constitutional argument remains the same. In the last four years, Scotland has in no sense been 'governed according to Scottish ideas' and Scottish reaction to this has been made clear in the election, with the Conservative Party registering its second-worst vote this century. Never has a British Government so decisively lacked a Scottish mandate and, on all sides, never has the notion of constitutional conflict been so dominant.

The divergent basis of Scottish political consent is unlikely to deter Mrs Thatcher from her campaign of selling State and local authority assets, running down public services, and accelerating defence preparations. The labour movement's reaction to this will be one of bitter and increasingly non-parliamentary resistance, while the supporters of the Alliance will be little inclined to defend a political system which gives their voters such derisory represent-ation. Scotland isn't a country given to direct action. But it still has, in North Sea oil, the life-support system of a decrepit British economy woefully lacking in signs of structural innovation. As the agitation for self-government gets under way again, a critical underlying question must be: will the legalistic constraints on Scots political action still hold, or will forms of political action associated with nationalism elsewhere in Europe take over?

4
Coping with Carlyle
(1992)

Rediscovering the Scots Enlightenment
background of Thomas Carlyle uncovers a
stock of notions common to liberalism,
nationalism and scientific socialism in the years
before 1848. This essay which first appeared
the *Times Higher Education Supplement*, argues
that the energetic element in Marx comes out
of Carlyle's vivid perceptions. Carlyle at home
seems humane and justly indignant,
abroad 'a damn'd mischievous North Briton'.

When I was a student at Edinburgh in the 1960s I used to notice a small but persistent advertisement in the gloomy entry to Old College. 'Entries are invited,' it read, 'for the Thomas Carlyle Essay Prize' – on some minatory theme like 'Carlyle and the Absolute'. Were any entries ever received, I wondered, and if so where? In some mahogany solicitor's office in the New Town, with a brass plate polished to anonymity, to be scrutinised by a committee of retired headmasters?

Carlyle seemed, to my social democrat generation, a dinosaur of Victorian reaction. If there were tempting references in Engels' *Situation of the English Working Classes*, we settled for his dismissal: 'Grumbling against the tide of history, which has left him high and dry'. Carlyle on the Irish in *Chartism*, the very title of that *Latter-Day Pamphlet* on 'The Nigger Question', Carlyle on democracy in *Shooting Niagara*, all those glowering volumes of *Frederick the Great*: a few quotes explained and condemned.

But in 1970, when preparing the Industrialisation and Culture section of the Open University's first foundation course, I encountered 'Signs of the Times'. What a warning this was to anyone working for the *dernier cri* of the 'steam intellect societies':

> 'Instruction, that mysterious communing of Wisdom with Ignorance, is no longer an indefinable tentative progress, requiring a study of individual aptitudes, and a perpetual variation of means and methods, to attain the same end; but a secure, universal, straightforward business, to be conducted in the gross, by proper mechanism, . . . with such intellect as comes to hand.'

This was different – a disturbing intellect whose observations had sharp contemporary relevance. Since then, the critic of the 'cash nexus', of 'mechanism', of 'the Condition of England' seems to have become unavoidable. The collapse of 'scientific socialism', and the rise of the 'alternative religion' of market forces, obviously reawakens interest in Carlyle's pre-Marxian critique of them. His 'European mind' – his fascination with French and German history and culture – restates itself within a project of European unity which again stresses Scotland's links to the continent.

As a central interpreter, Karl Marx isn't what he once was, and there's been a lot of crowing over this by the *Times* columnist school of political thought, the Scrutons, Amiels and Levins. But the young Marx of grand phrases and savage laughter was far more incendiary than the dry mathematical dogmatist of the later years. Like Carlyle, he used the compactness of metaphor and irony, scepticism and moral urgency, to fuse 'scientific' explanation to the imagination; he created a humane *consciousness* of problems otherwise too vast to comprehend.

Of the two, Carlyle was certainly the more pessimistic: 'The English coachman, as he whirls by, lashes the Milesian with his whip. The Irishman is holding out his hat to beg.' The 'cash-nexus' degrades, but it also divides. The affluent worker will tend rather to hate and fear the desperately poor than to express solidarity with them.

'English' and 'Milesian' now stand for different things – 'affluent' and 'underclass' in contemporary Britain, 'Wessis' and 'Ossis' in Germany, the 'developed' and the 'developing' world – but the lash goes on.

In my own case, research for a book about political fiction, *The Centre of Things*, showed that Carlyle, despite his contempt for the novel's 'long ear' and the 'national palaver' of parliament, more or less animated the great Victorian 'novel of public affairs' from the 1840s to the 1880s: Disraeli, Trollope, Kingsley, Dickens, George Eliot and Meredith. On his always audible prompting the novel, in particular the political novel, rose in Kathleen Tillotson's words 'to a status in literature and life which it has hardly yet lost'. His injunctions were still resounding in DH Lawrence a century later. Yet his style – however violent, personal and uncouth – helped give British politics new autonomy and energy, and swung British social thought to German from classically-derived models, while his 'interdisciplinary' signifiers, derived from fashion and contemporary politics, seemed to make him truly the first post-modernist.

Take blue jeans. In explaining the collapse of the Communist order the words blue jeans came up as frequently as, say, Chernobyl or Solidarnosc. They were the easy symbol for what Eastern youth wanted – they incorporated American culture, sex, informality, classlessness, freedom. But the interesting thing was that, as the 1980s wore on, the image restructured itself. Denim became fashion. What had been the uniform of the drudges became the 'designer jeans' of the dandies, and started to project something quite different from the gentle pacifism of 1968. They appeared on scowling model-girls, all hips and padded shoulders, on their hunky studs, with two-day growths and the air of blackshirt hit-men of the 1920s. 'Power-dressing' reflected fashion as international big business. By the time the refugees came through the unravelling curtain, jeans were definable in terms of class – the Ossies wore the wrong sort, were 'instantly recognisable in their stone-washed jeans'. Albanians in their 'unfashionable flared nylon trousers' were the end. Indicative of a new confrontation which might have reassured him, this insight was beyond Marx. It would not have been beyond the author of *Sartor Resartus*.

Lawrence, however, called Carlyle a 'philosophical maniac', and Meredith defined the Carlyle problem shrewdly enough when he said he caused 'an electrical agitation in the mind and joints', but was in matters of legislation, 'no more sagacious nor useful nor temperate than a flash of lightning in a grocer's shop. . . ' The insights petered out with *Latter-Day Pamphlets* – a more positive book than it's usually reckoned to be, pushing out ideas about government which the more tactful tones of Matthew Arnold made more acceptable a decade later – and the grumbling took over. But the flashes of lightning *were* illuminating, more so than many of Marx's strictures. Marx could not have foreseen Stalin or Saddam; Carlyle could.

This wasn't prophecy of a Nostradamus kind – though the man who tackled Cagliostro understood such charlatanry – but the outcome of an immersion in the Scots enlightenment: not the 'flat threshing-floor of logic' which he condemned in the mechanism of Hume and Adam Smith, but the understanding of society in Adam Ferguson, and the diffusion of intellect throughout the country. This 'enlightenment' was to be overwhelmed by the social and economic forces it had released: the social balance altered; men no longer properly in control. Carlyle became the Cassandra of print-capitalism. Journalism, his 'working church of our modern age' was able to interpret, to warn, but not to influence, as the machine pelted along its iron track. As reporter, academic and conference-groupie, over fifteen years or so, I take the point. 'Kenning' should have replaced 'can-ning'; information technology should have been mobilised against the fearsome problems that face us. Instead we have *Dallas*, bimbos, and Jeffrey Archer.

Observe the crisis of Carlyle's times, that remarkable body-swerve whereby capitalism, in the 1840s, avoided the doom predicted for it. In *Latter-Day Pamphlets* he let fly at George Hudson, the Railway King of York, whose manipulation of the Railway Mania in 1844-45 made him a power in the land. When the Mania ended in 1848 Hudson's mushroom schemes collapsed and he went into exile. 'How much could one have wished that the making of our British railways had gone on with deliberation; that these great works had made themselves not in five years but in fifty-and-five!'

Carlyle wrote when 'Suffrage' decided to laud Hudson for personifying its drive to wealth. 'His worth, I take it, to English railways, much more to English men, will turn out to be extremely inconsiderable; to be incalculable damage, rather!' But Hudson at least got his railways built. A system of 5,000 miles was laid down between 1845 and 1850, an almost incredible mileage, given the absence of concrete, dynamite, earth-movers, etc. It has taken the Germans twenty years to build two hundred miles of high-speed lines, and Britain five years to decide not to build a high-speed link to the Channel Tunnel, but during this period billions of pounds have surged into London office developments, often undertaken on giant rafts floated above decrepit railway stations. Offices have been provided for 1,600,000 office workers, while most studies expect computerisation to cause their number to *decline* by 300,000. Railways are at least a form of transport. An empty office block is an empty office block.

Environmental horrors – heatwaves, pollution, Chernobyl catastrophes – now underline the global crisis, just as cholera advertised urban congestion and lack of sanitation in Carlyle's day. Yet fact and suffrage can still be ludicrously at odds, particularly in the dislocated politics of the United Kingdom. The project of European unity coincides with industrial and social changes as vertiginous as those of the 1830s and 1840s, when transport took over from textiles as the motor of industrial development, a fact of which Britain's economic controllers are only fitfully – at best – aware.

Perhaps poets are more sensitised. Hans-Magnus Enzensberger's *Europe! Europe!* with its sharp observation and boisterous wit brought sense and involvement – however provisionally – and provided the essentially poetic qualities of insight, empathy, role-playing, parody: the material of culture, not the 'facts' of materialism. Carlyle made sense to the Victorians, not least Marx and Engels, because he created resonant images, and enjoined effective action. Indeed, Carlyle went further by opening himself to the unexpected, the irrational, the non-material. He noted the way men thought they acted, and how he felt when writing about them.

Carlyle offered writers and reformers a secularised religious impulse, maintaining evangelical fervour when the agenda changed. After a period when Britain had been cut off from Europe, he was cosmopolitan. He insisted in 1837 on the irreversible impact of the French Revolution, and in *Oliver Cromwell* (1845) he equated Britain's own civil war with it, something which also stressed the 'industrial revolution' whose consequences had still to be faced.

Carlyle's 'philosophical mania' implied an exploding galaxy of radical ideas, kept together by sheer energy and viscerally appealing to a readership which was cosmopolitan – Scots, German, American: Jeffrey, Goethe, Emerson – rather than metropolitan English. This dynamism persisted in his first London years, when his friends the Bullers and John Stuart Mill aligned him with the philosophical radicals, and attracted to him nationalists like Mazzini and the future Young Irelanders Charles Gavan Duffy and John Mitchel. Erudite, friendly, and brilliant in conversation – Dr Johnson a century on – his reaction to 'mechanism', his search for a new national identity, could only be contagious.

Marx and Engels were essentially passive, believing that the tide of history, of economic change, would carry their ideas to fulfilment. What the 'hidden hand' of *laisser-faire* did in the previous generation, dialectical materialism would do in theirs. Assisted by two vastly destructive wars, which derailed any logical development of capitalist industry, various states that called themselves 'scientific socialist' took control over half the world's population. These have now split apart in ways that showed the subordination of the 'new socialist man' to the old Adam: their élites wrecked by laziness, mediocrity and corruption. On the other hand the market economies, with their vast demand for natural resources, their economic inequality, the tasteless affluence of their wealthy and the crushing mediocrity of their popular culture, present no optimistic prospect.

With his insistence on balancing the great impersonal forces against the uniqueness and peculiarity of history, the role of individuals in historical change, and on analysing the physical and mental processes of conveying information, Carlyle still offers sharp, alarming perceptions. Was this because he stood for twenty years or so – between 1830 and 1850 – at the nodal point of so many disciplines which were then interacting in a way that, in the Western world, could scarcely be paralleled today?

Economics, politics, print-capitalism, religion, poetry fused into the movements which he recognised – in advance of practically all of his contemporaries – as altering totally the world in which he lived. He went on to plant concepts like the 'cash-nexus', the 'industrial revolution', 'mechanism', the 'condition of England' – in the national and indeed European consciousness. His remarkable prose was a sort of choric mosaic of excerpts from Scots Calvinism and Common Sense, German idealism and French Saint-Simonianism, thrown together as an existential 'gospel of work' which many besides the liberal John Morley used as a route out of the 'great gulf which is fixed round our faculty and existence'. His style, violent, personal and uncouth though it often seemed, not only helped give British politics an autonomy and energy which Marx and Engels had never expected, but reified British social thought round a Germano-English rather than a classically-derived culture. It incorporated 'interdisciplinary' signifiers derived from fashion and contemporary political discourse, which seemed to make him truly the first post-modernist.

Taken in conjunction with the reappearance of civil society, Carlyle gives the 'modernisation' of Scottish society in the late eighteenth and early nineteenth century an immediate contemporary relevance. He saw Europe in a *Zeitbruch* – what Saint-Simon called a 'critical period' between two plateaus of more gradual development. In a more imaginative – but also more febrile way than Marx – he probed the totality of that society's adaptation. With his background in Scotland, society had to Carlyle a presence much more powerful and moulding than the atomism which Marx inherited from Smith and Bentham. If its logic was more problematic, its resources in religion and social solidarity were much greater, not for antiquarian reasons or a superficial patriotism: Carlyle is where the 'matter of Scotland' dialogue was broken off in the early nineteenth century, and I believe that dialogue to have been of much more than purely Scottish interest.

Civil society has again appeared on the agenda; 'the demon of mechanism' is smoking and thundering in far from metaphoric ways; the 'monstrous ocean-moan of *ennui*' is as paralysing as it was in the 1830s.

After a hiatus, the Carlylean impulse is still at work today, in the remarkable novels of his fellow-Scot Alasdair Gray, who gives himself these lines in *1982 Janine*, when a group of actors are trying to put on a political play:

> 'Bluster has no effect on the British public when
> uttered with a regional accent. You've got to be
> damned hard, and dry and incisive. Use an Anglo-
> Scots accent. The Scotch do change their accents when
> they get into positions of power.'
> 'Thomas Carlyle didn't!' said the writer loudly.
> 'As far as I know Thomas Carlyle was never in a
> position of power,' said the actor, 'fortunately for
> Britain.'
> 'You English are cunning bastards,' said the writer, and
> walked out.

5

The Father of European Federalism?
– Lorimer invents Europe
(1997)

James Lorimer ought to be remembered as someone who coupled Scotland's sense of nationality to the international peace movement and the cause of European federalism, of which he was truly the pioneer. Originally carried in the _Scotsman_, a revised version of this essay appeared in _History Today_.

In a dull election, two issues became salient which threatened to accelerate the collapse of the United Kingdom as a state. One was Europe, the other the future of Scotland. The first divided the Conservative Party as disastrously as Free Trade had done before the débàcle in 1906. In 1992 John Major's 'soap-box' defence of the British constitution had helped his unexpected success. But an attempt in 1994-97 by his young Scottish Secretary, Michael Forsyth, to play cultural nationalism against political nationalism – notably by shipping the Stone of Scone back North – only provoked the home rulers.

Opinion polls showed the Scots to be more pro-European, and indeed more republican, than any other part of the United Kingdom. Forsyth, going for broke, preached the teaching of Scottish history in the schools. Garlic against the European vampire? But the more the Scots remembered their history – and not necessarily the _Braveheart_ bit of it – the less British they felt.

Scotland had always been the absentee of European nationalism. Although countless novelists and poets of 'unhistorical' nationalities – Manzoni, Petofi, Mickiewicz, Topelius – modelled themselves either on 'Ossian' MacPherson or Walter Scott, churning out epics or historical novels justifying their people's claim to statehood, the Scots got as far as print capitalism and, apparently, stuck. They seemed quite content to cash in on access to the British (never English) Empire, defend cultural distinctiveness, and leave it at that. The Czech historian Miroslav Hroch's three stage typology of the formation of European national movements – élite mobilisation, the creation or capture of institutions, the mass movement – didn't seem to work. Or did it?

> 'I to the hills shall lift my eyes.
> From whence cometh my aid.'

Thus sang the Covenanters, the Scottish Calvinist radicals, given in the 1680s to assembling in mutinous conventicles on the moors. High above Edinburgh, on the summit of the Castle rock, stands one symbol of Scottish separateness, intellectual and political – the Scottish National War Memorial. Built in the 1920s in the rich late gothic which was influenced by Scotland's 'auld alliance' with France, its architect was Sir Robert Lorimer (1864-1929), next to Charles Rennie Mackintosh the greatest of his generation, the reviver of the Scottish vernacular style. The names of 100,000 dead, 13% of British casualties (Scotland then had 10% of the British population) commemorate a tragedy of Scottish and European history which would have particularly grieved Lorimer's father, had he lived to see it.

James Lorimer, Professor of Public Law at Edinburgh University, and Laird of Kellie in Fife, is better known in Germany than in England, and suggests a different sort of nationalism from that which Hroch surveys – civic rather than ethnic, and always alert to international relations. Perhaps uniquely Scots? Lorimer was one of the founders of modern International Law, and in two substantial volumes of *The Institutes of the Law of Nations* which he published in 1884 he created that bogey of English, though not

Scottish, patriotism. the first proposal for a federal Europe.

Lorimer was born in Perthshire in 1819 but, like so many Scots during and after the 'Enlightenment', was partly educated abroad, at the Universities of Berlin, Bonn and Geneva as well as Edinburgh. This reflected the cosmopolitanism of a Scottish juridical tradition which prided itself on its affinity to Roman Law rather than the Common Law of the English. Nowhere in his work are there the limited horizons that one associates with the utilitarianism of such Victorians as Sir William Holdsworth or Professor AV Dicey. In fact, the opposite. In the decade of the 1880s, which found British imperialism at its zenith (Burma and Egypt annexed, Gordon martyred at Khartoum) Lorimer's Europeanism went out from a strong sense of the political community of units smaller than the nation-state. He wrote in his *Institutes*:

> 'The notion that the progress of the Anglo-Saxon race
> can only take place by the expansion of England
> appears to me to belong to the exclusively English, or
> rather I would say London, school of thought. The
> Londoner conceives that steam and electricity will
> stamp out any traces of separate national life which
> still linger in Scotland or in Ireland.'

The England of Sir John Seeley and Sir Charles Dilke talked of its global destiny, and founded the Imperial Federation League in 1884. Lorimer's European project was radically different. Ideas for an international peacekeeping body had come from Henry IV of France in the seventeenth, and from Leibniz, Rousseau and Kant in the eighteenth century. But by the 1870s the rise of nationalism had sidelined them. Even when Lorimer's friend the Swiss-German jurist Johann Kaspar Bluntschli (1808-1881), co-founder with him of the Institute of International Law in Ghent in 1873, proposed a confederation in his *Europa als Staatenbund*, in 1871, it was to be German-dominated and heavily-armed.

Lorimer – disarmer and (qualified) democrat – was more radical – rather to Bluntschli's alarm, who regarded his federal scheme as 'an international republic'. The Scotsman worked out in some detail 'how to find international equivalents for the factors known to national law as legislation, jurisdiction and execution'. Lorimer would preserve peace through a European superstate. This was to have a Senate and a Chamber of Deputies. The six great powers – Britain, France, Austria, Italy, Russia and Germany – would each get five life Senators and fifteen elected Deputies; the smaller countries a lesser number. The ministry would be fifteen-strong; five of its members would be Senators and the rest would include one representative from each great power. These would be balanced by a civil and criminal judiciary under a European Attorney-General. The seat of government would be Geneva; the language of government French.

The executive of the United States of Europe would command a small police-force type army and a General Staff of proto-Eurocrats granted wide powers

> 'The cosmopolitan service would become the most
> ambitious career in which young men of talent could
> engage; it would appeal to the imagination far beyond
> diplomacy or the Indian Civil Service, and would
> speedily be embraced by those who were most gifted
> by nature and most favoured by fortune.'

Securing European peace was at the head of Lorimer's agenda – natural enough given the wars the continent had endured since 1848. But his scheme wasn't, like earlier attempts, bound by existing power-structures. The European legislature would decide what was national and what was not. It would create unity through great public works projects – 'architectural structures, both sacred and secular, of prodigious magnitude and grandeur' (this was the decade of Sir Edward Watkin's first Channel Tunnel scheme).

But it would also gradually dissolve the old great powers:

'Its tendency would be to protect and give freer scope
to ethnic peculiarities, whilst their anti-national action
would add to its strength.'

Among the political communities of the future were his own people,
the Scots:

'There seems every reason to anticipate that Scotland,
at no distant period, will lay claim to that local
autonomy for which Ireland has never ceased to cry
out, and which her own incapacity for self-government
can alone justify us in refusing her.'

Lorimer was not always 'politically correct'. The stress that he put
on bureaucracy reflected the Scottish Enlightenment's concern with
the importance of civic virtù: that, in the words of his close friend
the 'modernist' presbyterian theologian Thomas Erskine of
Linlathen (1788-1870), 'good government is preferable to self-
government'. But though Lorimer published in 1857 a pamphlet
Political Progress Not Necessarily Democratic, critical of franchise
extension without provision for educated minorities, he was
refreshingly free of Victorian racial prejudice. He contemplated
the Anglo-Indians as the successors of the Anglo-Saxons: 'they may
conquer their conquerors as the Anglo-Saxon heiresses conquered
the Norman nobles'.

Was Lorimer's United States of Europe an impractical utopia?
The losers tend to get written out of history. Up to the 1960s
young Scots were taught at school about Cavour and Italian unity
(a Good Thing) and Bismarck and German unity (a Less Good
Thing), despite the appalling consequences of both. Federal
schemes, like small nationalities and city states, were ignored,
though after nearly fifty years of successful European cooperation
the perspective has been changing. Space is being made for
federalism and diffused sovereignty. In this Scots, such as the Liberal
statesman James Bryce (1838-1922), proponent of the League of

Nations, the Tory FS Oliver (1864-1934), who proposed a British federation, played besides Lorimer a disproportionate role.

But the man who followed most closely in Lorimer's tradition was the polymathic regionalist Sir Patrick Geddes (1854-1932), who erupted in Edinburgh just at the end of Lorimer's career with a fusion of architecture and communitarianism, which he embodied in the Outlook Tower, a fascinating range of buildings, also on the Castle Hill, part social laboratory, part student residence.

Lorimer was more than a random precursor. He was the disciple of two remarkable Scots. The first was Erskine, with his humanistic ideal of a 'teaching Christ' and of politics as a religious vocation, the friend of Carlyle, Madame de Staël, Guizot and the Christian Socialist FD Maurice. The second was Sir William Hamilton (1788-1856), the last great master of the 'Scottish School' of deductive philosophy, still influential in France and America when utilitarianism was carrying all before it in Britain. Lorimer carried on the deductive tradition, and fought so hard for the autonomy and broad philosophic curriculum of the Scottish universities that he became the hero of George Elder Davie's influential study of Scottish higher education, *The Democratic Intellect* of 1961.

Equally presciently, he advocated proportional representation and female suffrage. As contemporary Scots historians have been clearing away the 'tartan and tourism' overlay from a Victorian past which seemed stifled by dreary sectarian conflicts, Lorimer, like Carlyle, or the geologist and journalist Hugh Miller, the philosopher JF Ferrier and the woman suffragist Marion Reid, has re-emerged as a figure with something original and challenging to say. In the legal philosophy of Professor Neil MacCormick, who holds Lorimer's old chair at Edinburgh, or Judge Edward David of the European Court in Luxembourg, the themes of international law are salient, as are those of evolving conventions which mediate between the civic and the international.

But James Lorimer was not simply a jurist. Unreliable as a literary critic, whose judgement on *Wuthering Heights* – 'the only consolation which we have on reflecting on it is that it will never be generally read' – became legendary, he did better as antiquarian and conservationist. In 1878 he took over the derelict Kellie Castle in Fife, but instead of 'modernising' it along the lines of Prince Albert's Balmoral – the fate of so many old houses in Scotland – he and his architect John Currie revived the functional 'Franco-Scottish' craftsmanship of the seventeenth century, and started his son's influential career. Kellie is still one of the gems of the National Trust for Scotland. The 'Scotland in Europe' theme – so popular with Nationalists in the 1990s – was taken up again by Sir Robert's disciple, Robert Hurd, uncle of the former British foreign secretary Douglas Hurd, in an influential manifesto *Building Scotland* (1943) which united the causes of modern and vernacular architecture, social planning and small nationalism.

With the 'democratic' dawn of 1989-90 ending in ideological confusion and the reassertion of national egoism, Lorimer's legacy provides an example of a small nationalism that is grounded in respect for law and civic identity both at home and abroad, and also has a cultural content which is both local and international – and exciting. Lorimer mourned the blinkered vision of nineteenth-century nationalism:

> 'When rational men cross the frontiers of the separate
> states of which they are citizens, (must they) of
> necessity leave their wits behind them and in all their
> more important relations with each other, revert to the
> condition of savages or sink to that of fools?'

Lorimer's concept of 'positive' international law, disarmament, and a common European culture, ought to appeal to those faced with the post-Maastricht impasse, who need to realise that a settlement must involve both an imaginative commitment to Europe, and a concept of 'subsidiarity' which gives real power to regions and culture-nations such as Scotland. The alternative of a recrudescent militarised nationalism is likely to give us more war memorials, like his son's – if there's anyone around to put them up.

6
The Golden Age of the Carpetbaggers
(1982)

Stimulated by Roy Jenkins' electoral campaign
in Glasgow Hillhead in 1982, this *Scotsman*
piece surveyed the rich history of English
politicians making their way in Scottish politics,
and the conditions which allowed this curious
combination of native ideology and foreign
representation to happen. Jenkins turned out,
in fact, to be the last of the line.

One summer afternoon, about a century ago, three young men climbed a hill in Fife and looked out over the Kingdom and across the Firth of Forth to the Lothian coast. 'What a grateful thought,' observed Augustine Birrell, 'that there is not an acre in this vast and varied landscape which is not represented at Westminster by a London barrister.' One of his companions, Richard Burdon Haldane, MP for East Lothian and coming man in the great Liberal Party, was to become Lord Chancellor. The third, a Yorkshire-born product of Balliol, climbed, as Disraeli put it, 'to the top of the greasy pole': Herbert Henry Asquith, MP for East Fife and Prime Minister, 1908-1916. Birrell's phrase must surely have recurred to the mind of Roy Jenkins, Asquith's biographer, as he campaigns in the unfamiliar streets of Glasgow Hillhead. And not, perhaps, entirely reassuringly. Asquith was the last man who led a Liberal government. When he lost East Fife in the 1918 election he was returned for Paisley, in the first of several illusory Liberal revivals. He lost Paisley in 1924, and although that election laid the first Labour government low, it destroyed the Liberals completely.

Asquith's election for East Fife in 1886 inaugurated the golden age of the 'carpet-bagger' in Scottish politics; his dismissal from Paisley almost, but not quite, ended it. Whether Mr Jenkins will be able to revive the genre is, of course, a current preoccupation.

The term 'carpet-bagger', meaning a politician living out of a suitcase, originated in the American West, and gained currency after the Civil War as a means of describing the Northern politicians who were returned by the briefly multi-racial electorates in the states of the defeated South. It has since been extended to embrace career politicians who gain election, in the normal democratic manner, for constituencies with which they have otherwise no connection. The carpetbagger is not imposed by a patron, although he might be assisted in his nomination by a local oligarchy or interest group; he is a product of electoral deference, not of coercion.

So we can't really talk of carpetbaggers in Scotland before the 1832 Reform Act. Until then virtually every Scottish constituency – there were only 4,500 electors! – was sewn-up by one patron or another, and in the late eighteenth century most of them (Dr Bruce Lenman has estimated 36 out of 45) were subject to the nomination of Henry Dundas, 'the Scotch Dictator' who boasted that it was in his power 'to prevent the return of (even) one Member for Scotland hostile to the government.' MPs approved by Dundas had often about as much connection with their constituencies as Vatican functionaries have with their titular sees in Greece or Asia Minor. To try on the other hand, to muscle in on this 'huge rotten burgh' was to court almost certain bankruptcy, as the father of Elizabeth Grant of Rothiemurchus found out.

1832 was the millenium of the Scottish Whigs; the electorate rose to 65,000, and the first generation of MPs tended to be Scottish lawyers or landowners. The arcane controversies of Scottish politics, and of religious politics in particular, tended to put southerners off. Thomas Babington Macaulay became MP for Edinburgh in 1838, and spent a miserable time in the seat, increasingly pestered by men he regarded as sectarian bigots, until he was thrown out in 1847. From about this time Scottish affairs became even more religion-dominated, as a result of the Disruption of 1843. The Scots preoccupation with 'controversial divinity' was assumed, however, to lead to electoral honesty, a quality praised for example by Alexander Russel, the editor of the *Scotsman*, when he appeared before commissioners investigating the otherwise pretty dirty campaign of 1868. One of the losers in that year, Anthony Trollope, who had taken on the primeval corruption of Beverley in Yorkshire, was not so sure. In his novel *The Three Clerks* (1858) he produces a rascally Scots MP called Undecimus Scott, who inveigles the ambitious civil servant Alaric Tudor into putting himself up for the burgh of Strathbogie – an enterprise whose failure through Undy Scott's treachery brings about Tudor's ruin.

An even more prejudiced view of Scots political morality came from the high Tory William Edmonstone Aytoun. In his tale 'How we stood for the Dreepdailly Burghs' (1845) Aytoun threw his Flashman-like hero, Augustus Dunshunner, into a 'grouped burgh' constituency pullulating with examples of venality, intrigue and hypocrisy:

> 'Hark ye, Dunshunner, more than half of the Scottish burghs are at this moment held by nominees!'
> 'You amaze me Bob! The thing is impossible! The Reform Bill, that great charter of our Liberties. . . '
> 'Bravo! There spoke the Whig! The Reform Bill, you think, put an end to nomination? It did nothing of the kind; it merely transferred it. Did you ever hear of such things as CLIQUES?'
> 'I have, but they are tremendously unpopular.'
> 'Nevertheless, they hold the returning power. There is a clique in almost every town throughout Scotland, which leads the electors as quietly, but as surely, as the blind man is conducted by his dog. These are modelled on the true Venetian principles of secrecy and terrorism. They control the whole constituency, put in the member, and in return monopolise the patronage

of the place. If you have the Clique with you, you are almost sure of your election; if not, except in the larger towns, you have not a shadow of success.'

The Dreepdailly Burghs – which cries out for television adaption – dramatised a feature nearly unique to Scotland: the segregation of burghs from their surrounding countryside into 'districts' or 'grouped burghs'. Three such still survive: Stirling, Falkirk and Grangemouth, Dunfermline, (with Cowdenbeath and Lochgelly) and Kirkcaldy (which includes Burntisland, Kinghorn. and Leven); before 1914 there were 14, the most spectacular being the Wick district, whose southernmost burgh was Dingwall, and whose northernmost was Kirkwall in Orkney. Such burghs were often run by juntas on the principles Ayton described; and could thus suit a 'money-bag' candidate prepared to square their leading figures. There was little outright bribery but Elizabeth Haldane, RB Haldane's sister and a shrewd observer of nineteenth century Scotland, noted that before the Ballot Act of 1872 local merchants could keep their customers in line by offering them long-term credit so long as they voted the right way.

The further north you got, the rougher the politics became – even after the ballot. James Bryce, Professor of Civil Law at Oxford, tried to get in for the Wick District in 1874 against Sir John Pender, a telegraph magnate unseated from Totnes for bribery in 1868. Bryce a 'moderate radical' had some local connections, and was backed by Wick and Thurso; Pender, nominally a Liberal, squared the Duke of Sutherland's interest at Golspie, bought over the Provost of Kirkwall, and in the *John O'Groats Gazette* launched a smear campaign against his high-minded opponent – Bryce consorted with Communists, was an atheist, etc. Pender won.

Bryce subsequently got in for Aberdeen South in 1885, and his electors felt honoured by a visit twice every year during which the great constitutional theorist 'occupied himself delivering addresses on political, literary or educational topics, and always setting apart one day for callers who might wish to see him on business of any kind.' Deference had taken over from expectations of patronage.

Patronage had probably reached its apogee in the late 1840s, when Arthur Anderson, MP for Orkney and Shetland, combatted an economic downturn in the island economies by staffing the Brazilian Navy with Shetlanders. But although he was the chairman of the P&O steamer company he was a Shetlander by birth and so not, strictly speaking, a 'carpet-bagger'.

Between 1874 and 1886 there was a change in the Scottish political climate, and one which made it easier for 'carpet-baggers' to get elected. There were several reasons for this – North-South communications were steadily improving; agricultural depression after 1873 made it more difficult for the traditional landed élite to serve in Parliament; a supply of relatively safe Liberal seats vanished in 1884 when householder suffrage was extended to Ireland; and Gladstone demonstrated in 1879-80 that the Scots were apparently prepared to put the quality of their MPs before the representation of local interests. The change thereafter was rapid. Edinburgh, which between 1880 and 1882 swapped its two local MPs for two southern barristers may have been a little premature, but by 1885 Oxford was twice as well represented as Edinburgh University as the *alma mater* of Scottish Liberal MPs, and twenty-five years later over 50 per cent of them had London addresses.

Paradoxically, this development occurred just when Scottish affairs were being given more publicity, through land disturbances in the Highlands, and when, in 1885, the position of Secretary for Scotland was revived. Yet even radicals tended to live in the South, and visit their constituencies fairly infrequently. Dr Gavin Clark, founder-member of the Scottish Labour Party and Crofter MP for Caithness, 1885-1900, was almost an archetype of the Hampstead Lefty. The Scottish Labour Party, however, was a protest *inter alia* against carpetbagging. Its leading light, Keir Hardie had contested North Lanark in 1888 partly in protest at the importing of a Welsh barrister Wynford Philipps into a constituency of whose problems he was totally ignorant, and the Radical-Liberal pressure-group the Young Scots Society, founded originally in 1900 to oppose the Boer War, also made this a major plank in their campaigning.

Yet still the carpetbaggers came. Gladstone remained in Midlothian until 1895; his biographer John Morley sat for Montrose Burghs from 1896 to 1908. What with Asquith, Birrell, Haldane and Bryce, when the Liberals broke through in 1906 almost half the elected members of the Cabinet sat for Scottish seats.

They were able to live the quiet life because Scottish business – and even domestic business as a whole – had been very limited. In any peacetime budget the civil estimates only amounted to around 25 per cent, compared with over 75 per cent today. Things changed during the Liberal Government of 1906-14 with increased welfare legislation. Scottish business grew until the Scottish Secretary could no longer be a peer yet Scotland was slow to adopt the 'new Liberalism', with its concentration on redistributive social reform. Scots radicals of this stamp would tend to call themselves socialists and write for or read Tom Johnston's *Forward* rather than CP Scott's *Manchester Guardian*.

The First World War effectively destroyed the Liberal Party. In Scotland it had been the party of power for so long that, once separated from office, its local organisation – which usually consisted of a solicitor in each of the more important burghs, simply crumbled away. From fifty eight seats in 1910, the Liberals had only nine in 1924. They took with them the carpetbaggers, or most of them. Labour rose from three seats in 1910 to seven in 1918 and twenty nine in 1922. Little islands of Liberal support survived the deluge here and there – mainly on the East Coast. Tony Benn's maternal grandfather, DT Holmes, might have been wiped out in 1918 at Govan but his father William Wedgwood Benn held Leith as a Liberal until 1927. Michael Foot's brother, elaborated from Dingle into Dingle Mackintosh Foot, held Dundee from 1931 to 1945.

Because Scotland was still politically unstable – demonstrated by Dundee's dismissal of Winston Churchill in 1922 – it did not pick up many aspirant Unionist Cabinet members, who could usually find convenient, safe and undemanding berths in the Home

Counties. Unionists in the inter-war period tended to be native Scots, and a pretty dim lot they were: there is nothing more useless at Westminster than a Scots lawyer, and after the Unionist landslide in 1931 there were lots of them. Any byelection, however, has a magnetic effect during unstable periods, and two in particular brought the press up in droves.

In 1933, Lord Beaverbrook – the *bête noir* of the Conservatives – put a candidate of his own up against the National Liberal in East Fife, and in the course of an exceedingly tortuous campaign, appeared in the constituency with his entourage and, disliking his own candidate, apparently produced a Liberal as well. Eric Linklater, standing lucklessly as a National Party of Scotland candidate, incorporated aspects of the contest into *Magnus Merriman*. Beyond changing Beaverbrook's sex, he needed to do little to make it into high farce.

In February 1936 the Government had to get a seat for Malcolm MacDonald, Ramsay's son and then Dominion Secretary, and picked on Ross and Cromarty. Like a jam jar to a wasp, this attracted Randolph Churchill, standing in for his father as chief nuisance to the Baldwin Government. The candidates and their machines descended on the puzzled crofters, who were more concerned about the worst winter in decades. Pretty soon the weather overtook Churchill and MacDonald and the Labour candidate Hector McNeil. The election became an exercise in mutual aid between politicians preoccupied more with surviving the contest than with winning it. MacDonald won, but the parties seemed thereafter to become very leery about picking Scottish seats for such contests. Unless your candidate was blatantly Scots, it was much easier to elevate some suburban nonentity to the peerage than to try to come to terms with strange Scottish causes and wild Scottish weather.

Labour were on the whole careful not to foist entirely alien MPs on the Scots although this happened periodically with union-sponsored candidates. The pendulum has swung the other way, particularly in Glasgow with the heroic figures of James Maxton and John Wheatley followed by a succession of obscure local councillors. Even so, the Scottish cities have established different traditions. Aberdeen, with a history of socialist activity going back to the 1890s, and strong local Labour control, has rarely had a resident Labour MP. Hector Hughes, who represented North Aberdeen in 1945, was an Irish barrister. Adopted in the final weeks of the 1945 campaign, he succeeded a Welsh barrister, Garro-Jones, fighting off a challenge from Prof. CEM Joad of *Brains Trust* fame. Dundee's choices have been even more exotic. In 1939 this large and left-wing Labour Party chose VK Krishna Menon, the leading figure of the Indian left (not entirely surprising, given Dundee's close Indian connections). Menon proved too left wing for Transport House who expelled him in 1940 for sharing platforms with Communist speakers. He was succeeded by the scarcely less bizarre figure of John Strachey, an old Etonian who had been a Labour MP, 1929-31, then dallied with Sir Oswald Mosley's New Party before emerging as the most prominent Communist fellow-traveller of the 1930s. 'Comrade X', George Orwell called him, 'Author of Marxism for Infants. He would be ready to die on the barricades, in theory anyway, but you notice that he still leaves his bottom waistcoat button undone.' The Dundee comrades were to find, almost as soon as they elected him, that Strachey was moving to the right. During the campaign he got on better with his opponent, Dingle Foot, than with his supporters. As his biographer Hugh Thomas wrote, 'After the day's electioneering they would dine together in a private room screened from their supporters, and (once elected) Strachey and his wife walked along the train to where Robert Boothby was waiting for them in his sleeper with a bottle of champagne.'

Strachey died in 1963. Since then only a handful of 'non-resident' Englishmen have sat for Scottish constituencies. In the present Parliament only 10 per cent of MPs have main addresses in London. The local problems induced by persistent recessions, the decline of the political agent, the baffling consequences of local government reform, all mean that MPs must devote at least a day a week to constituency affairs – not the two days a year that Bryce got away with. It is scarcely perhaps a prospect that appeals to Roy Jenkins, who was not well known as a Birmingham MP during his last period in the Commons. On the other hand, having a front-bencher, actual or potential around the place stimulates interest in Scottish problems, whether his party likes it or not. Sir Alec Douglas-Home's election for Kinross turned out something of a godsend for the Labour Party in 1963. On balance, in terms of actual impact, our centralised political system means that there has been little to choose between the Liberal high-flyers of the pre-First World War epoch and the ex-councillors who followed them. The first rarely thought about Scotland; the second may have come to realise that Parliament rarely thinks about them.

7
Decoding Buchan
(1989)

In retrospect, this piece from the *Scotsman* can be seen as one of the earlier rehabilitations of Buchan, whose reputation has grown in step with the decline and fall of his party. What emerges is a complex figure and one whose career mirrors the Scots bourgeois identity. The power that Toryism had once enjoyed in Scottish society rested on a humane, undogmatic pragmatism and these foundations rapidly decayed after 1979.

I must have read my first book by John Buchan, *The Thirty-Nine Steps*, at around eleven, and remember identifying with Hannay fleeing across the Galloway moors, the Black Stone's aircraft wheeling overhead. Even at that stage it was the writer's engagement with his landscape – my landscape – of the Southern Uplands that mattered: the peat-hags, the bleached grasses, the endless, convex hills with their ribbons of roads and dykes. Thereafter Buchan novels became as much part of my regular habits as pipe-smoking, wearing old tweeds until they fell apart, walking everywhere. You see before you, in that sense, a Buchan enthusiast.

But, initially, rather a guilty one, or at least someone disposed to differentiate between a 'good' and a 'bad' Buchan. The good Buchan was the man with the ability to suggest the grey distances of the Border hills or the smell of wood-smoke from an inn at evening in the Bavarian woods, and the anticipation of an omelette, ham and steins of cool beer. This and the possibility of *something happening*, the prospect that the road, smelling of an early-morning shower, would lead to 'escapes and hurried journeys'.

The 'bad Buchan' was the habitué of West End clubs, where men with hyphenated names, titles and remarkable reputations got together to save civilisation (themselves) from Communistic agitators, cosmopolitan intellectuals, and the lower races. I remember Alan Bennett in *Forty Years On* capturing this with lines like, 'If the King of England should marry a divorced woman, that would be a feather in the cap of an organisation of communists and international pederasts: I mean the Labour Party.'

Nor did Buchan on sex seem very instructive to those of us trying to catch up after a Scottish adolescence. All Buchan could offer were girls with boyish figures to whom 'getting in the club' meant getting Archie Roylance to admit that they had bags of pluck, and were as good as the chaps who were members. At the beginning of *A Prince of the Captivity* there occurs the line (anent the errant wife of the hero), 'There were always plenty of men eager to mount her' – meaning 'to loan her a horse' – but you see what I mean.

So although I'd read and admired Janet Adam Smith's fine biography, Buchan tended to remain what the Germans call *Unterhaltungsliteratur* – entertainment literature – until into the 1970s. I remember flipping through David Daniell's *Interpreter's House* when it first came out in 1976 and thinking that he took Buchan a bit too seriously by drawing parallels with Bunyan's imagery. But almost immediately I left Britain for Germany I was commissioned to do an essay on Scott, and found Buchan's biography not just a model of what a critical biography should be, but one which suggested a man of immensely wide reading and judicious selectivity, with an eye for the obscure gem, like that remarkable introduction to *The Chronicles of the Canongate*, which Buchan considered 'equal in its clarity and autumnal vision to Turgenev'. *Walter Scott*, of 1932, proved to be like a mirror, which showed Buchan's output up at a different, more suggestive angle.

An influence here was the work of a contemporary Scots critic, Dr Douglas Gifford, and in particular his essay on *The Master of*

Ballantrae. In analysing this – and in particular the credibility of Ephraim MacKellar – Douglas stressed the Scottish tradition of the unreliable narrator and the structural irony that this device creates. It seemed obvious that after Stevenson (both as literary theorist and active author), Barrie, and the revived James Hogg, the twentieth-century Scots novel had to be treated very carefully indeed – and particularly the novel with first-person narration, in which Buchan excelled.

The final thing that got me under way was my interest in political fiction. The spy novel occurs on the fringes of this genre, but themes to do with political ideals and behaviour and organisation occured frequently enough in his novels to suggest that Buchan ought to be considered a major performer. During and after 1983 I re-read most of the 'contemporary' novels with an interest which grew with every book I picked up. This took me back to the secondary literature, to my own reading in the history of Buchan's Scotland, and the following deductions from the evidence on offer began to emerge.

One: Buchan was an enormously erudite and allusive writer and the allusions were not inserted for fun. They work at a deeper level than the 'good read' of the text.

Two: Buchan's attitude to the boundary between the civilised and the primitive was much more complicated than his character Lumley's 'a thread, a pane of glass' in *The Power House* (1913), which Graham Greene believed to represent Buchan's own views.

Three: The business of story-telling – the praxis, if you like – was very important to Buchan and was bound up with a detailed formal knowledge of philosophy, psychology and anthropology.

Four: Buchan's own efficient, undemonstrative personality masked considerable tensions and ambivalences, personal and political.

Five: In a cultural sense, these crystallised in his ambiguous attitudes to Scotland, Britain and the Empire.

Six: Buchan had a highly-developed facility for irony and wit, a delight in double-bluff and an ability carefully to conceal his tracks.

Let me give some examples in support of each.

One Buchan's allusiveness: 'You think that civilisation is as solid as the earth you tread on. I tell you it is a thread, a pane of glass.' This is perhaps the most famous line in all of Buchan, though we must remember that it's the view of an arch-villain, not of the narrator, Edward Leithen, himself. Now, where did it come from?

I'd seen it somewhere before, in another contemporary novel, also about politics. In a bizarre and alarming scene at the end of HG Wells' *The New Machiavelli* (1910), in which Tory politicians discuss the collapse of civilisation while a London house burns about their ears, Mr Evesham (a thinly-disguised Arthur Balfour) speaks: 'But what is civilisation? A mere thin net of habits and associations.'

Is Lumley Balfour, to whom *The Power House* is dedicated? Lumley's conversation is everything that Buchan said Balfour's was – ingenious, super-cerebral, ruthless. But the allusion goes even further back, to Disraeli's last novel, *Falconet* (a name Buchan would later use for a character), where a nameless Nihilist uses a similar line about modern civilisation 'resolving itself into its constituent parts'. We know that Buchan wanted to write a study of Disraeli, viewing him (I think) with a kind of fascinated horror as an example of Lumleyite 'pure intellect' let loose in politics. If we study Disraeli's own reading-matter we end up with Carlyle's *Characteristics* of 1831 and his vision of the 'thin crust' of civilisation giving way and plunging France into the raging inferno of the revolution and the terror.

So, *Two*: 'The civilised and the primitive' is a recurrent theme in Buchan but, as Dr Daniell has stressed, it is the starting-point of further complexity, not a simplifying formula. In *The Three Hostages* (1924) Hannay encounters a psychologist, Dr Greenslade, who assures him that 'the civilised is far simpler than the primeval'. Unlike Herbert Spencer, who argued that society evolved from the 'homogenous' to the 'heterogenous', Buchan believed that the 'elementary and lawless' subconscious remained as a complicating and irrationalising factor.

The theme, as I say, is constant and can be related to the juxtaposition in nineteenth century Scotland (more than most places in north Europe) of the advanced and the primitive: the railway porter who could chant the old ballads, the sailor returning from a modern steamer to a community still controlled by Old Testament religion. The contrast was not one which necessarily led to destructive tensions, or demanded (as contemporary imperialists tended to insist) a form of élite-led modernisation to protect it. Lumley is, after all, brought down by Leithen, a Scots lawyer, and a North Country Labour MP, neither of them exceptional and both representatives of the dull reliability of the two-party system.

Matters changed after World War I and Buchan realised that social breakdown had unleashed an enormous potential for atavistic destruction, through the rise of individuals unlimited by traditional social constraints. Civilisation really was under threat. I think he realised this peculiarly acutely because he had been at the centre of wartime intelligence and propaganda, which acted on lines of total *Realpolitik*, and thus were a sort of barometer, indicating the precipitate decay of old conventions.

After the war, in part fortified by a crash course in psychoanalysis, he set out in quest of a new point of social balance, in which ritual, locality and leadership would be used to balance the class politics of industrial society, and such atavistic threats to it.

Three: One of Buchan's chief tools in this enterprise was his grounding in philosophy and anthropology, and the influence in particular of his fellow-Scots James George Frazer, Andrew Lang, and the anthropological school associated with his own Free Church of Scotland. This took the form of a concentration on the rituals of rebirth and kingship, and on the reconciliation of the 'animus' of rational, calculating man with an 'anima' or 'back-self' of more intuitive, traditionary qualities and 'nature'. The consequences of not attempting this reconciliation were made patent in the character of Dominick Medina in *The Three Hostages* (arguably an updating of Disraeli) and the collective schizophrenic madness of the parish of Woodilee in *Witch Wood* (1928). His attempts at reconciliation are to be found in *John MacNab* (1930) and *A Prince of the Captivity* (1933).

This recourse to myth was not, in this period, unique. The fascination with psychoanalysis and anthropology is a common theme in the Scottish Renaissance, constantly recurring in Edwin Muir, Neil Gunn and Lewis Grassic Gibbon. Buchan's ultimate point of rest, in *Sick Heart River* (1940), when the autobiographical Sir Edward Leithen decides to stay with the Hare Indians and organise their hunting, at peril of his life, replicates the same idea of a 'golden age' of human and ecological balance, to be found in Gibbon and Gunn.

Thus Buchan's position is both ecologically 'holistic' (can we equate Peter Pienaar with JC Smuts?) and casts back to the philosophical system-building of the Scots tradition – away from utilitarian atomism and what (I've no doubt) he would have denounced as the linguistic nit-picking of the logical positivism which was coming to underlie English cultural life.

Four: Given Buchan's views about the England which sustained him, it would be very surprising if our auld acquaintance the *Doppelgänger* didn't make his appearance at this point. Buchan after World War I was so eminently the epitome of Unionist capitalist rationality that something has to show up. In Buchan's case the support offered to the infant Scottish renaissance through his editing of *The Northern Muse* (1924) and his championing of MacDiarmid's first vernacular collection, *Sangschaw* (1924). And in Buchan's subsequent prose there's a strong and quite subversive Scottishness which seems actually to increase as he's more and more incorporated into the establishment (or, perhaps, as he *fails* to be incorporated into the establishment, as he made little mark on the Commons compared with the much younger – and equally 'literary' – Walter Elliot).

Was he, in fact, as well-adjusted as Janet Adam Smith and Catherine Carswell made out? Was his persistent ill-health totally physical, or was it partly psychosomatic? Did his Jungian remedies

the pilgrimage leads *away* from England – just as it has done with another writer who has made the spy novel into a commentary on the 'Condition of England', John le Carré.

Six: I called this essay 'Decoding Buchan', and you'll see by now the double-meaning of this title. It may also give you some idea why I've found the man and his work increasingly fascinating. One Chinese box, once opened, reveals another, and so on; but the range of the man, his continuing popularity, the way in which he remains a key to our understanding of the peculiar national experience of Scotland in the epoch of Union and Empire, makes it important to crack the enigma.

Buchan's was an odd and in many ways an unsatisfactory career, and he seems to have realised this, in a tight-lipped way. He had recognised the role that creative writers had played in the Scottish identity – Scott most of all, and MacDiarmid in his own day – but his own interventions had limited success. But neither had he succeeded in English politics, while his translation to Canada (which he probably could have managed in the 1920s) came as his health was failing.

So my hunch is that, in his latter novels, he communicates his critique – of his own career, of the causes he served – in code. The imagery, as ever, is that of the test. The competitor, in apparently good shape, is the British character. The landscape to be struggled over is faultlessly drawn, but the code suggests a further, subterranean dimension: the green roads, the caves, the secret places of *Midwinter* (1923). And the competitor?

There's a short story, *The Loathly Opposite* (1928), which he wrote about cryptographers in World War I – I think one of the first ever stories by any writer which deals with the 'shop', the hard graft of intelligence work – in which the leading British decrypter envisages his German opponent as a ruthless, sensual woman. Long after the war a colleague discovers the German to be a humane and sensitive medical man, the death of whose young son 'Reinmar' in the 'starvation months' led to his making the mistake which enabled the Englishman to crack his cipher.

The German doctor now has the Englishman under psychoanalytic treatment, but will not unmask himself. The Englishman needs the illusion, the 'necessary lie', if his character is to hold together. This seems to me to reveal as much about the Britain of his day and, perhaps, of ours, as it reveals of Buchan.

8
The Jacks Case:
a Scandal of the True-Blue Clyde?
(1997)

The Unionist scandal of the Jacks case
betrayed a sense in which the World War I
deprived Scottish Liberalism of its ethical
virginity and its unionist high-mindedness.
From that point it isn't far to the
accommodation with right-wing régimes in
Italy and Germany which the bosses
of cotton and chemicals managed in the
interwar years – something not taken
sufficiently into account in explaining the
Scottish bourgeoisie's
apprehension about democracy.

Ten months into world war. Army chiefs – hopes of spending Christmas in Berlin long forgotten – are raging about the shortage of shells to pound their entrenched opponents. Lord Fisher, the brainy, neurotic First Sea Lord, is screaming for the head of Winston Churchill, the naval minister. On 26 May 1915 HH Asquith's Liberal government is forced into coalition with the Unionists, with the Unionist leader Andrew Bonar Law becoming Colonial Secretary and Deputy Prime Minister. By an effective coup culminating on 6 December 1916 the ministry is taken over by the 'Radical and Welsh Home Ruler' David Lloyd George. A five-man executive heads a largely Conservative administration and wins the war.

On 19 October 1922, following a Unionist parliamentary

revolt, Bonar Law replaces Lloyd George as premier but, already ill, soon resigns. Long hours and endless cigars take their toll. He dies of cancer in 1923. At his funeral his old enemy Asquith remarks, rather more than *sotto voce*, 'They have buried the unknown prime minister alongside the unknown soldier'. Despite Law's dour competence in office, the reputation sticks.

National unity is purchased at the cost of peace in Ireland, as the new ministers are the *ci-devant* zealots of the Ulster revolt against Home Rule. But the immediate cost is borne by the Tory *bête noir* Winston Churchill and, after a persistent press campaign – notably in Lord Beaverbrook's *Express* and Lord Northcliffe's *Daily Mail* – by Lord Chancellor Haldane. The reformer of the army between 1906 and 1911, partly German-educated and unreconstructedly Hegelian, he is accused of pro-Germanism and in May 1915 is hounded out. Asquith and Foreign Secretary Grey fail to defend him.

Yet Bonar Law triumphs in the shadow of the Jacks Case, a now almost-forgotten scandal.

The Scottish image of the war is proletarian. Glasgow wifies out in the streets, protesting against rent rises: 'We are fighting the Huns at home!' The shop stewards – Kirkwood, MacManus, Bell – deported or imprisoned. John MacLean standing in the dock, denouncing bloody-handed capitalism. The red flag in George Square. There is another story.

The Jacks case is a thriller of mahogany boardrooms and lawyers' chambers, of men in heavy morning-coats and stiff collars, of first-class carriages out of Central Station. But the threat that it posed, and the way in which it was neutralised, impinged on Scottish and Westminster politics, as the Clyde industrial region, and its aggressive capitalists and manufacturers, squared up to the munitions business, their trade union opponents, and the prospect of war-borne wealth and power.

War broke out on 3 August, which found the Norwegian steamer *Themis* crossing the Atlantic, with a cargo of 7359 tons of iron ore. The ore (part of a contract for 250,000 tons over five years) was the property of the Nova Scotia Iron Company, but the agent for the cargo was the Glasgow firm of Jacks and Company, the firm of the Laws, a family with strong Canadian Maritimes connections. Jacks was effectively a commodity broker in what was the centre of the world iron trade; as important in its time as the Rotterdam 'spot' market in oil is today.

Radio was new and the *Themis* hadn't got one. After an attempt to turn the ship back by semaphore signals at Dungeness failed, it docked in neutral Rotterdam on 7 August. Its cargo was then transferred between 11 August and 3 September to Rhine barges by Jacks' Rotterdam agents Van Uden and Co. 4443 tons was then towed up-river to the Rheinhausen Steel Company at Duisburg and 2916 tons to Alfred Krupp of Essen. By this time the German army was in Brussels. A cheque for £17,000, the result of this transaction, was remitted to Glasgow by 16 August, and banked on 18 September, after the critical Battles of the Marne and Aisne had subsided to leave a rigid Western Front.

Under the Trading with the Enemy Act, the British government intercepted the cables between Glasgow and Rotterdam, and the Glasgow Procurator-Fiscal decided to prosecute Jacks and Co. Andrew Bonar Law, outside his Westminster role a very active Glasgow capitalist – Director of the Bank of Scotland and the Clydesdale Electricity Company – had ceased to be a Director in 1902, but still used the firm as his deposit bankers and retained a large financial interest (holdings of £40,000 in the period 1913-15). Its chief partner was his elder brother John (Jack) Law. By the spring of 1914 the Procurator-Fiscal had Jack Law in his sights. Were he to be put on trial, his brother feared that his own career would be brought to an end. Three weeks before the formation of the Coalition he told the Commons on 6 May 1915,

> 'He (John Law) has been accused of this great crime, but to be accused does not necessarily imply guilt, and if it should be proved that he has been guilty I should

not be willing to continue in public life and I should at once resign the position that I now hold.'

Bonar Law's apprehensions were well founded. A letter to him from from his Glasgow solicitor EH Robb, of GH Robb and Crosbie ran,

> 'I am very sorry to say that the affair, notwithstanding all our efforts, is not well and I am very much afraid a prosecution is inevitable.'

Robb, however, went on,

> 'I have taken other steps – perfectly discreet – to bring pressure on Munro and there is still hope but not much. I fear the temptation to Munro and his satellites to be in the limelight will be too strong for them.'

It was not. Charges were never brought against Jack Law. Two partners in the firm, Hetherington and Wilson, were put on trial at the beginning of June 1915 and on 15 June found guilty. Both were sentenced to six months imprisonment and a fine of £2000 (about £200,000 in our money). Despite Robb's apprehensions, the Fiscal accepted Jack Law's defence, that he had had no part in the business for two years, having 'tapered off' his activities, mainly concentrated in Middlesbrough anyway.

Why this deliverance? Particularly as Robb thought that the Lord Advocate, Robert Munro MP, would make a dead set at Jack Law. There was left-wing pressure, headed by the veteran (though also ultra-patriotic) socialist HM Hyndman, and the Irish Nationalist MP Lawrence Ginnell. This came to a head on 26 June, but was greeted by a united and hostile house. This contrasted with the venomous anti-Haldane campaign conducted by the *Daily Express*, which culminated in 2600 letters of hate-mail descending on Haldane's London house (to be disposed of by the kitchenmaid). Bonar Law's admission that what Jacks and Company had done was normal business practice, which he fully defended, was never questioned, or even publicised.

In October Law, now a minister, wrote to Sir George Cave urging the War Trade department not to prosecute the firm,

> 'in spite of what has happened I think they (the partners) are as honourable as other men. . . and though I think they were guilty technically I really believe that ninety-nine business men out of a hundred would have done as they did.'

And that was that. The Jacks Case slipped out of notice, and has remained there, although the circumstances of the toppling of Haldane, Churchill and Prince Louis of Battenberg have endlessly been discussed, and Bonar Law's entourage – FE Smith, Max Beaverbrook, Lord Carson – was anything but retiring. The official papers in the Scottish Record Office, newspaper reports, Lord Blake's *The Unknown Prime Minister* (1955) and the Bonar Law archives are uninformative. But the circumstances of the case suggest two factors which could have taken the pressure off the Law family: the internal politics of the Scottish legal establishment, and the labour conflict on the Clyde, already under way.

The Laws feared the Lord Advocate, but from Robert Munro's own *Looking Back* (1930) – I have Beaverbrook's copy of this deeply boring work – Munro was plainly an admirer of Law himself. Munro was a pawky, ambitious lawyer. Liberal MP for Wick Burghs in 1914, he followed Lloyd George into the Coalition and ended his career as a Conservative and Lord Alness. But Scottish legal politics, as John Buchan shrewdly remarked, were about positions, not about principles. In 1914 Scottish Tory lawyers were impressive, Liberal appointees were not, and against Munro was a Tory legal establishment which was also, unsurprisingly, the Law family's legal allies: John Clyde KC, MP, and Andrew Dickson KC, Dean of the Faculty of Advocates.

The story of Scottish administration has been that of the expansion of the Scottish Office and its executive departments at the expense of the Lord Advocate, the *quondam* 'Scotch Manager'. But the events of 1914-15 flung this into reverse. To transform the Defence of the Realm Act into an effective executive measure for war production, the posts of Attorney-General and Lord Advocate became of critical importance. So Munro came directly into the firing-line, when the 'tuppence an hour' engineers strike took place in the second fortnight of February. On13 March the shell shortage broke, and within a week, on 17-19 March, government and most of the unions signed the Treasury agreements and set up the joint management-labour Clyde Armaments Output Committee. But militant management, represented by William Weir of Weirs of Cathcart, broadcast lurid tales of drink and incompetence, and was seconded by Lloyd George.

Minister of Munitions from 19 May, Lloyd George had already been active behind the scenes, as Chair of the Shell Supply Committee, in informal negotiation with Bonar Law and FE Smith. In prospect was a government reshuffle when the expected coalition was formed. Not long after this the Munitions Directorate for Clydeside, under the autocratic Weir, replaced the joint committee. On 13 July 1915 Clyde, Jack Law's advocate, became its Counsel. He would shortly be faced with the menace of the Fairfield strike, the debut of the Clyde Workers' Committee, which the Directorate coped with by policies of imprisonment and deportation so ruthless that they were condemned by the former Unionist Scottish Secretary Lord Balfour of Burleigh.

The Red Clyde episode didn't do any harm to Munro and Clyde. The outcome of Lloyd George's ousting of Asquith in late 1916 was that – on Bonar Law's insistence – Clyde became Lord Advocate and Munro became Scottish Secretary, retaining this position until 1922. The Public Records are limited and legal papers seemingly non-existent, but my hunch is that the Jacks case gave the chance for a deal to be done between Unionists and conservative Liberals within the Scottish legal establishment. This wouldn't just let John Law off the hook, weaken the Asquithians in the Scottish Office and further Munro's career. In immediate terms, 1915-16, it facilitated both the creation of a very powerful legal team for use against the leaders of the Clyde workers, and consolidated the Clydeside bourgeoisie, Liberal and Unionist.

Most studies of the Red Clyde have concentrated on the strength or otherwise of the workers' movement, and the enforcement of dilution and intensified work patterns by the employers. But the deportations and imprisonment which were crucial in breaking the shop stewards' power by 1916 were *judicial* measures. Weir, Clyde and later Munro himself became the Kirkman Finlays, Braxfields and Dundases of this counter-revolution. So, as well as the questions which remain outstanding about the case – was John Law in fact guilty? Did he have an alibi? What was the response of the jailed men and the fate of their families? And there is the wider issue – how much did this consolidation enable a right-wing élite to take over a supposedly radical country?

Behind this was the manoeuvre of two sorts of industrial politics and ideas of internationality, and further in the background, an awareness among the bosses of growing instability within the heavy industries of Clydeside. The sudden slump of 1906-09, as yet unresearched in terms of industrial history, had pushed shipbuilding unemployment to 21% and radicalised employers into seeking solutions to high unit costs. This took the form of rationalised production – the introduction of the Taylor and Bedaux systems of 'scientific management' – and a much more determined confrontation with the unions. The region's Liberal politicians, who had only recently made progress against the Orange-Tory majority, were also aware of intensifying Labour Party organisation and the threat to a dominance which had been based on a small and controllable electorate. These motives underlay the discreet cross-party negotiations which followed the constitutional crisis of 1910, in which can be seen the outlines of the Lloyd George coalition.

In parallel to these were moves to rationalise international competition, sea transport in particular. In the mature shipping world of the Edwardians, threatened with overcapacity and declining profits, conferences had carved up the main shipping routes, and in these the major figures were Sir Ernest Cassel and Alfred Ballin. Both men were German Jews and were behind the attempts to negotiate an Anglo-German *entente* on naval and colonial matters, the climax of which was Ballin's arrangement of Viscount Haldane's mission to Berlin in February 1912. Out of this came the German realisation of the failure of their *flottenpolitik*: the loss of the 'naval race'. This had two, contradictory, effects. There was a more benign atmosphere in colonial policy, in which Britain and Germany agreed to dismember the Portuguese empire. There was also an increased army aggressiveness, as the German General Staff realised that Russian rearmament menaced its Schlieffen Plan strategy of a war on two fronts, and began planning for a rapid declaration of war.

On the British side there was another mutinous group: the 'outs' in Edwardian politics, with their own form of internationalism. We know very little about Bonar Law's ideology, save that he was an enthusiast for Carlyle, the great conduit of 'Germanism'. But Jacks and Company didn't just do business with the Ruhr. Dr William Jacks, Bonar Law's close associate for a quarter of a century, was a Liberal-Unionist MP and enthusiastic pro-German (he endowed the German chair at Glasgow University) whose 1904 biography of William II was received enthusiastically by its subject. Jacks died in 1908 but his younger partner appears to have shared this enthusiasm. It was to protestant Germany that Ulster turned as Home Rule loomed up. On 24 April 1914 the Larne gun-running involved weapons being imported from Hamburg for the use of the Ulster Volunteers. Although kept in the dark by Edward Carson until the operation was complete, Law thoroughly approved of it.

In the spring of 1915, assaulted by both his military leaders, Lords French and Fisher, Asquith was desperately anxious to preserve his autonomy. The Jacks Case meant that Law had something to cover up. The Scots lawyers and his press allies helped to limit the damage, but this meant that Law entered the Cabinet only in a rather lowly position, that of Colonial Secretary. He stayed there until the overthrow of Asquith, when he became a very effective Chancellor, responsible for putting the Bank of England under state control (a measure reversed, ironically by a historian of the Red Clyde).

Bonar Law made Haldane's exclusion an absolute condition of the coalition. This was to have pregnant consequences when Haldane edged towards Labour by the end of the war. He became Ramsay MacDonald's Lord Chancellor in 1924, inaugurating that managerial leftism which has endured to the present. By then the Red Clyde – Wheatley, Maxton, Kirkwood, Buchanan – had made its mark on Parliament. But Labour's inheritance was an industrially-exhausted Clydeside. The ultimate irony was that Bonar Law himself became one of its major victims. As a result of the slump of 1921, Jacks and Company collapsed. The forgotten scandal preceded the unknown premier into the shadows.

9
MacDiarmid, Socialism and the Democratic Intellect
(1981)

MacDiarmid, the auld Superscot,
once parted from the engaging private man,
could exude an atmosphere in which anything
went – fanaticism, brutality, and plagiarism
amounting to literary banditry.
Yet in this tribute first written for the *Scottish
Labour History Journal* it is argued that the
'gowden lyric' was social, and at its best – the
cusp of the 'Drunk Man' – democratic and
religious as well.

Hugh MacDiarmid (Christopher Murray Grieve, 1892-1978) died at the beginning of a bitter winter. Its events would not have disconcerted him. He had always viewed devolution as an expedient to preserve the hated Union of 1707. About the policies of the Thatcher régime he would have shared the opinion of the old Fenian John O'Leary, Yeats's friend, 'I was in the hands of my enemies: why should I complain?' Yet lines of his from *To Circumjack Cencrastus* (1930), seemed a supremely apposite valedictory:

> Lourd on my hert as winter lies
> The state that Scotland's in the day.
> Spring to the North has aye come slow
> But noo dour winter's like to stay
> For guid,
> And no' for guid!

O wae's me on the weary days
When it is scarce grey licht at noon;
It maun be a' the stupid folk
Diffusin' their dullness roon and roon
        Like soot,
        That keeps the sunlicht oot.

Nae wonder if I think I see
A lichter shadow than the neist
I'm fain to cry: 'The dawn, the dawn!'
I see it brakin' in the East.'
        But ah
        It's juist mair snaw!

On that grim election-day in May 1979 it was not difficult to think of him 'smilin' underfit' in Langholm kirkyard.

As a political activist MacDiarmid was lively, unruly, and almost wholly ineffective. From the ages of sixteen to thirty-six he was a member of the Independent Labour Party, and from sixty-five to his death he was a monument of the Communist Party. Yet at no stage was his socialism ever orthodox, and in his own, as well as in the public mind, he was identified with Scottish nationalism of a very emphatic sort. His connection with political Nationalism was, however, brief. In 1928 he helped found the National Party of Scotland, along with Roland Muirhead, RB Cunninghame-Graham and John MacCormick. He was expelled from it in 1933 by MacCormick, as part of the purge of radicals which preceded the NPS's fusion with the moderate Scottish Party in the following year. In 1934 he joined the Communist Party, was expelled for 'nationalist deviation' in 1937, reinstated on appeal in 1938, but expelled again later that year. When MacCormick left the SNP in 1942, MacDiarmid rejoined, but was expelled again in 1948. He contested several elections for his various parties, vigorously and with an almost total lack of success. With reason: his grasp of practical politics was just about as bad as his notorious platform style. MacDiarmid the public speaker was well-nigh excruciating: extremism of opinion coupled with a leaden recitative about most matters other than the one in hand, from an armful of much-thumbed press-cuttings: an image strangely at odds with the courtly charm of the private man. But political activism and personality become, in the long run, only of historical or anecdotal interest. What will survive is MacDiarmid's remarkable cultural achievement, and poetry which is among the greatest written in the twentieth century.

Yeats, Eliot and Pound are probably the only other comparable figures. MacDiarmid would not have disagreed with such a judgement, nor would he have devalued the work of any of the others. But the comparison raises problems in assessing the work of MacDiarmid as a socialist poet. The other three were men of the right: Yeats the Ascendancy authoritarian, dallying with the Irish Blue-shirts; Eliot the clerical Legitimist; Pound the propagandist for Mussolini. For all his revolutionary affiliations, much of MacDiarmid's most ambitious poetry often appears as arrogantly cerebral and elitist as anything they wrote, while too often his overtly 'socialist' poetry is commonplace in ideas and technically poor. In the opinion of some commentators – notably Norman MacCaig – MacDiarmid's socialism simply acted as an intellectual catalyst, like Yeats's occultism and authoritarianism, something which ultimately purged itself from his greatest work, leaving the clarity of the 'golden lyric':

> Better a'e gowden lyric
> Than a social problem solved. (1930)

And yet, surely, to accept this is to devalue MacDiarmid's cultural significance, as someone who believed that he was bringing his poetic gift to bear on the great problematics of his time, and whose ideas, work and life have an ultimate coherence which goes beyond poetry and socialism and Scotland. To do this it's necessary to go back to the philosophical groundwork of his poetry, and then look at the way it comprehended the shifting social and political relationships of the country in which he wrote his greatest work.

Contradiction – often, it seemed, of a most wilful kind – was central to MacDiarmid's *Weltanschauung*. Many of his opinions and loyalties seemed mutually irreconcileable. He was aristocrat and democrat, nationalist and cosmopolitan, communist and social crediter. When the torpid intelligentsia of Scotland wouldn't argue with him he created another persona and argued with himself. His most bitter public controversy, with Edwin Muir over the use of Lowland Scots, was fought – venomously – over a cause he seemed to have deserted several years earlier. Not surprisingly, he institutionalised this, in an unpronounceable phrase which he borrowed from Professor Gregory Smith and fathered on the Scottish intellectual predicament: the Caledonian *Antisyzygy* – the Scottish unrest. In part this was emotional: a vitalist response to the smug consensus which governed Scottish literary and educational life. But there was also logic to it. The philosophical tradition of Scotland – which MacDiarmid read himself into at the Langholm library and at school, and later as a student in Edinburgh – had been deeply affected by Hegelianism. Its basic premise was that empiricism – the reduction of reality to facts and sense-perception – was itself unreal, as the importance of such facts was always contingent on their overall context and on the fact of change. The dialectic, the continual contrasting of one world-view with another, and their fashioning into a synthesis which was itself challenged, registered the reality of change. It was the power of this as a social explanation which had impressed Karl Marx in the 1830s, and MacDiarmid replicated this process. Although he was to revel in his materialism, he did not arrive at it through orthodox 'scientific socialist' analysis, but by following Marx's own path to a new synthetic world-view. Hence the interaction of philosophy and poetry in MacDiarmid carries the same sort of emotional as well as intellectual charge as the work of the young Marx.

To MacDiarmid at the end of World War I it seemed that this unrest was manifest, both in the commotion of Europe after the

Russian revolution, and in the predicament of society. This was only partially connected with the economic problems which beset Scotland; it was also a reaction to the suppression of political experimentation by the establishment. Before the war radicals like his friends on Orage's *New Age* could look forward to a future in which syndicalism or guild socialism or decentralisation of various sorts would play important roles in British politics. Now an era of central mediocrity began – the age of Baldwin and MacDonald – which mirrored the artistic vacuum of a metropolitan culture dominated by such as Galsworthy, John Masefield and the Bloomsbury claque. For MacDiarmid a Scottish antithesis was a necessity, and with good reason, given the similar reactions of other writers from the provinces of the English-speaking world – Joyce, Yeats, Pound and Eliot. In this context compromise – even that implied by conventional left-wing politics – was fatal to the dialectic, and thus to any hope of progress:

I'll hae nae hauf-way hoose, but aye be whaur
Extremes meet – it's the only way I ken
To dodge the curst conceit o' bein' right
That damns the vast majority o' men.
(*A Drunk Man looks at the Thistle*)

MacDiarmid's Anglophobia is thus ideological rather than actual, as indeed is his Scottish nationalism – in 1926 his *Albyn, or Scotland and the Future*, placed the southern boundary between Humber and Mersey. At this stage, anyway, he looked for cultural salvation to revolutionary activity, nationalist and socialist.

In the early 1920s, the period of possibly his greatest lyric poetry, his politics were at their most effervescent and ambiguous, and he has been accused of sympathy for fascism. He was certainly influenced by right-wing thinkers. He must have read Maurras and Barrés while in France at the end of World War I, and been attracted towards their gospel of French provincialism. He also seems to have accepted the Italian Futurists' characterisation of Mussolini as a kind of indigenous Lenin, but although he pamphleteered for 'A Scottish Fascism' in 1923 he had nothing to do with the actual Scottish Fascists who, under the Earl of Glasgow, were strongly right-wing and aided the government in the General Strike. MacDiarmid, of course, took the opposite line and, in *A Drunk Man looks at the Thistle*, published later in 1926, commemorated it, movingly yet ironically, as a premature synthesis of the Scottish dialectic:

> I saw a rose come loupin' oot
> Frae a camsteerie plant.
> O wha'd hae thocht yon puir stock had
> Sic an inhabitant?
>
> For centuries it ran to waste,
> Wi' pin-heid flooers at times.
> O'ts hidden hert o' beauty they
> Were but the merest skimes
>
> Yet while it ran to wud and thorns,
> The feckless growth was seekin'
> Some airt to cheenge its life until
> A' in a rose was beekin'.
>
> A rose loupt oot and grew, until
> It was ten times the size
> O' ony rose the thistle afore
> Hed heistit to the skies.
>
> And still it grew till a' the buss
> Was hidden in its flame.
> I never saw sae braw a floo'er
> As yon thrawn stock became.
>
> And still it grew until it seemed

The haill braid earth had turned
A reid reid rose that in the lift
Like a ball o' fire burned.

The waeful clay was fire since mair
As earth had been resumed
Into God's mind, frae which sae lang
To grugous state 'twas doomed.

Syne the rose shrivelled suddenly
As a balloon is burst,
The thistle was a ghaistly stick,
As gin it had been curst.

Was it the ancient vicious sway
Imposed itsel' again,
Or nerve owre weak for new emprise
That made the effort vain,

A coward strain in that lorn growth
That wrocht the sorry trick?
-- The thistle like a rocket soared
And cam' doon like the stick.

It is invidious to extract one section from a poem as multi-faceted as *A Drunk Man*, but the strike 'ballad' is surely a pivot of MacDiarmid's political development, just as the General Strike episode in *Cloud Howe* is the pivot of Lewis Grassic Gibbon's *Scots Quair* trilogy. Indeed there is a strong parallel between the failed transmutation of thistle into rose, and Chris Guthrie's miscarriage. Both are metaphors for the new world that the Scots working class tried, and failed, to bring into being. It is surely important that the two greatest literary commemorations of the strike both come from the side of the strikers, and both come from Scotland. Yet both were also in a sense valedictories on the end of a popular radical

tradition. Thereafter the themes which preoccupy MacDiarmid –
and the fictional young Ewan Tavendale in the *Quair* – are those of
a scientism which rigorously distinguishes between subject and
object, exemplified by the obsession with the cold crystallate
vocabulary of geology, the wisdom of trained leadership, the faith
'that will cut like a knife'. Carlyle and Calvin are here, as well as
Lenin, and with them seems to come a new dialectic, provided,
perhaps, by Yeats's image of stone and water, resolution and
imagination, in *Easter 1916*:

> Hearts with one purpose alone
> Through summer and winter seem
> Enchanted to a stone
> To trouble the living stream.

Although the strike was the work of the 'British' institutions of the
working class, MacDiarmid registered its collapse as a victory for
'England' and the notion of politics that it represented:

> The vices that defeat the dream
> Are in the plant itsel',
> And till they're purged its virtues maun
> In pain and misery dwell.

He propounded a new antithesis: a combination of radical
nationalism and Leninism. For if he resembled another great
Dumfriesshire sage of a century earlier, Thomas Carlyle, in his sense
of witnessing a *Zeitbruch* – a culture-shift – he also continued
Carlyle's cult of the hero. Lenin replaced Cromwell.

Possibly MacDiarmid exaggerated, but the predicament he
invoked Lenin to resolve was real enough, and MacDiarmid's
perception of it may have been more realistic than that of most
Scottish labour leaders. 1926 was a critical episode in the dissolution
of the Scottish skilled working class – MacDiarmid's own class –
and the failure of the strike was followed by the accelerated

absorption of its 'organic intellectuals' into the professional classes, while its rank-and-file sank into the ranks of the unskilled. In the long term this was to damn any prospect of socialist, as opposed to 'Labourist' development in Scotland. MacDiarmid understood this intuitively and split with an increasingly organisation-bound Labour movement which was content to substitute trade union bureaucracy and municipal hegemony for socialist goals. An anti-imperialist nationalism seemed to offer some prospect of distinctive and imaginative socialist development. The Scandinavian analogy was made much of by left-wing nationalists during the 1930s. Yet the compromises MacCormick and his *confrères* made to create the SNP in 1933-34 were designed to fit Scotland into an imperial framework, and appeal to dissatisfied Scottish traditionalists. There was little place for MacDiarmid in such a movement, and MacDiarmid's reincarnation of John MacLean as the Scottish Lenin, and his movement towards the Communist Party, created a further antithesis. The pitting of an authoritarian élite against the growing misery of the country.

MacDiarmid was a critic of industrialisation but unlike Ruskin or Yeats he did not want to reverse it. As he wrote in *The Seamless Garment* (1932):

> Want to gang back to the handloom days?
> Nae fear:
> Or paintin' oor hides?
> Hoo d'ye think we've got
> Frae there to here?

Modern technology, apostrophised by Lenin in his definition of Bolshevism as 'electrification and power to the soviets', demonstrated man's command over the physical world. To MacDiarmid, however, only a new man – a Lenin – could understand it as well, and this understanding was necessary if modern technological civilisation was not to turn out self-destructive. Again, he went back to Carlyle, and the vernacular, for what he regarded, in *Lucky Poet* (1943) as the crucial distinction between 'can-ning' and 'kenning' being able to do and being able to understand.

The ambition, of course, was vast, much greater than anything Lenin had done, as MacDiarmid was not slow to remind him:

> Unremittin' relentless,
> Organised to the last degree,
> Ah, Lenin, politics is bairns' play
> To what this maun be.

But thirties Scotland was a bad place to start from. MacDiarmid had worked hard throughout the 1920s, as a critic and literary entrepreneur, to coax an authentic literature into existence. *Contemporary Scottish Studies*, published in the Educational Institute of Scotland Journal between 1925 and 1927, was as concerned to nurture real talent as it was to attack pretension and parochialism, with MacDiarmid consciously playing the part of Georg Brandes in late nineteenth century Scandinavia. Partly through this, the quality of Scots literature did improve enormously – Neil Gunn, Grassic Gibbon, Naomi Mitchison, Edwin Muir were by 1934 all producing work of a quality unanticipated a decade earlier. But provincialism and the eye for London opinion, persisted – exemplified by Muir's *Scott and Scotland* (1936) which denied the possibility of a vernacular revival. This was an extraordinary opinion, coming after the success of Gibbon's novels, and showed an ignorance of MacDiarmid's achievement which goes some way to justifying the violence of his response. But the result of this bitter clash – which showed MacDiarmid in an unattractive and implacable light – was to distance him (literally as well as metaphorically, for he was now living in Shetland) from literary leadership in Scotland, and contributed to the evolution of the personal style of his later poems and prose which, like the later Carlyle, was idiosyncratic to the point of being impenetrable.

Even here, however, there is a parallel with another early nineteenth century writer, revolutionary and artisan, much of whose 'world-vision' poetry is personal to the point of dottiness, but whose greatest work combines a sense of the greatness of the ordinary individual with an intuitive understanding of society and the natural world. Roderick Watson has considered that these lines from William Blake's *Marriage of Heaven and Hell* summarise remarkably MacDiarmid's work:

> 1 Man has no Body distinct from his Soul; for that
> call'd body is a portion of Soul discern'd by the five
> Senses, the chief inlets of Soul in this age.
> 2 Energy is the only life, and is from the Body; and
> Reason is the bound or outward circumference of Energy.
> 3 Energy is Eternal Delight.

In the course of a long career MacDiarmid produced an enormous amount of poetry, good and bad, and endorsed some opinions that most of us find unacceptable. It can't all be excused by his own skill in deflating himself:

> I am like a volcano, producing heat and light and also
> a great deal of rubbish.

Anyone who writes on the grand scale, like Wordsworth, runs the risk of unevenness, and even the best of MacDiarmid's longer poems have their belly-flops; as in the 'Second Hymn to Lenin':

> The sailor gangs owre the curve o' the sea,
> The hoosewife's thrang in the wash-tub,
> And whatna rhyme can I find but hub,
> And what else can poetry be?

Yet at his greatest – and this is the real justification for his use of Scots – language and ideas are 'a' ae' oo'':

> Woven owre close for the point o' a pin
> Onywhere to win in.

The violence of his defence of his vocabulary is understandable. MacDiarmid is not a poet who uses his skill to compel acquiescence in opinions we would otherwise find untenable. TS Eliot does. As a result aspects of the 'Second Hymn to Lenin' repel, while 'Little Gidding' is seductive, although also an apologia for absolute monarchy. Language, like MacDiarmid's recurrent image of intellectual effort – water – is clear, and cannot lie.

In MacDiarmid inappropriate language and false ideology betray one another. Take, for instance, that much-anthologised horror 'John MacLean' (1932). Historically this doubtless contributed to the mythicisation of MacLean, nominated by MacDiarmid as the Scottish Lenin, but MacLean's own ineffectiveness seems only to be dramatised by the phoney grand manner of the verse, its best line stolen from Yeats's 'Meditations on Civil War' (written to a quite antithetical programme) and finally flopping to somewhere near MacGonagall:

> Royal honours for murderers and fools:
> The 'fount of honour'
> Is poisoned and spreads its corruption all through,
> But Scotland will think yet of the broken body
> And unbreakable spirit, MacLean, of you,
> And know you were indeed the true tower of its strength,
> As your prison of its foul stupidity, at length.

As MacDiarmid himself said in the context of the public school Communists of the 1930s, 'You cannot light a match on a crumbling wall.' The contrast with 'The Dead Liebknecht', his earlier translation of Rudolf Leonhardt is, implicitly, one of poetic quality as well as politics:

> His corpse owre a' the city lies
> In ilka square and ilka street.
> His spilt bluid floods the vera skies
> And nae hoose but is darkened wi't.
> The factory horns begin to blaw
> Thro' a the city, blare on blare,
> The lowsin' time o' workers a'
> Like emmits skailin' everywhere.
> An wi' his white teeth shinin' yet
> The corpse lies smilin' underfit.

MacDiarmid's poem, partly through the power of its Scots, partly from its effective echoes of Blake's 'London', creates a brilliant vision of the dehumanising industrial city, but, in the last two lines, allows us hope: the dead leader has learned, and acted, and taught, and his work will be carried on. This poetry is both great, and committed: it uses ordinary language to create the possibility of extraordinary action.

Even a poem like 'Empty Vessel' – often cited as the apotheosis of the 'Gowden Lyric' – is socialist, if socialism has room for the greatest dialectic:

> I met ayont the cairney
> A lass wi' tousie hair
> Singin' till a bairnie
> That was nae langer there.
> Wunds wi' warlds to swing
> Dinna sing sae sweet,
> The licht that bends owre a'thing
> Is less ta'en up wi't.

Here is the painful tenderness of the girl mourning her dead child, there the great social movements, the power of reason. Any socialism must find room for both. We ought to feel proud that we had MacDiarmid to tell us that.

10
Walter Elliot: the White Marxist
(1983)

Walter Elliot, not George Davie, coined the
phrase 'democratic intellectualism', and is
therefore a legitimate godparent to the
Scottish cultural revival of the 1980s.
But as this *Scotsman* essay shows,
the man himself would not have acquiesced
in any easy definition of 'democratic'.

On 1 May 1930, Beatrice Webb invited three young Conservative
MPs to one of her famous mutton suppers. '*Laissez faire*,' wrote
the grande dame of socialism triumphantly afterwards, 'is as dead
as ditchwater and stinks in the nostrils of all politicians.' She was
particularly impressed by one of the party:

> 'The Scot was the dominant figure – a big loosely
> made man trained as an MD . . . with good manners
> and personal charm, an ugly but pleasing face, homely
> but well-bred manner . . . Elliot suggested that
> customs were to be considered as one among many
> ways of bringing the commerce and industry of the
> country under control.'

'Elliot' was Captain Walter Elliot, MC, MP for Glasgow
Kelvingrove, one of the few Scots politicians to play an originative
role in British government in the twentieth century.

There is much in Elliot to celebrate. If he didn't exactly look
the part of a Renaissance man, he had many of the necessary

qualities. He was scholarly, witty, imaginative, conscientious and brave. Life with him, according to his widow, meant 'never a dull moment, and never an angry word'. He comes alive in his friend Colin Coote's affectionate biography, and remains, twenty-five years after his death, an immensely attractive and appealing figure.

Elliot had a successful 'departmental career' in three offices. As Minister of Agriculture from 1932 to 1936, he laid the foundations of the marketing and subsidy system which was, in time, to diminish, from about 70% in 1930 to 60% in 1950, Britain's dependence on imported foodstuffs. As Secretary of State for Scotland from 1936 to 1938, he founded Films of Scotland and the Scottish Special Housing Association and boosted the Empire Exhibition in Glasgow in 1938. Finally as Minister of Health, 1938-40, he had to help organise the evacuation of women and children from urban areas in the event of war and created a network of emergency hospitals in areas distant from bombing in Scotland including Killearn, Law and Peel which proved a valuable endowment for the postwar NHS.

There is also a more poignant aspect. Elliot entered the Cabinet as a young man; he was only 51 when he left it, and he never held office again, although he remained an MP until his death in 1958. Now there's a point of more than biographical interest here, as Elliot represented something relatively rare until the 1980s, a Scottish politician, sitting for a Scottish constituency, who gained prominence outside the Scottish Office.

At the beginning of this century Scottish constituencies accomodated about a third of Britain's senior politicians, many of whom were themselves Scots. Since 1920 this has changed – unquestionably for the worse. Between 1800 and 1923 six prime ministers, foreign secretaries and chancellors of the exchequer were Scots or had Scottish seats; between 1922 and 1980 only three. The Scottish connections of some of these men were all but nominal, and they were rarely sighted outside election time, yet they were at least 'friends at court' and they were not replaced by local talent.

On the left James Maxton and John Wheatley were

exceptional. The rule has been a succession of run-of-the-mill former councillors and trade union officials, headed by uninspiring Scottish Office ministers. Nor were matters much better on the Right; among the ranks of the landowners and advocates whom the Unionists chose to represent a peculiarly crisis-ridden capitalism.

But this isn't the full story. During the First World War, when the old Whig state crumbled under the pressure of supplying munitions and putting the generals under restraint, there was an enormous influx of Scots businessmen into government, men such as William Weir, Joseph MacLay, James Lithgow, Auckland and Eric Geddes, Andrew Duncan, and Robert Horne. Their impact was dramatic in creating the interventionist state, but it was also temporary. They remained businessmen first, distrustful of all but a limited degree of state action, and after the war they tended to return to industry, not in most cases to Scottish industry but to the large-scale London-based companies which were a feature of the time, and which in their turn made greater and greater inroads on Scottish economic autonomy.

In the long run this did Scotland little good. But on the political fringe there was another area of Scottish involvement which drew on new scientific and technological discoveries and their application. RB Haldane, the assiduous Fabian who eventually became Lord Chancellor in the first Labour Government, could be called its godfather, and it pulled in, between the wars, figures like John Reith, John Grierson, Lord Boyd Orr and Haldane's own nephew JBS Haldane.

Elliot belonged to both worlds. He didn't at all conform to the earlier 'carpetbagging London barrister' image (though his wife Katharine was the half-sister of Margot Asquith, he didn't marry until six years after Asquith's death and so can't be classed with that distinguished cousinhood). He was wealthy enough to be politically independent-minded, but he was also a medical man and a trained scientist and a man whose intellectual expertise and sheer curiosity influenced his politics. Like so many of the Lloyd George generation he also sat loose to party ties, although in Elliot's case this heterodoxy was balanced by the enthusiasm he felt for the political game itself. Whether Westminster fully appreciated his skills is more debatable.

Walter Elliot was born in 1889, the son of a successful auctioneer in Lanark. His grandfather had been a great sheep-farmer and the story goes that he once saw a refrigerator at an exhibition in Glasgow, realised the likely impact of frozen Australian and New Zealand carcases on his business, and retrenched just in time to avoid financial ruin. An uncle provided a cautionary tale by going bust trying to transmute base metals into gold. But both conveyed the impact of scientific advance on economics which became a major theme in Elliot's political thinking. At Glasgow university Elliot studied medicine alongside his friend Osborne Mavor, 'James Bridie': a friendship cemented in lampoon, cartoon, lots of drink, radical-ish politics (Elliot was then a Fabian) and strange knowledge. In *Mr Bolfry* the saga of 'Wee Stumpy Stoorie' the liver fluke which breeds through a succession of million-to-one chances, was Elliot's doing.

He went from university to war. As an unarmed medical officer, he won two MCs on the Western Front. Towards its end, he was wounded in the foot and, while invalided, accepted an invitation to stand for Lanark as Coalition Unionist candidate. He was supposed to have wired back, 'Yes, which party?' – not as opportunistic as it looked, as distinctions between Coalition Liberals and Coalition Unionists were pretty vague anyway – and was elected in November 1918.

The Lloyd George coalition was the sort of government that Elliot, in principle, liked. A lot of the support that Conservatives gave it was purely self-interested, and evaporated once the postwar boom turned into a slump in 1920, but he maintained his enthusiasm in the hope of further action on housing, public health and Ireland. The last case shows how completely he had broken with prewar Conservatism – in 1914 the party of Bonar Law was prepared to connive at military mutiny and drive the whole country into civil war over Home Rule. Now Elliot exerted himself to the utmost as a backbench MP to bring British repression in Southern Ireland to an end, and to facilitate the creation of the Free State. In August 1922, when the Conservatives ended the coalition, Elliot stood out for Lloyd George, without avail.

The architect of Conservative independence was Stanley Baldwin, that misleading combination of English squire and Celtic mystic, and Elliot was favoured by Baldwin's desire for a moderate domestic policy. Baldwin made him Under-Secretary at the Scottish Office and even wrote a foreword to Elliot's 1928 essay *Toryism and the Twentieth Century*. This was a highly individual performance which can scarcely have had much influence on Tory backbenchers whom Bagehot had once christened 'the best brute vote in creation'. Its historical bits are no better than the sort of thing that Disraeli regularly flung into his novels, but the final chapter shows a perception of the reorientation of European social thought in the early twentieth century which was very rare in 1920s Britain. Elliot argued that advances in the sciences, particularly theoretical physics and psychology, had overthrown the materialistic ethos both of nineteenth-century liberalism and of Marxism. The material universe was no longer reducible to hard fact, nor were people's actions governed by rational calculation. In this situation the democratic Conservative, committed to the reform of existing institutions, was better placed for political effectiveness than the doctrinaire radical. In fact, he could be a much more drastic reformer.

There was a tradition of right-wing state socialism in the Conservative Party, chiefly, associated with Viscount Milner, the great imperial proconsul and a valuable member of the War Cabinet, 1916–18. Elliot knew various of Milner's colleagues, notably FS Oliver (another Scottish borderer) and Leo Amery, but there was nothing particularly Bismarckian about his own views. His attitudes to the working class was cooperative. He sat for a largely working-class constituency, Glasgow Kelvingrove, and got in (usually only just) on a vote which testified to the variety of views within it.

He realised the divergence between socialist theory and actual political behaviour, but he also respected the logic of revolutionary socialism. It wasn't to be dismissed or banned, but combatted by the different logic of science and technology. Elliot once referred to himself as a 'White Marxist', someone who understood Marx and argued against him on his own terms. His approach was twofold: the classical economics on which Marx based his system had been subverted by the rise of economic nationalism in the late nineteenth century. Governments would no longer let the laws of the market take their course, they would intervene. And secondly, when they intervened, they would commission the benefits of modern science – as the First World War had abundantly proved.

The Tory Party has never been particulary receptive to ideas, and in the 1920s the Labour Party, dominated by trade-union bureaucrats, wasn't much better. Not surprisingly, Elliot found himself mixing with similarly isolated Liberal and socialist intellectuals. He was a welcome guest at the *New Statesman*, and even played a part in installing Kingsley Martin as editor in 1931. In 1930 these catholic political tastes nearly bought him to grief, when in December 1930 he broke ranks to commend the plans of Sir Oswald Mosley – then a radical leader of the Labour Party – for economic recovery through protection and public works funded by deficit financing. Baldwin rebuked him, but when he became the effective head of the National Government in August 1931, he made Elliot Financial Secretary to the Treasury, and a year later raised him to the Cabinet as Minister of Agriculture.

Elliot was one of the few successes of a ministry which was less a coalition of all the talents than a lowest common denominator of agreement between Britain's less imaginative politicians. He was faced with an emergency, as the collapse of world demand after the Wall Street crash meant that Britain was being flooded by cheap foodstuffs and a fall of 50 per cent in agricultural prices threatened to put British farmers out of business.

Once Britain had come off the gold standard and was committed to protection, however, Elliot could choose from a wide range of measures. He had inherited from his Labour predecessor

Christopher Addison legislation allowing marketing boards to be set up to regulate British prices and production. The most famous of those he set up was the Milk Marketing Board of 1933, which also tied in with his programme to combat child malnutrition by supplying milk to schools at low prices. But marketing was not enough in the case of wheat or beef, which were still threatened by foreign imports.

Here Elliot used combinations of bilateral agreements with major producer countries (which ensured them guaranteed if restricted markets), quotas and subsidies. Not all of these schemes worked; indeed many of the criticisms of the Common Market's agricultural policy first saw the light in the early 1930s. However, by 1936, Elliot had hauled agriculture back from the brink, and production actually rose over this period by 15 per cent.

In 1936 Elliot went to the Scottish Office. Two years later he became Minister of Health. In itself this was unusual – the Scottish Office has buried more statesmen than it has created, and the condition of Scotland – with an unemployment rate of 19 per cent (five points over the UK level) – was daunting to any politician. But Elliot had already played some part in creating Britain's first approach to a regional policy, the Special Areas Act of 1934, and he tried to exploit this legislation to set up machinery to remodel the Scottish economy. He developed the Scottish Economic Committee which Sir Godfrey Collins, his predecessor, had sanctioned. It responded to the Barlow Commission on the distribution of industry by drafting an ambitious rationale for Scottish economic planning, and enquired into the Highland economy, light industries and the impact of rearmament. From its leading members came the organisation which set up Hillington industrial estate and the Scottish Special Housing Association.

Elliot gave a further boost to the Scottish economy by the £11 million Empire Exibition project, held at Bellahouston Park, Glasgow, in 1938. Timed to coincide with the launch of the *Queen Elizabeth*, it also managed to coincide with the wettest summer on record, and more ominously, with the Munich crisis. The latter meant that the exhibition's underlying aim – to give a boost to the diversifying of Scottish industry – was frustrated. Rearmament, not new light industries, activated Scotland's economy as Europe moved towards war.

In May 1938 Elliot went to the Ministry of Health, just at the moment that Chamberlain's policy of appeasement reached its crisis over Czechoslovakia. Elliot was not by inclination a 'man of Munich' and came very close to resignation as that tragedy dragged itself out through the summer months. But largely because he did not believe that Chamberlain secured 'peace with honour' – or with anything else – he stayed on. With war seemingly inevitable, and the fear universal that 'the bomber would always get through' he organised with his friend and fellow Scot John Anderson the evacuation scheme whereby three-and-a-half million people, mainly women and children, were moved to country districts in the first weeks of the war.

When Churchill formed his war coalition in May 1940, Elliot was dismissed. Was Munich held against him? Possibly, but several of his former colleagues, far more culpable, were retained – Halifax, Kingsley Wood, RA Butler. It's more likely that he didn't fit – at least into Churchill's notion of giving Attlee and Arthur Greenwood responsibility for domestic policy (at which they did not turn out to be very good). He had the chagrin of seeing lesser men in positions he could have filled with imagination.

He did not complain but made what he could of a range of lesser jobs, became an adept broadcasting propagandist, chaired the Public Accounts Committee, ran a Royal Commission on African education. A decision of his, on a night of heavy bombing on London, saved the eleventh century Westminster Hall when he switched the fire services from the doomed Victorian House of Commons. Tom Johnston, the Labour journalist who became Scottish Secretary had been a collaborator in the past. He made good use of him in his Scottish Council of State, where he shone out among the elderly ex-Secretaries of State, moving the Council strongly towards housing reform and industrial development.

At the end of the war, in contrast to Churchill's anti-socialist pyrotechnics, he was campaigning for 'a partnership between the State and industry at home, and between Britain, the United States, and Russia abroad'. Against the sweeping Labour tide, he nearly survived. He lost Kelvingrove by only 92 votes.

Again, one of his friends came to his rescue. John Boyd Orr, elected in 1945 for the Scottish universities as an independent with socialist and Scottish nationalist leanings, gave up his seat to go to the Lords, and incidentally, let Elliot back. In a contested election he won overwhelmingly – gaining the votes of several thousand graduates who were fundamentally opposed to his party. Back in the Commons and on the front bench he became health services spokesman, and Aneurin Bevan's leading antagonist.

Elliot did well in opposition, and was responsible – with Lord Woolton and RA Butler – for the modernisation of the Conservative Party. Yet when Churchill returned to power in 1951 he offered Elliot only minor office. Elliot refused. He remained on the back benches until his death in 1958, still fascinated by the 'endless adventure' of politics, still managing to be a paradoxical combination of reliable party man and sponsor of consensus measures. He protested with Bertrand Russell against nuclear weapons and urged a Highland Development Board on the government. Alone among Scots Conservatives, he was prepared to make common cause with Labour in urging new initiatives to cope with the decline of the Scots economy.

Elliot was never a man with a one-track mind. Besides agriculture, health and Scottish affairs, he involved himself in Commonwealth politics (where his views on Africa anticipated those of Iain MacLeod) in European unity, in Zionism, the United Nations and in women's rights. The last two were further enlivened by the career of Katherine Elliot. She was a UK delegate to the UN in the 1950s, and in 1959 became one of the first four women life peers, and the first woman ever to speak in the House of Lords. Which, happily, she still does.

Elliot wasn't a Scottish Nationalist, but he never considered himself English, believing that the ingenuity of his fellow-countrymen was there to leaven British politics. This was not always welcome at Westminster, however. Lloyd George told the young Harold Macmillan that the Commons could digest only one good idea at a time, while Elliot, 'Who could, if asked, talk the hind legs off a donkey about the finances of Saturn' was inclined to force-feeding. 'He talks too much,' was Churchill's reason for excluding him from the Cabinet in 1951 – an old man's judgment at a time when new ideas were vitally necessary. Elliot was not the first Westminster Scot to suffer for valuing intellect and imagination more than discretion, as the career of RB Haldane had shown. Nor, given the Labour establishment's treatment of John Mackintosh, was he to be the last.

11
The Four Lives of Tom Johnston
(1982)

Tom Johnston was in the early 1980s more
venerated than properly understood.
This centenary tribute in the *Times Higher
Education Supplement* argued that he had to be
seen within the matrix of imperialism and
British socialism as well as that of
the home rule cause.

The Right Honourable Thomas Johnston CH was born over a hundred years ago on November 2, 1881. The fact that his centenary was established only recently – the 'official' entries give his year of birth as 1882 – exemplifies the mythic quality of Johnston's career as socialist and patriot, and above all as 'the greatest Secretary of State'. Like so many of his contemporaries, James Maxton, John MacLean or John Wheatley, he has tended to attract reverence rather than research. A reappraisal of his life and times may show a more complex character who had the potential to succeed in fields wider than the Scottish Office but was frustrated by the rules of the British political game.

Johnston achieved success in four fields – journalism, history writing, politics and administration. He had much of the energy of the polymaths Scotland produced at the time of the Enlightenment and by specialising in any one of these fields he could probably have made himself the master of it, not out of genius but out of a capacity for organising and synthesising the knowledge of others.

He never carried his work as historian beyond the salutary

task of demolishing (as far as that was possible) much of the romanticism which cluttered the view of Scotland's past. He always wanted to return to the field but was frustrated, not only by mounting public duties but by the very motivation which had impelled him into it in the first place. History to Johnston subserved his political programme, and in the first years of his career this programme was projected by journalism.

As editor of *Forward* for almost thirty years from its foundation in 1906, Johnston was one of the greatest socialist journalists Britain produced. He began *Forward* when he inherited a small trade paper as a student at Glasgow University, during the brave days of James Bridie, Walter Elliot and James Maxton. *Forward*, launched significantly enough in one of Miss Cranston's tea rooms in Glasgow, exemplified that high-minded alliance of civic improvers, intellectual socialists, home rulers and skilled workers which made up the Clydeside radical scene at the zenith of the river's prosperity.

It published Shaw and Wells, besides giving a platform to figures as disparate as Ramsay MacDonald, John MacLean and James Connolly. Its circulation has never been accurately charted – alas as an efficient journalist, Johnston destroyed practically all his letters once he replied to them – but it seems usually to have been more than 10,000 and when it circulated his great assaults on *Our Noble Families* he wrote in his *Memories* that it went up to more than 30,000.

Forward's first two decades were its greatest, enlivened by its suppression in late 1915 for reporting what happened when Lloyd George – 'Boys, I'm a socialist like yourselves' – tried to sell the Munitions Act to the Clydeside shop stewards. *Forward* was not in fact as antiwar as the various Marxist sheets also circulating along the Clyde, but it did articulate the progressive disenchantment with the war, not only of skilled labour, but also of upholders of the old liberal-radical tradition.

The influence of this was seen in the general election of November 1922, after the collapse of the postwar boom, when

Scottish Labour representation went up from seven to twenty-nine MPs. *Forward*'s mixture of socialist uplift and hard-nosed exploitation of specific issues, notably housing, indicated areas where Labour had captured the initiative from the discredited forces of the centre and right. In housing in particular the schemes propounded in its columns by John Wheatley became the foundation of his successful Housing Act, the only domestic achievement of the first Labour Government of 1924.

Johnston, who entered Parliament in 1922, did not get office in that administration. As a backbencher he had delivered a fierce attack on Asquith, and Asquith's support was essential to sustain MacDonald in power. By the time he did reach the cabinet in 1931, MacDonald's next administration was tottering towards ruin. In the meantime he had become a member of the Empire Marketing Board, a quango which provided great scope for cooperative ventures between reform-minded Conservative and Socialist politicians, resulting notably in the documentary film movement.

Out of this stemmed his belief that certain key areas of economic reconstruction could be tackled by consensus action, a conviction strengthened by the disastrous adherence of Labour when in office to an incompatible mixture of fundamentalist socialism and *laisser faire* economics. In this Johnston, who called himself a 'moderate extremist', was joined by 'middle opinion' figures as diverse as Harold Macmillan, the future Lord Sieff, and Walter Elliot, his Scots colleague, a Unionist with a strong belief in state intervention in industry and welfare. In the thirties Johnston and Elliot were to cooperate in setting up the Saltire Society, an attempt to regenerate the cultural and economic life of Scotland, and in the reorganization of the Scottish Office.

In the late 1930s Johnston became more and more identified with Scottish issues. Ultimately in 1939 he became Regional Commissioner for civil defence, a step which seemed to mean the end of his parliamentary career. He had come close to the highest office in the Labour Party, only to see it snatched from him. He lost his seat in Labour's débàcle in October 1931, and only just failed to get back at a byelection in early 1932. Had he returned at that point he, and not the retiring Attlee, would probably have succeeded George Lansbury in 1935 as leader of the Labour Party. This setback seems to have contributed to his increasing interest in Scottish devolution. In 1938 he became president of the London Scots' Self-Government Committee, a left-wing pressure group, and in a note of dissent to the official Gilmour Committee in 1939 he recommended regular sittings in Scotland of the Scottish Grand Committee. His commitment to home rule ought not, however, to be exaggerated – he was more concerned at the isolation of the Scottish Office from political groups within Scotland, and from Scottish opinion, than with schemes for fundamental legislative devolution.

Like many another moderate socialist, he visited Soviet Russia and was impressed with what he was allowed to see of the operation of a 'planned' economy. Together with his interest in problems of colonial government, this meant that his approach was more one of imaginative administration than of democratisation.

Johnston's finest hour began in February 1941, when he got Churchill to make him Secretary of State for Scotland. He turned down the substantial salary (although he was never a wealthy man) and insisted on taking the job on his own terms, which were more or less that he should be able to proceed with Scottish reconstruction during the war itself, policy being vetted by a Council of State composed of all surviving Secretaries for Scotland. The Council, of which Elliot was, next to Johnston, the most active member, met regularly until mid-1943, and created no less than 32 committees to investigate aspects of Scottish postwar economic and social policy.

Its achievements were threefold. It prepared Scotland for the crucial strategic role it was to play in the final years of the war, as the great marshalling yard for American aid to Europe; its positive action on Highland electrification gave a pledge that economic reconstruction would not be shelved after the war; and it secured in Central Scotland important extensions of medical provision in anticipation of the creation of the National Health Service.

Patriotic fervour in Scotland during World War Two should not be exaggerated. The country had suffered terribly during the depression and morale among important groups of workers was low. Agitation by nationalists was persistent and latterly quite effective. Johnston used it to persuade Cabinet committees to grant him increased autonomy and more money. By setting up the Scottish Council on Industry in February 1942, he created a powerful pressure-group to urge the direction of industry northwards.

His advisory committees were a mixed bag. The moderation of his extremism seemed sometimes to be leading him almost to embrace the 'noble families' he had once abused – perhaps the committees were more a gesture of unity within the Scottish establishment than a new and radical departure. But the Advisory Committee on Education produced a report in 1947 which remains the most authoritative survey of twentieth century Scottish education.

Johnston withdrew from Parliament at the end of the war, but not before using his impressive reputation to help Labour win the 1945 election, an important factor given the overwhelmingly anti-socialist bias of the Scottish press. He turned the tables neatly on the Unionists by arguing that they were dragging politics into areas like industrial development and health care, where he had secured consensus. Then he left for a productive old age directing the Scottish Tourist Board, the Scottish division of the Forestry Commission and most notably the North of Scotland Hydro-Electric Board between 1946 and 1959. He died in 1965.

Johnston was a legend as early as 1945. Churchill lavished praise on him only a couple of days after his notorious 'Gestapo' speech, and I can find no instance of him being attacked by Unionist candidates, although their MPs were in the majority throughout the war, and Johnston threw his prestige solidly behind Labour. Subsequently he was to become critical of Labour's dogmatic centralisation and his pugnacity saved the Hydro Board from absorption by a London-based nationalised industry.

The tragedy was that Johnston's skill as a departmental minister (a peculiarly Scots forte, with impressive twentieth century practitioners like Haldane at the War Office, Wheatley at health and Elliot at agriculture) was not transmitted to his younger colleagues; nor was the Scottish Office's competence firmly extended into the economic sphere. Johnston captured the initiative for St Andrew's House, at a time when the general flow of legislation was towards centralisation; but the resulting Scottish establishment was rather conservative, and lacked much of the imagination of prewar Scottish semi-governmental groups like the Scottish Economic Committee, 1936-39.

Had Johnston not concentrated on Scots affairs he might well have become Labour's colonial spokesman. Churchill reputedly offered to make him Viceroy of India. There is an analogy between his colonial interests and his success in propelling Scotland in a socialist direction while the bulk of its elected representatives were still conservative. Devolved administration is a pretty good approximation to enlightened colonial government, and the Scottish Office is an effective machine. Whether Johnston would approve of its use by a Secretary of State – supported by only 22 of 71 Scottish MPs – to reverse his policies of collectivisation by stealth is another matter.

12
Lunchtime MacBooze
(1988)

Idiosyncratic press barons have been supplemented by cash-seeking accountant-editors and reporters reduced to goggling into their VDUs in smoke- and booze-free open-plan offices. When this article on the archetype of the Scottish journalist came out in the *Scotsman*, Lunchtime MacBooze's days were numbered.

When John Buchan wanted, in *Castle Gay*, to present a symbol of the new Scotland, relevant to 1930, he made Dougal Crombie, ex-Gorbals diehard, a journalist with socialist and nationalist views. In 1880 Crombie would have been a missionary, in 1900 a soldier, in the early 1920s, perhaps, a socialist politician. But, in the Scotland of the depression years, Buchan's opinion was not unique. In the same year Compton Mackenzie would tell Scottish newspapermen that national revival depended on their efforts. Thomas Carlyle had, a century before, called books and journals 'our new Church'. The new priests were coming into their own.

How come all these high opinions? The journalist has not, as a rule, occupied an exalted position in British political life. Most people know Humbert Wolfe's lines:

> It never does to bribe or twist
> Thank God! the British journalist.
> But, seeing what the man will do,
> Unbribed, there's no occasion to.

Parliamentary memoirs or novels treat journalists as at best a necessary evil, and otherwise as a conduit for gossip, malice and betrayal: a regard reciprocated by the reptiles themselves. 'The relation of the journalist to the politician,' the late Vincent Hanna wrote, 'should be that of the dog to the lamp post.'

The Scottish public tend to agree with him. Politicians of all parties are deeply suspect. A Scottish poll in 1987 discovered that only 2% of those surveyed would trust an MP to help them make up their mind on a political decision, while over 16% would trust television commentators, and 24% newspaper journalists. There are charismatic – or would-be charismatic – politicians of course but these have tended, like Winnie Ewing, Jim Sillars and David Steel, to put their message over to the Scots as journalists. The curious episode of the Scottish Labour Party of 1974-76, which many believed to be journalist-created and journalist-run, might not at first glance bear this out, as it collapsed in ignominy, but participation in it hasn't done the careers of Tom Nairn, Jim Sillars and Neal Ascherson any harm.

Still, the media tide of 'soft' nationalism which accompanied Jim Sillars' Govan victory receded pretty rapidly when he followed a party-based strategy over the Scottish Constitutional Convention. Such a strategy – perhaps mistaken – was still legitimate, but press comment got highly judgmental. The distance between journalist and MP seemed as great as ever.

Why should this be? The low evaluation of MPs has obviously got something to do with their perceived ineffectiveness, in a country which habitually returns a big majority from the 'wrong' party. Cabinet ministers got a somewhat higher credit-rating, 9%, because they were presumably seen, at least by members of their own party, as having 'got somewhere', and to be 'doing something'. But why should Scots journalists be as popular as, say, clergy and schoolteachers?

This seems to have been the case since newspapers and periodicals first started to offer opinion as well as digests of information, and the radical press confronted the concentrated power of the 'Scotch manager'. In the absence of freely elected Scots MPs, Peter McKenzie's *Loyal Reformers' Gazette* took on particular importance, as did Hugh Miller's *The Witness*, during the struggle to create the Free Church. Dr Willie Donaldson has argued in his remarkable *Popular Literature in Victorian Scotland* (1986) that in the mid-19th century radicalism – and the vernacular – colonised the rapidly-expanding popular press, largely through the success of the Dundee-based papers of John Leng, of which the *People's Journal*, with its huge circulation, was the most important. This commercialism did not, as in England, liquidate radical journalism so much as change it from a class to a Scottish press.

Radical journalism was however in decline by the end of the century, under pressure from the sensationalism of the halfpenny press. This disadvantaged the more high-minded Scots journalists working in England, but in Scotland there was a compensating rise of more specialised periodicals, like the religious, literary and woman's weeklies founded in the 1890s by the 'King of the Kailyard', William Robertson Nicoll. The more doctrinaire left chimed in with *Forward*, founded by the ILPer Tom Johnston and the radical Liberal Roland Muirhead in 1906, and John Buchan's *Scottish Review* (1906-7) appealed to some of the *intellectuels* (Buchan seems to have coined the term in a Scottish context). But if journalism was less prestigious than it had been – and despite the country's Liberalism, the Scottish press was Unionist where not imperialist – it remained the main training and occupation of the most distinguished writers of the period – Neil Munro, George Douglas Brown, Andrew Lang, Buchan himself.

The first world war brought the Liberal era to an end. Censorship, news rationing – only four war correspondents were given (qualified) access to the western front – and press manipulation curtailed journalistic freedom, and with the younger generation absent, there was little discussion of the social problems that gripped wartime Scotland. But after the war a quite different social and intellectual situation supervened, something dramatised by the 'Condition of Scotland' books – almost totally journalist-written – which appeared practically every year in the interwar period.

There is a paradox about these years. The Scottish press remained Unionist and became increasingly English-controlled, yet journalists seemed to seize a greater degree of autonomy than ever before. In the 1920s a series of amalgamations removed competing papers from virtually every Scottish town except Glasgow and Edinburgh – to the detriment of the Liberal party – and in 1928 Beaverbrook newspapers set up in Glasgow with the *Scottish Daily Express* and *Evening Citizen*. Yet greater interest was taken in Scottish politics than ever before.

Editorials might be Tory but features and news coverage were alert to the rise of the literary and political nationalist movements, and two of the leading figures in the nationalist cause, George Malcolm Thomson, assistant to Beaverbrook, and JM Reid, editor of that curious hybrid, the Glasgow *Bulletin*, an up-market tabloid angled at a woman's readership, had alter-egos as nationalist journalists. Thomson wrote three important 'Condition of Scotland' books in the 1920s and 1930s and covered Scottish affairs at Westminster for the *Scots Independent* as Charles Ryswick or 'Caledonius', and Reid published frequently on history and nationalist themes as 'Colin Walkinshaw'. Helping to set the tone also was the figure of 'Alias MacAlias', Hamish Henderson's great Scottish *doppelgänger*.

The newspaper connection proves that this wasn't just the Scottish psyche in trouble but a means whereby journalists either got more money or wrote about what they wanted to write about. To cite the greatest of all, for example, Christopher Grieve contributed countless articles to the press under all his pseudonyms, both directly and through the Scottish Secretariat, founded by Roland Muirhead in 1924, as a mechanism for spreading nationalist propaganda in the provincial press. The 'radical' phase of nationalist politics, from the founding of the National Party of Scotland in 1928 to the creation of the Scottish National Party, was largely the creation of journalists. It received a sort of journalistic Viking funeral in Eric Linklater's immolation as National Party candidate in the 1933 East Fife byelection – a contest run by and for the press – and was immortalised in his *Magnus Merriman*.

What pushed the old Tory press off-balance was the total collapse of Scottish economic confidence after 1929. This politicised one old-style cultural nationalist, William Power, in particular, and Power (besides running the *Scots Observer*) was a major actor in setting up the Scottish National Development Council in 1931, the Scottish Party in 1933 and the Saltire Society in 1936. Not surprisingly, one of the first things the SNDC did was to set up its own periodical, *Scotland*, and its offspring, the Scottish Economic Committee, bankrolled not just 'hot metal' journalists but the country's first documentary film-makers.

Both were given a mighty boost by the Empire Exhibition in Glasgow in 1938, and by the end of the decade St Andrews House in Edinburgh had its own press corps under William Ballantine. It was symbolic that administrative devolution was given a powerful push by the appointment in 1941 of the greatest of all radical Scots journalists, Tom Johnston, as Secretary of State. Johnston achieved a lot but, drawing on the assistance of colleagues like Alastair Dunnett and Forsyth Hardy, his 'Scottish Council' (of Ex-Secretaries of State) gave the impression of having achieved even more.

As well as promoting devolved administration in the mixed economy, the press continued the cultural function of printing poetry, short stories and critical essays which, in a financial sense, probably sustained Scottish literary activity more than book publishing – it paid better and it drew attention to, and stirred up controversy about, the books that were published. In the Scottish renaissance being presswise was essential, and furthered some authors (who knew how to play the system) more than others. Grassic Gibbon, Compton Mackenzie and Eric Linklater were 'professionals' (ex-journos, all of them) while MacDiarmid, after success in the 1920s while a journalist, seems to have become an all-time loser when he moved to the lonely mountain of prophecy.

In his *The Unspeakable Scot* (1900) TWH Crosland reserved a particular venom for Scots journalists. Because of their didactic style he referred to them all as 'Doctor' – Dr Nicoll, Dr Archer, and so on. This element of prestige has, however, lasted, at a time when most metropolitan journalism makes the *Sunday Post* look like *Le Monde*. But four factors make its overall effect ambiguous rather than positive.

First, there's the language question. Willie Donaldson has shown how, in the popular press of the nineteenth century, comment and political polemic was carried in the vernacular, but the journalism of the Scottish renaissance was from start to finish Anglophone. To get its point over to a wide audience it automatically chose English, even when it was promoting the Scots tongue. This problem is found throughout Europe, even with a dialect like *Schweizer-Deutsch* which is prominent on TV but absent from the Swiss press. Yet much of the energy of Scots popular speech – now to be encountered in plays, poetry and political pop and folk music – is weakened in standard English and entirely emasculated in the Newspeak of the tabloids. The loss is great. James Bridie once commented that few languages could equal Scots for terms of abuse – 'thowless, blowtering nyaffs; feckless, donnart, doited, havering gowks; daft, glaikit, foutering taupies, snuitet gomerals'. Perhaps now, when politics have taken the form of a bitter cultural struggle, a popular journalism which develops this native talent is needed.

Second, at the 'quality' level journalism is necessarily responsive to the market, not to the maturation of any great world-view. (And if we didn't think the Scottish renaissance was about profound philosophy, after Ronnie Turnbull & Craig Beveridge's *Eclipse of Scottish Culture*, we ken noo). Meeting deadlines pays, but it blunts long-range thought. The European practice – familiar in *Spiegel* or *Le Monde* – of the detailed inquiry or 'think-piece' followed by book publication is unknown, although Tom Johnston produced most of his books, including *Our Noble Families* (1910) in this way. Relevance is measured in days rather than weeks; once the piece is filed and read, it's forgotten about.

But even this version of journalism is embattled. The real cancer of metropolitan journalism is not the gutter responses of the tabloids but the deformation of journalism by public relations. The advertising 'industry' has been the great – perhaps the sole – success of the Thatcher decade. It has cloaked the massive failure of government policy and the corruption of the establishment by manipulating public opinion on an unprecedented scale and assisting government pressure on the media. Scotland, which has suffered more than most regions from the outright criminality of financial circles, remains resistant to this new totalitarianism, but the continuing centralisation of media power and recent changes in the Scottish Office suggest that a 'gloves off' power-struggle is imminent.

Finally, journalism is not politics but a commentary on politics. It's a peculiar irony that, over the years, Scottish journalists of quite remarkable quality – James Margach, Bob Carvel, Jimmie Naughtie – have crowded the English off the ringside seats, while actual Scots politicians have been dismal performers. Moreover, the Scots have never been just 'sketch writers'; when Margach made his by-line 'A Student of Politics', he meant it. Yet the country's terrible dualism seems somehow bound up in this breach between discussion and action. The critics are blessed with understanding but cursed with the failure to transmit it to the actors. The actors are self-preoccupied and unable to see beyond the immediate contours of the political game. The first must become tolerant, the second tractable – and soon.

13
Awful Scotch Fellows
(1991)

This *New Statesman* piece was
an antidote to the 'heids o' depairtments'
narrative of the Union.
Why leave it when you could
exploit the English instead?
Reading the record seemed to suggest
that a lot of good English authors – from Jane
Austen to Anthony Powell – didn't like the
Scots much and, politely and subtly, said so.

A few weeks ago an Oxford friend went near-apoplectic when the name of Norman Stone came up. The name of Oxford was being besmirched by this reactionary, opportunist, self-publicist, etc. Certainly, I envy Stone the money he's reputedly banking, but I have a certain guilty pride that both of the gladiators of the quality London Sundays, Neal Ascherson and Stone, are Scots. Which is the more characteristic?

Ascherson seems to represent *Scotus Viator*, a somewhat rueful 'progressive' pilgrim through what Thomas Hardy called 'the graveyard of dead creeds', but one who believes that you've got to keep on thinking and planning, fitting facts into some consistent pattern, otherwise the sleep of reason will supervene. Stone on the other hand is a buccaneer apologist for the *status quo*, flattering the chauvinism of an eccentric former prime minister through his Bruges Group and his Radical Society while skipping off into private convictions which don't make him 'one of us' at all – his admiration for federal Germany, his apparent belief in Scottish home rule. A throwback to those courtiers who used to surround Beaverbrook, and as odd a union of opposites as five Cabinet Scots – MacKay, Lang, Lamont, MacGregor and Rifkind – with only ten Scots Tory seats behind them.

A century ago the French political scientist Emil Boutmy was intrigued to find that the so-called United Kingdom consisted of four nations existing in a state of permanent irritation with each other. Stone – and the reaction to him – conjures up a cockiness evident even earlier in Hugh Miller's remark that among the English 'the preponderance of enjoyment lies on the more credulous side. I never yet encountered a better-pleased people. . . unthinking, unsuspicious, blue-eyed, fair-complexioned, honest Saxons.'

The English, conversely, have always suspected Scottish literary and political entrepreneurs, even when they've adapted themselves completely. 'That awful Scotch fellow who outwrote everybody' was the political scientist James Bryce making his Oxford debut. Posh London papers still pillory John Buchan as a snob and anti-semite and incarcerate him along with literary gorillas like Dornford Yates and Sapper. And that engaging bunch of weirdos, the Adam Smith Institute, seem now to be carrying the can for Mrs Thatcher's misdeeds.

The high ministerial count is evidence of a political convention which operates in Scotland's favour – Scots can fill 'English' ministries while Englishmen in the Scottish Office have been as rare as hen's teeth. The second half of this convention doesn't work for Wales, whose most successful recent Secretary of State was Peter Walker. The Welsh Tory, moreover, can slip effortlessly into the persona of Reigate Man, as Geoffrey Howe, Michael Heseltine and Michael Howard have done. Moreover – witness the vapourings of Bernard Levin and Kingsley Amis – English literary gents are allowed to be rude about the Welsh; they have to be much more discreet about the Scots. A buffer is evidently provided by an Anglified upper class which is present in Scotland, and largely absent in Wales. Torquils, Jamies and Fionas turn tartan at the right season, roughly coinciding with the annual northward migration of the royals, who have always given Wales a very wide berth.

Anti-Scottishness was never as widespread as anti-Irishness or anti-semitism, but it's still there, particularly in the literary *canon* which serves the English as a surrogate constitution. Ireland brought out the worst in the 'unthinking Anglo-Saxons': the poison poured by dons and journalists on Irish home rulers – a pacific and fundamentally assimilationist bunch – between 1880 and 1914 has, given the recent record of English justice, stuck. Even that solid socialist JB Priestley on the Liverpool Irish in *English Journey* (1935) doesn't make pleasant reading. But the Irishman could also inspire English writers to affection – think of Trollope's Phineas Finn or Thackeray's Major O'Dowd. The Scot, apparently, did not.

In *The Unspeakable Scot* (1900) the journalist and critic TWH Crosland deployed a robust yah-boo style – 'if you can without inconvenience to yourselves stay at home, please do so' – and (with Lloyd George in his sights) set about the Welsh in *Taffy* (1912). Crosland followed on a tradition which had been around since the days when the ambitions of Lord Bute prompted John Wilkes to publish his *North Briton*, Dr Johnson snarled about the Scots to Boswell, and Cobbett complained about the inhuman utilitarianism of 'Scotch feelosophers'. There were good grounds for this. Unreformed Scotland, before 1832, was Britain's biggest rotten borough, and its MPs were suitably reptilian. Jane Austen rarely makes political allusions of any sort, yet her most unappealing figures are Crawfords, Elliots, Dalrymples, offspring, perhaps, of the nabobs and placemen whom the Dundases had promoted, now battening on the riches of the English south.

'Englishness' has always been notoriously hard to define – definitions, anyhow, are not the sort of thing chaps go in for. But one circuitous approach is to nail down the un-English – those who, in the old Clubland thrillers, have clothes a shade too well cut, features too regular. In this sense the Scots can know the rules of the game – 'In his own way Jock's very reliable' – but they have them off by heart, they aren't instinctual. They talk too much, and they don't *feel*.

Considering the importance of soldier or explorer heroes in

the Scots pantheon, and that Carlyle wrote the basic text of 'history as the lives of great men', there is a curious dearth of heroic Scots in the great tradition of Victorian fiction. There are lots of Scots bores, crooks and madmen: Crotchet and MacQuedy in Peacock, M'Choakumchild in Dickens, and a particularly rich bag in Trollope. Think of Undecimus Scott promoting dodgy companies in *The Three Clerks*, Robert Kennedy trying to kill Phineas Finn, or the awful Mrs Proudie humbugging her way through Barchester. In Thomas Hardy's *The Mayor of Casterbridge*, his hero Michael Henchard is a Sophoclean figure, yet also personifies an epoch of English history, agriculture-based provincialism, which was ending. Against him is set a typical 'enlightened Scot'. Donald Farfrae could be straight out of John Galt – clever, sentimental, but bloodless and calculating, in no way heroic. If the English are the lions, the implication runs, the Scots are the foxes.

By the end of the century, through Stevenson and Douglas Brown, the Scots had kick-started their literary imagination back into life, but the dualism that resulted didn't make them equable companions south of the border. Scots produced such apparently cosy fantasies of Englishness as *Peter Pan* and *The Wind in the Willows*, but were they ever really trusted? Or were the fantasies themselves – 'boys who wanted never to grow up', little, furry, all-male worlds – a sort of critique? Rudyard Kipling, half-Scots and in his proconsular authoritarianism, successor to Carlyle, commemorated the imperial Scot in 'MacAndrew's Hymn' but in *Puck of Pook's Hill* (1906) appended 'A Pict Song' to his tale of the Romans on Hadrian's Wall:

> . . . we gather behind them in hordes,
> And plot to reconquer the Wall
> With only our tongues for our swords.
> We are the Little Folk – we!
> Too little to love or to hate.
> Leave us alone and you'll see
> How we can drag down the State!

The Picts were obviously not just the Irish. By their persistent radicalism – particularly obvious in 1906, when scarcely a Scottish Tory MP survived – the Scots had put themselves beyond this elective Sussex-man's own wall.

An 'English' monument of similar dimensions to Hardy's is Ford Madox Ford's *Parade's End* tetralogy, his 'meditation on the public events of a decade' centred on World War I. Here the 'English Tory' hero, Christopher Tietjens, is a Henchard-like figure of inarticulate power and responsibility, the human counterpart to the symbol of his family, the Groby Great Tree which dominates their Yorkshire mansion. Marinated in the English past, where 'a man could stand up on a hill', Tietjens is brought down by the machinations of his Scots civil service colleague, Vincent MacMaster. Instructed by the government – Lloyd George, of course – to falsify military statistics, MacMaster complies, while Tietjens refuses, and is sent to the front, perhaps to his death. MacMaster ends the war as Sir Vincent, civilian head of his ministry; his new wife has climbed from a Fife manse into London literary society by marrying a wealthy but insane English clergyman. MacMaster's career parallels in some ways that of another product of a Fife manse, John Buchan, whom Ford and his friend Conrad regarded as a bounder, and who ended World War I in a similarly exalted position in the Ministry of Information. To the 'English Tory', even the Scot prepared to play on his side was a morally suspect performer.

In 1936 George Orwell wrote to Anthony Powell, who had sent him an eighteenth century squib about the Scots, 'It is so rare nowadays to find anyone hitting back at the Scotch cult. I am glad to see you make a point of calling them 'Scotchmen' not 'Scotsmen' as they like to be called. I find this a good easy way of annoying them.' Orwell probably had AG MacDonnell's arch but on the whole affectionate *England, their England* (1933) in mind, and it took him some time, and a period of residence in Scotland, to become more tolerant. Powell himself, in his classic *roman fleuve, A Dance to the Music of Time*, made his symbol of 'power' rather than 'feelings', Kenneth Widmerpool, a Scot. Widmerpool's real name is Geddes, and his father made his money by selling manure. From there, evidently, it was downhill all the way. This Fabian Society version of Wagner's Alberich intrigues his way through big business, the army, the Labour Party and, maybe, the KGB. Various 'feelings people' perish through his agency until, in an episode very similar to the fate of Ignorance in Bunyan's *Pilgrim's Progress*, he is dragged off to hell in the final volume by a necromancer, Scorpio Murtlock.

'Power people' don't win friends, only underlings, and, once out of the country, the 'achieving Scot' could present an unappealing side. Alastair Kerr, the anti-hero of JD Scott's *The End of an Old Song* (1954), celebrates his successful assault on the New York financial scene by burning down the family mansion. But 'power people' don't usually write novels, tending more to journalism, or Whitehall corridors. Victorian London had more than its fair share of tough Tory editors like JD Cook of the *Saturday Review*, and in the Thatcher years such Scots as avoided the 'dependency culture' stigma have tended to pop up as 'hundred and fifty percent' journalist-radicals of the Thatcher-approved sort.

Neither group fitted into the 'English' frame. Rejecting Scottish devolution might be seen as a plus-point for unsentimentality. But Sir Iain MacGregor, Michael Forsyth, or 'our boys' at Rupert Murdoch's, Andrew Neil, Charlie Wilson and the inimitable Kelvin MacKenzie, have been anything but ingratiating, swithering between a centralised, authoritarian British nationalism, and letting the Scots go their own way. The recent Murdoch ideology of right-wing republicanism, moreover, accompanies a feeling that the Cabinet Scots have been political trimmers, liberals who went with Thatcher when it paid, and felled her when it didn't.

Thatcher herself – the ultimate 'power person' – apparently shared Kipling's methodist patriotism and unease, but hit the English establishment like Mrs Proudie colliding with Barchester Close. Craving establishment acceptance, she devalued the honours system far beyond what Lloyd George and Harold Wilson had done, yet wanted to evangelise it with the 'Judeo-Christian tradition' that marked her Sermon on the Mound, and the simpler precepts of the Scots enlightenment. Hence that bizarre desire to be accepted *as* a Scot.

The other enlightenment tradition – of society and civic action – plainly bewildered her; her boorish parliamentary supporters deepened the gulf. But without Thatcher, and 'minimal government', Anglo-Scottish coexistence becomes more difficult. Douglas Hurd (whose thriller *Scotch on the Rocks* didn't help matters much) once wrote that voluntary social activity was an English rather than a Scottish principle. In England there is less inter-penetration of state and civil society, so a state expanded at the expense of local power is possible. Not in Scotland. Charter 88 argued that the English could profitably develop the local state – through the example of the Scottish Constitutional Convention. But in view of the government's assault on local responsibility, regardless of European or Scottish developments, Benjamin Jowett's retort to John Stuart Blackie seems more apposite. Asked what he thought of Scotland, the Master of Balliol replied, 'Sir, we never think of you at all!'

Section Three
A Spear Carrier Speaks

14
Peace and War in Steelopolis
(1998)

One of the few ways of making sense of a
period of sustained technological and social
change is to start with family history and
biography – trying to work out what was
'typical' and what was exceptional.
The drift of the author's own 'extended family'
– originally chronicled in a *London Review of
Books* diary – may cast some light on the
distinctive nature of Scottish industrialisation
and the retreat from it.

There is a photograph of me on VE day in 1945. I am sitting in a
pram in the Clyde Park in Motherwell. My mother has thoughtfully
decorated the pram with Allied flags. I am all of six months old,
and already the veteran of one political campaign. In April my
mother had voted for Dr Robert MacIntyre as Scottish National
Party MP for Motherwell, the first and for a long time the last
Nationalist in Westminster. He would lose the seat in the General
Election of July, by which time my father had returned from Canada,
where he had been training to be a fighter pilot, something he
never – thank God – had to be.

Six months later we would be living in a 'Pre-fab' in Watling
Crescent. This invention of the new Labour government,
hammering swords pretty rapidly into phoughshares, was a neat
little house, built on the assembly-line of the Blackburn aircraft
works at Dumbarton, and delivered by a big blue low-loader truck
which, hardly a year before, had been carrying bits of bombers.

Watling Crescent couldn't have been more different to the grandparental houses, Harvie Crossfield and Russell Broomside. Both were big Edwardian villas, but Crossfield was built with two two-room flats on the first storey, while Broomside, in red sandstone, had been the manager's house for Broomside Pit, which lay in woodland a hundred yards away. Papa Russell had helped install its winding engines, green hissing monsters, forty years before.

Motherwell was a town of two storey houses. Anything higher would have fallen down because of the subsidence which the pits had caused. Subsidence had, before my time, carried off the gigantic Hamilton Palace, which my aunt could remember standing empty in the early 1920s. Dalzell House, deserted by the Hamiltons of Dalzell, looked likely to follow it.

The Harvies were a federal unit of one of those ramified Lowland clans which the French – or rather Franco-Scottish – sociologist Emanuel Todd argues were peculiar to the Celtic periphery of Britain: 'authoritarian families' where attitudes and policies tended to be hammered out by discussion rather than loyalty. According to Todd, the English family was close, essentially nuclear, but also subject to emotional explosions which could blow it apart. The Scots and Irish families remained at greater distance but generally managed to keep on speaking terms. There was a Harvie-Notman-Aikman-Watt cousinhood which ramified through what George Orwell would have called a lower-middle-middle-class stratum (teachers, office managers, Free Church ministers) in west-central Scotland, sending branches into the higher strata. There was a mirror image, slightly weaker, on my mother's side, which connected with the North-East, a famous recruiting-ground for teachers.

The framework which accommodated both was Motherwell, and its rapid industrialisation in the second half of the nineteenth century. The population of the town went up from 4,000 in 1860 to over 70,000 in 1910, if the surrounding villages were counted in. With steelworks, mines, foundries and two railway rolling stock works, it was the nearest that Scotland got to Germany's Essen.

Both family groups represented an artisan-professional class ingested to provide a sort of instant social overhead capital. So far as I knew, no-one had actually done unskilled manual work, of the sort that propelled Motherwell forward – and hardly a soul had seen the inside of a pub. The Harvies had been small farmers in Dalserf, who had made the transition to industry by moving the four miles to Motherwell. The Notmans had been railwaymen, the Russells blacksmiths and the Petries slaters. But all of them were moving, often by working for the railways – across Scotland, into the salariat and professions, and abroad, a process which seems to have got going in the 1870s, roughly when steelmaking in Motherwell started through the entrepreneurship of the Colville family.

In the 1890s the Harvies and another Motherwell family, the Craigs, got together and formed a discussion group called the Octagon – evangelical, liberal, republican – whose doings were recorded in the *Motherwell Speaker* which my grandfather ran. Journalism was always a lure for the Harvies; the *Speaker* nearly ruined Grandpa. He became office manager at Colvilles; his brother built the elaborate Roman-revival red sandstone office; his brother Willie went to London as the private secretary of a Liberal MP, Sir Robert Laidlaw, and made a modest packet in Malayan rubber. Tom Craig became Manager of the Dalziel Co-op, then the second-largest in the country. John Craig, an iron-puddler's son, became the managing director of Colvilles, and ran the works until the 1950s. The Colvilles became Tories. One, briefly Secretary of State, ended as Governor of Bengal.

Grandma Harvie's brother-in-law Alex Aikman started as a naval architect, worked for various Clydeside yards, and ended up owning the Grangemouth Dockyard, which had built the first steamer in the the world, the *Charlotte Dundas* in 1802. It was a small yard specialising in slightly oddball ships – wine carriers, missionary ships, flatiron colliers which could sail under the bridges of the Thames.

On the Russell side, Grandma's sister Janet married another Huntly man Robert Hay, who became Professor of Metallurgy at the Royal Technical College (now Strathclyde University) in Glasgow. These were the days when the title meant a big house near Blantyre with the haunting name of Chanting Hall, and a bottle-green Armstrong-Siddeley, chauffeur-driven. There was also one Frank Guelph Cox, a distant relative of Grandpa Harvie, who started out as a hydraulic engineer in Wishaw and perfected a method of raising hulks by pumping them full of compressed air. In the 1920s he purchased much of the German High Seas Fleet, lying on the bottom of Scapa Flow, and sold several battleships for scrap. The stern lantern of the flagship, the *Kaiser Friedrich der Grosse* stood in the sitting room of Uncle Alex's summer house at North Berwick. In 1939 Grandpa Harvie felt sufficiently prosperous to sail aross the Atlantic to visit his brothers in Canada. He returned on the Donaldson liner *Athenia*. Then war broke out. On its return trip, the *Athenia* was torpedoed, the first sinking of the war.

West Scotland was an industrial Sleeping Beauty before Hitler awoke it – the shipyards empty, 40% unemployment in steel and mining towns like Motherwell. Then rearmament after 1934 began to revive the shipyards of the Clyde, and their suppliers. But they, and perhaps Scotland in general, were hit harder by the Second than by the First World War. British casualties were a third of those in the earlier conflict, which had killed three-quarters of a million; something which may account for that peculiar 'Dad's Army' sentimentality about 1939-45. Everywhere else, World War II was a hellish conflict, in which unthinkable barbarities were committed by everyone; in Britain it was – with Dunkirk, the Blitz, D-Day – a sort of ritual, painful, but still a celebration of nationality. Yet my father's best man was killed in Italy; one of his closest friends was shot down over Cologne. My mother's cousin died on an RAF training flight. I remember his mother, Aunt Janet, at Chanting Hall, a sad and seemingly insubstantial lady, in her dark, overshadowed garden; the overgrown tennis court where the cousins had played.

My father had been in the Peace Pledge Union in the 1930s, one of the majority of Glasgow students who elected the Rev Dick Sheppard as Rector in 1936. But he enlisted in 1939 and after a short spell as a private, became a sub-lieutenant in the Highland Light Infantry – the *Giftzwerge* who terrified German conscripts in the previous war. His battalion, under Colonel Herbert Waddell (who had captained the Scottish rugby team in the 1930s) was in training during Dunkirk. Thereafter the powers in Whitehall decided that the HLI ought to become a tank regiment. They tried, but they were terrible. The regiment was disbanded, Waddell, sidelined (though his son, Gordon Waddell, also a Scotland captain, went into diamonds, married the daughter of Harry Oppenheimer, and ended up carving up the world diamond market between South Africa and the Soviet Union). Father went to Canada and stayed alive. His cousin Tom, whose father had been a Christian Socialist of the Keir Hardie sort, tried to keep out of the conflict, but eventually enlisted as a Medical Officer. He served as a Surgeon-Captain at Monte Cassino and Lake Trasimene. He was hit while trying to tend the wounded, and died, gazetted MC. I bear his name.

Father's cousin George Watt had an altogether different war. His father had married grandfather Harvie's sister and owned an ironworks in Armadale, fifteen miles north-east. George Harvie-Watt, as he styled himself, became a London lawyer and businessman and in 1935 a Conservative MP. His way up seemed to be the Territorial Army, and he got elected to parliament for the solidly Tory London suburban seat of Richmond. In 1940 he was commanding flak batteries south of London when Churchill came to inspect, horrifying everyone by suddenly urinating in full view of all the assembled troops. 'Must water the horses,' he had said.

Subsequently Harvie-Watt was invited to become his Parliamentary Private Secretary. He was reckoned to be a Chamberlainite but amiable, keeping the premier in touch with a Conservative Party which distrusted its leader. Which didn't prevent him meeting periodically with Hugh Dalton and conspiring in a mild way to replace Churchill with some human dynamo like Sir John Anderson. In these dialogues Scottish affairs surfaced never at all. He got a baronetcy in 1945, stayed at Richmond for another decade, spoke rarely if ever, and became Chairman of Consolidated Gold Fields. I met him a few years before his death, when he had retired to Earlsferry in Fife. Had he ever returned to the West of Scotland? Not for years.

Father's sister Jessie qualified with an ordinary degree at Glasgow, couldn't find a job, and returned to take honours. She then taught for the county in various parish schools, being sacked at the end of each term and then re-engaged to save money. At one stage she taught in the mining village of Lesmahagow, mentally dominated by the astonishing family of the Cairncrosses. There were eight children, five of whom went to university, and three became professors. Sir Alec Cairncross became chief government economist; his brother Andrew (for a time in the 1940s my father's head of department) was a Shakespearian scholar and went to an American university as professor; the youngest brother became a Communist and a Russian agent within British Intelligence. After Burgess and MacLean, Philby and Blunt, John Cairncross was the 'fifth man'.

This 'intelligence' theme cropped up in two other areas. My mother had also gone into teaching – the Harvies were in full flight from industry – in the Catholic high school in Motherwell, Our Lady's. This involved crossing a line rarely approached by the rest of the cousinhood, liberal though they were – there was no Catholic within the ranks. One of her pupils was Cardinal Winning. She had been to Germany in *Olympiajahre* 1936, staying with a pen-friend whose father ran a paint factory in Finsterwalde. Papa Russell, director of Anderson Boyes, the coal-cutter company, visited Finsterwalde and Berlin in 1936 and was impressed, like a lot of conservative British businessmen of the time, by Hitler, autobahns, etc. Anderson Boyes were desperate for orders, and there was the Ruhrgebiet and Silesia to be considered as markets. After the war, Soviet-controlled Poland and the Ukraine, not to speak of China, seemed as promising. (In fact, because Coats-Patons controlled most of the European cotton industry, and ICI were part of an international cartel with IG Farben, the Scottish business classes were more implicated than those in the south with the European authoritarians. Anti-devolution views from business had something of a pedigree). My mother spent the rest of the war as a teacher in Rothesay, but her best friend Nan Gillespie went south, to Bletchley Park, where (among 10,000 other civil servants) she became a translator in the department which was, through the Enigma decoder, intercepting the communications of the German high command. She emigrated to the USA and married a Princeton academic called Vincent Buranelli. They made their money scriptwriting for Lowell Thomas, who had 'discovered' TE Lawrence, on the prompting of John Buchan, in 1916.

In 1969, when the British Open University was set up, I moved to Walton Hall, one of the out-stations of Bletchley. In Aspley Guise, near where I had my house, lived Peter Calvocoressi, Nan's boss, who in due course became my first publisher, and a central historian of the war. The Open University also brought me into contact with the Kettles. Margot Gale had been, prewar, secretary of the Scottish Union of Students and Robert MacIntyre's girlfriend at Edinburgh University. She was married for a time to Gabriel Carrit, an upper-class radical who became a Communist spy on the staff of the *Viceroy of India*.

Were these ramifications unusual? My hunch is that they were fairly frequently encountered within what the sociologist David McCrone has called the 'lieutenant class'. This Scottish public service bourgeoisie was moralistic and intellectual, and intensely ambitious. Its industrial success was a means to an end, rather than an end in itself – its ambitions fitted into the framework of Britain and its empire. Hence this pattern of relationships which stretched into the 'corridors of power'.

I think that these foregoing may help provide an objective correlative for two things. One is the salience of espionage and state intelligence within the Scottish middle class, commemorated in the fiction of John Buchan, Stuart Hood and Allan Massie. Because of the interlinking of business, politics, and what could be called an European outlook, the Scots encountered this world more. But the war also accelerated the country's subsequent decline. War's demands hit the middle classes particularly hard. Casualties were severe in two areas in which technologists were closely involved – ships and aircraft. The U-Boat war claimed many thousand Scots engineers, and the bombing offensive against German towns – appalling in its consequences for German civilians – also cost the lives of 50,000 aircrew, most of them well-qualified professionals. A good proportion of a new generation of managers and technologists was wiped out.

Great-uncle Tom Notman died in 1946. He was a Minister of the Kirk who had come over in 1929 with the rest of the United Frees. The death of his son Tom in Italy hit him hard, and although he moved from his Glasgow shipyard parish, Govan, where his assistant was John Brown, father of Gordon, to the parish of Applegarth and Sibbaldie in Dumfriesshire, he never recovered. At his funeral there walked behind his coffin his university friend James Maxton. 'You have elected me to protest,' Maxton addressed his hard-done-by Bridgeton voters in 1945, 'And I will protest until I die.' Six months later Maxton, too was dead. A first crack in the structure?

But up until the 1960s the cousinhood still cohered. There was an annual gathering on Boxing Day at Uncle Alex's house at Stirling, and he had hopes that I might follow him as a shipbuilder. As it was, I got introduced to Grangemouth Dock ward on the cusp of revolutionary, irreversible change. The launch of the *Eaglescliffe Hall* occurred just on the eve of the Suez crisis. She was an ore carrier for the Great Lakes – no more than a self-propelling barge, though oddly similar in proportions to the vast bulk carriers which were to revolutionise sea freight. These took to the water when the closure of the canal produced a tenfold expansion in ship size. Within ten years this development had wiped most of the Scottish shipbuilding industry out, Grangemouth Dockyard included.

But even before this, war had radically altered this class's relationship to Scotland. My mother's brother John fought his way through the Normandy landings and was one of the first British soldiers into the *Reichskanzlei* in Berlin. He did not come back to Motherwell, not for any tragic reason. It made better sense to run a chemist's in Cambridgeshire. And many of his comrades thought likewise. Emigration from Scotland, to Canada, Australia and above all England, ran at record levels for a couple of decades after the war, although the economy had reverted to its Edwardian state of health.

Little of the world of the cousinhood is left, and only a few elderly relatives keep in contact. Broomside still stands, though Crossfield was demolished to make way for a fourteen-storey block of flats in 1961, the year Ravenscraig went into blast. Uncle Alex's Sutherland House is now the headquarters of the Scottish Youth Hostels Association. The Conservative Party of Churchill and cousin Harvie-Watt, which held over 50% of votes and MPs in Scotland in 1955, lost its last MPs in 1997. Dalziel Co-op is a part of ScotMid, struggling against the hypermarkets, but its miniature industrial commonwealth in central Motherwell is practically derelict. The funeral business survives. So too does Dalzell House, now converted to luxury flats. And though Hamilton Palace has long vanished, William Adam's stables at Chatelherault, which the Duke wanted more magnificent than his French chateau, are once again a miniature Trianon, a great place for wedding receptions.

You look north, and see a huge tract of birch waving over the graveyard of scores of furnaces and foundries, collieries and power stations, hundreds of miles of railway, and a vanished revolution.

15
A Voice from the Débàcle
– the 1979 Referendum Experience
(1982)

1979 was humiliating for home rulers and
misleading for unionists: to write about it was,
to paraphrase Yeats, to pluck 'bitter wisdom
which enriched the blood'. Still a member of
the Labour Party when he wrote it, the
author's assessment of our
present governing generation was not
enhanced by the experience.

My treatment of Labour's 1979 Referendum campaign in the East
of Scotland must be qualified by my own point of view – that of a
fairly central participant. For someone to return to Edinburgh after
ten years and then take the chair at meetings of the Lothian Labour
Yes Campaign may suggest either a flattering degree of charisma,
or total institutional breakdown. In reality, it meant neither, simply
the great organisational axiom of British socialism – 'Last out of
the room becomes minutes secretary.'

Yet this personal experience does dramatise some basic
problems of the Labour campaign. Devolution was a new and
contentious issue for Scottish socialists, bound up, for those who
supported it through conviction, with original and somewhat
intellectual conceptions of politics. It was difficult to square it with
the traditional routines of the Labour Party. Though a distinctive
organisation with a momentum of its own needed to be created to
fight the campaign, party unity had still to be maintained in the
run-up to a general election. The question which must be asked in

retrospect is: did the inevitable compromise weaken the impact of the campaign and, because of tensions which grew throughout, ultimately imperil Labour's traditional solidarity?

The looming election undoubtedly circumscribed Labour's possibilities of action. Party divisions on devolution – with most local government members hostile – meant, so most pro-devolutionists argued, that to join a devolution coalition, like Yes for Scotland, would provoke intra-party conflict. But the allocation of funds and responsibilities to the election meant that there was precious little to use for a separate campaign in Edinburgh. With only South, West and East Constituency Parties in favour of a devolution campaign, Pentlands and North hostile, Leith torpid and Central neutral, Labour pro-devolutionists had to proceed very cautiously to create an organisation which would mobilise all available support in the constituencies without spurring the antis into action. But playing it by the book took time. While an Edinburgh branch of Yes for Scotland was organised on November 13 at a meeting in the Appleton Tower, George Square, the Labour Committee was not set up until a meeting on January 20, at the Trades Council.

The Yes for Scotland organisation, whose November meeting I observed, would have confirmed many Labour doubts. The meeting certainly reflected the ecumenical spirit of John MacCormick's Scottish Convention more than the SNP (and, as Yes for Scotland included the Communists, later to be represented on the Labour Committee through the Trades Council, there was some organic connection between the two bodies). But Labour's notion of 'solidarity' could not have responded to the inclusion of prominent Conservatives, nor to the active role played by several members of the breakaway Scottish Labour Party, nor, most crucially, to the Secretary of YFS's Edinburgh branch, Ian Hoy. The son of the former Leith MP, Hoy had, three years earlier, ostentatiously quitted Labour for the Conservatives, and cooperation with him would have been valuable ammunition for the antis. My own impression is that Hoy's own consciousness of the constraints of his position may have inhibited his own organisation, until quite late on, from building up the informal contacts which were ultimately made.

Constraints of a different sort affected the main personality associated with the Labour campaign in the East of Scotland, Gordon Brown. The former student Rector of Edinburgh University, editor of *The Red Paper on Scotland* (1975) and prospective candidate for Edinburgh South, Brown had been elected to the Labour Party's Scottish Executive in March 1977, and the next year became Chairman of its campaign sub-committee. In this position it was impossible for him to be unaware of the strong anti-devolution feelings of the Chairman of the Scottish Executive, Janey Buchan, and his desire to preserve peace on the Executive possibly made him pursue – and thus transmit directly to Edinburgh – an over-defensive line. No one worked harder than Brown for the Labour-devolutionist cause, but the tragedy was that explicitly anti-devolution groups like the Conservatives and Scotland Says No were all too frequently the least of his worries. His fears were, I think, enhanced by a debate with Tam Dalyell at the Trades Council Centre on January 23, when a majority, largely composed of councillors and veteran activists, was aggressively hostile and responded enthusiastically to Dalyell's amazing combination of the folksy and the Olympian – 'Yes, I'm glad you asked me that about extra taxation, Betty, because as Willy Brandt told me. . . ' At this level, Brown could not compete, however lucid and impressive his arguments, and the experience may have led him to overestimate the opposition, which was content to come to meetings, pass resolutions in the Labour group, and leave it at that.

The initiative for setting up an Edinburgh campaign committee came from South Edinburgh, where the secretary, Nigel Griffiths, had been empowered to co-opt members on to a 'devolution sub-committee'. This met on January 7 and, although only five strong, commemorated itself with a press release. (Subsequently, Brown was liable to transform almost any drink with his friends into a 'meeting addressed by' for the benefit of the papers and the bafflement of future historians.) It allowed Brown, myself and Griffiths to make informal contacts and find out how matters stood in other parties, and convene the first, and not terribly successful, meeting of pro-devolutionists in the Trades Council on January 20.

The problem was that both of us were burdened by other – although linked – commitments, Brown with his Scottish Executive worries and I with the publication of a pamphlet we had written jointly with Carol Craig of the University Politics Department. Originally stimulated by a perceived lack of simple explanations of the Scotland Act (the antis having vetoed an official government leaflet), this pamphlet emerged early in February in two forms: Speakers' Notes published by the Scottish Council of the Labour Party; and *The Voter's Guide to the Scottish Assembly*. Given the almost total uselessness of meetings and the pamphlet's low sale (about 60 per cent of copies printed), this was, on reflection, so much wasted effort. Further, on January 19, I left for Paris to brief Professor Francois Bedarida's seminar at the *Ecole Nationale d'Administration* and to lecture at the Sorbonne, both on Scottish nationality. Deserting the ship? Possibly; but it was for academic reasons that I was supposed to be in Edinburgh as a Fellow of the School of Advanced Studies, anyway. Returning North, I went along to the campaign's second meeting on January 27 at the Trades Council and, in Brown's absence at Scottish Council, found myself chairing it

The meeting was instantly faced with a problem: how to get into the Trades Council offices? This was solved only in a material way by the arrival of the Trades Council Secretary, Des Loughney. His predecessor, John Henry, a much-loved Labour Party stalwart and strong devolutionist, had gone to the STUC as Assistant Secretary, whereupon Loughney, a member of the Socialist Workers' Party, had been elected through a brief *entente* of the far Left. Although nationally the SWP was pro-devolution, its Scottish Committee was against, and Loughney's lack of enthusiasm was all too patent.

Similarly obvious was the absence of the Edinburgh Labour Party organiser, Joe Hill, who had been allowed by the City Party Executive to treat the Referendum as a special campaign, outwith his usual duties. Being hostile to devolution, he had nothing to do with it. The 'Lothian Labour Yes Campaign', as the meeting later constituted itself, gained the use of the Trades Council duplicator and of Ruskin House, and personal relations with the two dissenting officials were always friendly, but the Committee had virtually to set up an organisation from scratch.

That the meeting was a success cannot be attributed to a chairman who had been absent from Edinburgh Labour politics for a decade, but to the personal motivations of the members who were to take on leading roles and execute them with great competence. These personal factors meant that a neutral chairman was a positive asset.

Don Robertson, who took on the organisation of meetings, and Ian Millar, who did the same for street leafleting, had both been involved with the Scottish Labour Party, and in a sense were 'working their passage back'. Jim Boyack, who handled posters and leaflets, had always been a strong Home Ruler within the Labour Party. Trevor Davies and Ron Hurley, who handled publicity, were both English, and participated primarily out of a sense of party loyalty. Their enthusiasm meant that decisions in principle about funds, appeals, meetings, leafleting, headquarters and constituency contacts were rapidly taken, a timetable was worked out, and then the constituent elements devolved to individuals for executive action.

This left the problem of organisation in the various Edinburgh constituencies. East had been contacted, and informed us that they were well-organised. South and West could be left to themselves. In North, which was run by a far-Left crowd of antis, the moderate minority could be counted on to organise leafleting. A somewhat similar situation obtained in Leith. In Pentlands the party was hostile but the candidate, Arthur Johnstone, and a minority of members, were helpful and energetic, while we could count on increasing support in Central as its MP, Robin Cook, took a more and more prominent share in the Conservative-sponsored Scotland Says No campaign. For all of these constituencies as well as for some of the actively devolutionist ones, we had to arrange leaflets and posters.

Leafleting was crucial. There was neither time nor manpower available for canvassing – although this would have been valuable in yielding poster sites. And the supply of literature was less than masterfully handled by the central organisations of the Scottish Labour movement. The STUC leaflet was a crabbed little piece of typography, while the Labour Party one was an unmitigated disaster – less than 100 words along the lines of 'All say yes or Tinkerbell will die'. Even more tragic was the admirable special issue of *Highway* issued by the Transport and General Workers' Union: the size and format of a *Daily Record* sheet, only about 200 could be carried at a time, and in no way could it be used as a poster, despite its bulk.

As for posters, the beaming grin of Uncle Jim Callaghan coexisted ill with streets of ungritted frozen slush, the result of the public service workers' strike, while the STUC offering had to be read through binoculars at distances of over five feet. We printed our own. But however bad these publications were, our problem was that they never seemed to be where we wanted them. We asked for about 32,000 of the Labour leaflet and got about 15,000, while around the same number of *Highways* found their way to our headquarters at Ruskin House, frequently from union or party offices where they had simply been dumped. Some, for all I know, may still be there. Eventually, we got them all out before Referendum day, but only by making informal contact with Yes for Scotland and the SNP to ensure that Yes literature in general was well distributed throughout the city. For this I take responsibility, as well as for the fact that the last 2000 *Highways* (a late windfall) were actually distributed in Pentlands by Stephen Maxwell, the SNP candidate, and his helpers on the evening of February 28 when Labour was having its final rally.

Our publicity was well-organised. There were press releases, press conferences and every evening we would sit and feed Gordon Brown with 'new lines' for his Glasgow press conferences on the following day. To what end? My own view now is that it simply made our arguments too diffuse. Tam Dalyell, by hammering away ceaselessly at three or four points, remained the personality of the campaign, simplistic and deeply reactionary though I think the tendency of his 'anti-all-government' propaganda was.

As for meetings, God knows we tried. Our own promotion at the Trades Council on February 21 was, in terms of numbers, a near disaster although the standard of speaking – from Ronald King Murray, the Lord Advocate, and Hugh Wyper of the T&GWU – was better than what was to come in the final rally organised by Labour in the North British Hotel. The strikers had closed the Assembly Rooms, so the venue had to be moved to this ominously named palace. The speeches of Bruce Millan, John Smith and David Owen, stupefyingly dull, were dutifully applauded by a capacity audience of well-dressed Edinbourgeois. The only man in a kilt there proved to be hostile. I cannot recollect that a word of thanks was expressed by the platform party or the Transport House officials to any of the Edinburgh volunteers. But by that time we had other things on our minds.

Referendum day was, almost inevitably, an anticlimax. Jim Boyack and his squad got poster boards out to schools in Labour areas (no mean feat given the non-participation of half the constituencies) and I manned the Labour Party office at Ruskin House. But for most of the time there was little to be done as, without canvassing returns, we had little information on needs for cars, babysitters, etc. I spent more time dealing with a stream of foreign journalists and Bedarida's ENA students. Most of our effort was put into four hired loudspeakers which were transferred from car to car as these became available. We covered pretty constantly the main Labour areas and shopping centres, overlapping as little as possible with the other Yes loudspeakers. In the intense cold of the evening we concentrated on Wester Hailes and Leith. Yet phone queries from areas like Craigmillar and Dunfermline seemed to indicate that assurances of efficient campaigning in 'solid Labour' areas were false, and pro-devolution organisation non-existent. But by then there was nothing we could do. Polls closed at 10 and we all trooped over to the pub to watch ITN, where a poll suggested a lead for devolution in Scotland of 57%: 43%.

Angus Calder, who had been driving a loudspeaker car for most of the day, persuaded himself after several pints that it was 1945 all over again. Thus exhilarated we went home. Next afternoon, when the results came in, the Yeses had it in Lothian by a whisker – 187,221 to 186,421. A report from the count suggested that Craigmillar, an area of council housing, had polled 45 per cent; Morningside, a middle-class area, 75 per cent. While our efforts might just have managed to turn a narrow defeat into a tiny majority, they were patently useless in overcoming the relative apathy and indifference of the Labour heartlands.

Who was involved in the Labour campaign? Estimating numbers and judging social background is difficult, and the sketch that follows is based only on the details I kept of the 56 who helped at Ruskin House in the last week. Up to 30 more must have been involved in those constituencies which organised their own campaigns.

The two most significant groups were from the teaching professions (34%) and from the other professions (25%), among whom those involved in the media, public relations, voluntary bodies and publishing yielded 16%. The dominance of the teachers probably had something to do with the closure of schools and colleges, both through the strikes and on Referendum day.

The age distribution peaked in the early thirties (although it was significant that students took virtually no interest in the campaign, the University Labour Club being both hostile and moribund). Eighty-five per cent were Scots, 70 per cent were men and the overall political complexion – a very rough and ready subjective judgement, this – seemed to work out just to the right of the Tribune group.

Occupations of volunteers

1. Members of the teaching profession   19
   - a. University teachers   7
   - b. Higher education teachers 4
   - c. Schoolteachers   8
2. Members of other professions   14
   - a. Media, public relations, voluntary societies organisers 9
   - b. Other professions   5
3. White collar (secretarial, clerical)   5
4. Skilled trades   4
5. Union organisers   2
6. Housewives   3
7. Students   3
8. Unidentified or unemployed   7

Total   **56**

Constituencies of volunteers

South*	13
Central	12
West*	8
North	7
Leith	5
Pentlands	5
East*	4
Other	2
Total	**56**

* organised own campaign

Ages of volunteers

under 20	1
21–30	16
31–40	21
41–50	10
51–60	7
61–70	1
Total	**56**

Overall, a paradox emerges. Working-class areas seem to have voted for devolution, middle-class areas against, yet the support for the Lothian Labour Yes Campaign was overwhelmingly middle-class (almost 60 per cent of volunteers had degrees). The local working-class support that a general election involves – lapsed members turning up at temporary offices in housing schemes, offers of windows for posters, old ladies making tea – was almost totally lacking, although it was back in evidence at the General Election two months later. This was plainly the consequence of the failure to mobilise the constituencies as such. Our *ersatz* campaign, drawing strongly on individual expertise and enthusiasm and personal contacts and well-heeled enough to liquidate £400-odd in debts, generated roughly the effectiveness of a single constituency party at election pitch. It was physically impossible to do more, given the constraints under which we operated.

The most crippling of these and the one which, in retrospect, caused most bitterness, was the lack of strong leadership from the Labour Party organisation. At the very least, the fact that it delayed action until into the New Year meant that the chance of recruiting large-scale trade union and workplace support was virtually thrown away. Such support might not have amounted to much anyway – my own view – but by January it was too late to appeal to branch meetings for funds, manpower and factory contacts. Some of us would have gone further and demanded an early warning to dissident councillors, Party officials and MPs, that sustained opposition to devolution would lead to expulsion. At stake, after all, was not simply devolution but the only major piece of legislation the Callaghan government had carried, whose failure would more or less guarantee defeat at the Election.

Yet this necessary *Realpolitik* – every bit as much as the subtle arguments for a decentralised socialism – still ran counter to the traditional 'solidarity' of the Labour Party, despite the latter's destructive implications. It was evident however after Referendum and Election as divisions – both pro- and anti-devolution and left-right – continued to widen within the Party, that solidarity was wearing very thin.

In the middle of the campaign I ran into Norman Buchan at Waverley Station. He was sceptical about devolution, but reputedly rather less so than his wife. 'Yes', he sighed, 'Naomi Mitchison wrote to me that the one reason for voting for the Assembly was that it would be interesting to see what happened.' I agreed on that much. He went on, 'It would be interesting if you, or Donald MacCormick got elected, but it will be the old gang who run it.' Well, to revert to the personal: I would have been prepared to serve in the Assembly for a fraction of my salary out of conviction about the need to reconstruct Scotland's economy and society, and to experiment with new forms of democratic socialism – taking on the 'old gang' if necessary, but with some hope that the Assembly experience and its attendant publicity, would break them for good.

I finish this piece as a civil servant of another devolved government, Baden-Württemberg, enjoying resources and privileges far greater than I could have hoped for in Britain. This appointment may, I hope justifiably, denote some confidence in my own abilities, but it does nothing to lessen the bitterness that I feel at the dissipation by the old political order in Scotland of all the ability and altruism that was evident in the campaign for devolution.

16
Beyond Bairns' Play
– A New Agenda for Scottish Politics
(1982)

Written in the shadow of the Falklands War
this essay for the magazine *Cencrastus*, shows
that three years after the devolution flop,
things were needing to happen urgently
for Scotland's politics
to get beyond
the nursery stage.

I wrote *Scotland and Nationalism* in six months in 1976. The book was commissioned by Allen and Unwin, anticipating the passage of the Scotland and Wales bill in early 1977, and a good selling season during the subsequent referendum campaign. It did not happen quite like that. Although the book was well received and is still in print, having sold all but about 500 of an edition of 5000, this and other modest successes were not sufficient to save the job of my assiduous and kindly publisher in one of the periodic bloodlettings which afflict the business.

Six years and another book later my feelings about *Scotland and Nationalism* are mixed. It was written under intense pressure. I remember being so exhausted while working on the last chapter that I put part of it together from sentences scribbled on index cards while taking therapeutic walks in the woodland above my house at Woburn Sands. But this brought some interesting ideas to the boil, and there are times when, looking at it, I envy the energy of its author.

About its basic thesis I am now more sceptical. Like Ibsen's

Gregers Werle, I was out to kill the wild duck of Scottish nationalism: that conviction that the Union of 1707 had been fundamentally destructive; and to replace it with what I believed a more realistic thesis that certain essential qualities of Scotish nationality had been enhanced – even created – by the relation with England. What was now needed was a renegotiation of this relationship, achieved through devolution, which would alter the balance between the province and the metropolis in favour of the former.

Curiously, I found that this plea for devolution based on what I regarded as a rational analysis of historical experience was interpreted as being politically neutral if not hostile to the Scotland bill. The book was commended by violent opponents of devolution such as Tam Dalyell and Teddy Taylor, got a dismissive review from John Mackintosh, whose position was closest to my own, and I was nearly sued for libel by several nationalist zealots, one of whom alleged I was in the pay of the 'Scotland is British' campaign. Like Gregers Werle I learned the hard way that myths are not some parasitic growth on top of the political organism, but part of the organism itself. Setting out to shoot the wild duck had, after all, tragic consequences.

I don't claim this effect for *Scotland and Nationalism*. (It had, I think, absolutely no influence on the politics of devolution, beyond providing some cash to bail out one of the Labour pro-devolution organisations). But I do think that my own generation had Werle characteristics: aggressive rationalists who didn't really know the sort of material we had to deal with in politics, in Scotland, in Britain as a whole, and above all in ourselves.

Scotland and Nationalism was really a book written at the end of a period. It reeked of 'the lessons of 1968'; it assumed that libertarian-marxist intellectuals purged of false doctrine were going to ride the horse of nationalism as a new governing élite. 'What we think, we can,' as Louis MacNeice wrote in *An Eclogue for Christmas*, 'the old idealist lie'. Consciousness of the *geist* of modern Scotland, moreover, told us little about the political process in Westminster or, for that matter, in Scotland itself (where it had hardly existed until the late 1960s). The events of 1977-9 were a test for my generation, and one which, in political terms, we failed dismally.

In *Scotland and Nationalism* I assumed, and I think the assumption was common to most of my friends, that a general consensus on devolution existed, and 'conventional' party rivalry was more likely to further it than to destroy it. This assumption was almost totally falsified by subsequent political shifts. Labour used devolution purely and simply to preserve the two-party system. It was a weapon against the SNP, and as soon as the SNP started to lose, Labour shifted back to its traditional centralism or what was left of it after a decade and a half of party indiscipline had taken its toll. Few causes can ever have been fought with more disunity and less conviction.

The Conservatives saw their chance. As someone who counted himself expert on the politics of Irish home rule in 1886 I should have seen this one coming. Once the two-party game was back, Mrs Thatcher played it with skill and total lack of scruple, exploiting to the full Labour's tolerance of dissentients such as George Cunningham, Tam Dalyell, and Robin Cook, and swinging what was left of the Scottish Tory press strongly against devolution. Labour's response was simply to kick more own goals – the strike-wave of January-February 1979 was an almost wilful contribution to the destruction of the bill and the government.

In this situation, could the intervention of convinced nationalists, in and out of the SNP, have done much? Possibly not, but their (our) role was surely the most depressing of the lot. In part this was due to the adventure of the Scottish Labour Party, whose rapid rise and protracted death-agony consumed much of the energy of the home-rule left. In retrospect 'the magic party' was a terrible mistake, but it also exemplified weaknesses in the 'hard' nationalist outlook, and a fundamental and continuing immaturity.

An intriguing side to nationalism was the fact that, among the intellectuals, it accompanied the 'liberation' of the 1960s and

1970s. We played around with politics as we had experimented with our personal relationships – something all the more exciting because both had been constrained by the old order: the churches, the British party system. The results were rarely happy, personally or politically. Although such disruption may be a normal accompaniment to adolescence – and Scotland's renaissances have been bids for individual maturity as well as political independence – political organisation requires a regression to the family: a combination of competent organisation with some suspension of disbelief, some inclination to accept and enhance available leadership and doctrine. In our case destroying myths inevitably became 'destroying personalities'. Not a single one of the Scottish political figures of the 1970s has retained their authority, let alone laid claim to the sort of national leadership typified by Parnell, De Valera or even Gwynfor Evans.

It is odd how systematically the potential leaders of the major parties in Scotland have damaged their careers – from Jim Sillars on the left to Teddy Taylor on the right. Conservatives and Labour are led by boring administrators. William Wolfe, one of the most attractive figures in the SNP, and the architect of the party's revival in the 1960s has been disowned by his party for some undiplomatic remarks about Catholics – which he had the decency (characteristic of him but not of most politicians) to apologise for in public. There are only two success stories: Roy Jenkins, the Oxford élitist who captured an uncharacteristic Glasgow seat for a party which next to no-one in Scotland supports, and David Steel, the leader of probably the least Scottish of the major parties, whose voters in the Borders and the Northern Isles summarily rejected devolution in the 1979 referendum. The Social Democrat-Liberal alliance is led from Scotland, which does not support it, while Scottish politics are leaderless – the ultimate irony.

We were right, however, about some things. Scotland and England have quietly continued to drift apart. The absence of what the Germans call 'hooray-patriotismus' from Scotland during the Falklands crisis was surely significant. Labour won one byelection convincingly and the Conservatives polled scarcely 25% of the vote in the local elections, while their English average was 40%. Fourteen years ago the Scots were mourning the Argyll and Sutherland Highlanders – the dream of Empire appears to have faded at last.

We are also getting to grips with the structure of our subordination, in terms of the history and organisation of the 'effective parts' of our constitution – our administrators and our economy. In one sense our twentieth-century route to consciousness has, curiously, been following the classic Comtist pattern, from religious through metaphysical/poetic to scientific interpretation. But we now understand much better how our economy and our administrative state operate, what their potential for change and their limitations are.

A recent book, *Scotland, Multinationals and the Third World*, edited by Stephen Maxwell, (Mainstream, 1982) shows a range of reference far broader than the simplistic 'we wis robbed' nationalist economics of the late 1960s: a consciousness that a restoration of Scots manufacturing – let alone a Scots socialism – depends on new relationships being worked out with the countries which Scots-based firms traditionally exploited. In the same way we are beginning to edge away from the ever-fascinating topic of nationalism to discover why our voters (a) have traditionally voted on two-party lines, and (b) why this voting pattern has now been distorted beyond all correspondence with the south. Our consciousness of distinctiveness has spread from poetry and politics to society as a whole.

On the other hand the political class remains tiny. Probably less than 1% of the population belongs to a political party, and only about 10% of these are active members – 10,000 people, possibly, out of five million. Around them, some 200,000 have a reasonably informed interest in politics, expressed by the newspapers they read. Apart from that, our population's only political function is to react, in a vague and general way, to the initiatives of others. Not much different from England, maybe, but arguably the Scottish political class is proportionately bigger than it would be, outside of London. By now it is certainly better informed about the detailed requirements of politics than its southern counterpart.

The problem is partly one of extending political activity beyond the 'political class' to those whom it – and only it – can help, such as the young and the pensioners, women, the unemployed. It is also one of changing what we mean by politics to give it a more constructive social impact. Nationalist politics have always been bedevilled by the fact that in any practical sense they can only take effect when home rule comes. The increasing divergence between socialist ideology and socialist possibility is consigning Labour to a similar limbo. Attempts to marry the two, in the activities – otherwise commendable – of the '79 group, are doubly cursed by this impotence.

We have to think hard about a strategy for our politics. Politics grows on immediate success and need not have much to do with the attainment of long term goals. The 'new moral world' of the Independent Labour Party in the 1890s and 1900s was largely self-sustaining. In the 1960s, the steady increase of SNP branches built up a momentum of its own, which survived the setback of 1970. In a sense this is politics without 'politics', attractive enough for the machinery – slates of candidates, disputes, inner-party groups, etc. – to be discarded or not even adopted. No political party has sustained it for very long. Its real home is in the voluntary association. When I assess the effectiveness of the organisations with which I have been involved over the last two decades the real success stories seem to be those run by dedicated, competent organisers, such as Iain MacDougall of the Scottish Labour History Society, Tom Hart of the Scottish Association for Public Transport and Andrew Boyd of the Scottish Railway Preservation Society. All of these succeeded in part because they have a strategy of meeting definite objectives – producing a bibliography, improving a bus or rail service, restoring a locomotive – and in part because they are run (mostly) by consensus among the members and recognition of the authority that comes from reliability and sheer hard work.

In order to strengthen it, we have to envisage our national

movement in terms of a network of such organisations which can crossfertilise with politics, and whose individual enterprises can build up a momentum of success which will sustain political organisation. Strategically, this is equivalent to light attacks on an extended front, to confuse and overextend opponents, and probe the weaknesses of their defences, while we build up our strength. Bodies such as Scottish Education for Action and Development provide a paradigm of the educational/propagandist work which is necessary. There should be others in – at least – the following key fields. (I focus only on three linked areas where I can claim some special expertise. Others in the economic area are possibly even more important).

(1) Education

Here we are divided. We have a school system which is comprehensive and Scottish, but, effectively two higher education systems – the Scots-controlled colleges and universities. The spokesman of the latter profess opposition to the 'parochial' Scottishness they allege would come from local control. They have a poor case. The University Grants Committee is no longer the guarantor of academic liberty. It has turned nasty. Moreover, is there any longer plausibility in the case that Scottish control will lead to second-rate standards? Rather, we have a situation in which indifferent staff – often English – were recruited in the seller's market of the 'fat' Robbins years (when Scottish postgraduate provision was limited), and now choke off the appointment and promotion of the more talented. How many of the best young Scots historians, scientists, literary critics, economists, sociologists have got jobs at Scottish universities?

There is no case, save individuals' self-interest, against Scottish control of our entire education system, and its opponents realise this. It is time that a concerted campaign was launched to secure it, and meanwhile to develop a genuinely comprehensive, community-centred tertiary education system. Scottish teachers –

with their authoritarianism and their arcane politics – have far too long been the weak link in our intelligentsia. But a new generation has grown up to whom the old constraints do not apply. They must be encouraged and mobilised.

(2) Communications

This area is going to be vital, and technology has dealt us a good hand, if we have the nous to play it. Video, cable tv, local radio and citizens' band, word-processing, new printing techniques – all these are going to destroy very rapidly the traditional communication systems and the timid, tenured oligarchy which, in Scotland, dominates them. We've got to try to do two things with them to reach the uninvolved and to enable the diaspora, those of us whom lack of opportunity at home has scattered throughout Europe and America, to contribute ideas, organisation and lessons derived from political action in other countries. It was a paradox of the Scottish renaissance of the twenties and thirties that it was in media terms so conservative when Scots like Grierson and even Reith were establishing bridgeheads with new communications technologies. Such technologies are now available and cheap. We have to make use of them.

(3) Public health, perhaps. . .

During the Scotland vs. Russian match in the World Cup series, some fans were seen clutching a banner inscribed 'Alcoholism versus Stalinism'. Wit is a quality relatively new to the Scottish football supporter, and there's a problem here which almost justifies the ferocity of nineteenth-century teetotallers. Not the old 'drink is the curse of the working classes' scenario but the connection between the low level of Scottish political leadership and the tragic impact of alcohol. One can cite enough cases of men of real ability who have become politically embarrassing, or of others whose politics are left in the Abbotsford at closing time. The early labour pioneers were teetotal for good reasons – one can contrast the careers of Keir Hardie and Victor Grayson – and, however self-righteous the proposition seems, this sort of self-discipline is necessary, both for political effectiveness and as an example. Sly MacNeice again:

> Another drink: Cain has slain his brother.
> Another drink: Cain, they say, is cursed.
> Another and another and another
> The beautiful ideologies have burst.

Booze and high talk have gained us some fine insights – look at MacDiarmid – which any determined political strategy must accept. But the careful assessment of possibilities and priorities, the probing of opponent's weaknesses, the dismantling of hostile alliances – the politics which will save Scotland – has to exclude irrationality and indulgence. Third world nationalist movements identify booze and fags as components of the multinational system of control. We have every reason to do so as well, and in our acute national predicament, we haven't got the margin for error.

Our chance, as well as our problem, is that we are tied to a society which is really sick – the complacent promotion of the SDP as a party devoid of ideology, and its as rapid eclipse; the crumbling of the inner cities into self-destructive violence; the failure of the mainstream Labour movement to think strategically, or even try to move out of the tutelage of competing members of a discredited Oxbridge élite, such as Foot or Benn. The last year has seen the English left fall apart, even before the English as a whole kissed the rod over the Falklands and realised that they loved Big Sister.

Since completing *No Gods and Precious Few Heroes, Scotland 1914-80* (*Scotland and Nationalism*'s Hyde-like *doppelganger*) I have been working on élitism in British politics, on the complex interconnections between business, administration, culture and politics. The picture so far suggests that not only is 'Butskellism' dead, but the values of the two-party system as well. Mrs Thatcher does not represent traditional toryism but rational international capitalism. In the shape of the City of London and its associated activities this is now the most competent and well-organised section of the English economy, capable of a concerted action far beyond the potential of its industrial, let alone political rivals. It has, these days, little time for democracy.

I remember in 1973 talking to some Conservatives close to Mrs Thatcher and being struck by their unstinted approval of the *coup d'état* in Chile. They believed that only under an authoritarian régime could 'correct' economic measures be enforced. Would Churchill, or even Chamberlain, have reacted in this way?

With the waning of our world power, so too has gone our identification as the didactic bit of a democratic state. Something much more unpleasant and ruthless has emerged in its place. We are in the same Laager as the South Africans, the Galtieris and the Pinochets, and our media and our rulers want to keep things that way.

So far, not much difference in analysis from the Labour left? But the problem of Benn and Co is that they do not realise how implicated in this are their own power structures, and how much their efforts are constrained and dissipated by these. Left-centralism is no longer realism. We have to make use of our painfully-acquired rationalism to think out a future for Scotland; we don't do the British left any service by continuing to acquiesce in its fantasies.

And then we have to plan, and organise, and pay. The last is crucially important. We probably spend less on cultural and political organisation than our fathers did in the 1930s. While French Communists and German Social Democrats tithe themselves, we grudge paying political subscriptions which are scarcely equivalent to a bottle of whisky a year. A tithing system which involved the '10,000-odd activists' in Scottish politics would, if calculated on the national average wage, yield an income of about £100,000 a week, or £5million a year. Daniel O'Connell did not win Catholic Emancipation because people thought it a good idea, or morally right, but because the Irish peasantry paid a penny a week to finance the Catholic League. This priority must be ours.

> Unremitting, relentless,
> Organised to the last degree,
> Ah, Lenin, politics is bairns' play.
> To what this maun be.

MacDiarmid's plea for poetry characterised the scope and style of Scottish politics all too accurately. In the next couple of years we have to go far beyond bairn's play, or our sore-stricken country will be lost.

17
Grasping the Thistle
– a diary
(1986/87)

When in the mid-1980s Thatcherism got
uncoupled from the high oil price,
tough economies were in prospect
and Scottish policy became important.
By 1987 the likes of Kenyon Wright
were in action and Scots had started
'living a little dangerously'.
Published in *Cencrastus* in 1991,
this diary came out just before
the anticlimax of the 1992 general election.

Ken Cargill of BBC Scotland approached me in the Summer of
1986 with the proposal that I make a 50-minute television
programme on the present and future of Scottish politics for the
six-part series *Scotland 2000*. I'm not sure why the choice fell on
one of Scotland's remoter pundits – I teach at the University of
Tübingen in Baden-Württemberg – but the idea appealed to me.
Scottish politics seemed to be getting interesting again, after the
near-catatonia which had succeeded the devolution catastrophe in
1979, and after ten years at the Open University, where I made
several teaching documentaries, I was interested and reasonably
expert in the business of film-making. It was also likely that I would
have to revise my history of contemporary Scotland, *No Gods and
Precious Few Heroes*, so it would be useful to have an open line to
various well-placed sources. I drafted a treatment early in July and
sent it to Ken and John Milne, who became my producer. They

approved it and we agreed to start filming at the end of September.

On the first day of filming, in Glasgow, I decided to keep a diary. I hadn't intended to do so, but it seemed to make sense, for several reasons. One was simply therapeutic. I forget whether it was war or sex of which Hemingway said it was nine-tenths boredom and one-tenth terror, but filming can be like that, and you need something to keep you occupied when the crew (metaphorically) dump you in the broom-cupboard or the boot of the car, and proceed on mysterious purposes of their own. Secondly, this commission coincided with a fair amount of personal involvement in other projects in Britain and in Germany, not best calculated to keep the memory up to scratch. Impressions and intentions not noted down straight away might tend to vanish for good. But, most important, for the team as well as for me, the diary could furnish material about background, enable experimental comparisons to be made, and record off-the-cuff and off-camera exchanges with our interviewees.

As time went on, however, the diary became even more absorbing, as it began to record a complex weave of British, German and Scottish politics. This was partly because the intensity of each of these was growing in anticipation of general elections, boosted by the concentration of the media on such auguries as opinion polls and byelections. More than this, the Baden-Württemberg-Scotland contrast tended to point up one growing issue: the north-south divide in Britain and the collapse of Scottish manufacturing (Baden-Württemberg, the most prosperous region in Europe, derives over 40% of its GDP from manufacturing, Scotland only 25%). The filming also straddled the formal deregulation of the London stock exchange, the 'Big Bang', but what began as a fairly theoretical contrast between the 'industrial' economy of Baden-Württemberg and the dominance of 'finance' in the UK, took on its own dynamism, and a particular Scottish context, in the Distillers' takeover battle and its consequences.

Finally, there was the interest in seeing what my generation was up to. At forty-two, one begins, if one is sensible – and can stand the shock – to apply an historical calibration to one's own past. What seems still 'the other day' in fact occurred when my students were in their prams. The Hamilton byelection – the first major impact of Scottish nationalism – took place twenty years ago; twelve years (the lifetime of Hitler's Third Reich) have passed since the second revival of the SNP in 1974. My school and university friends, or at least contemporaries – David Steel, Malcolm Rifkind, Robin Cook, James Naughtie, Gordon Brown – are now in positions of political power, or are writing about politics, or rationalising them through historical explanation. This prominence is itself unusual, as twenty years ago the archetypal Scots MP was a dim, elderly trade unionist or town councillor, and it does stress with particular acuteness the choice between being Scots and being British politicians.

Such contacts are useful, but they emphasise my own situation 'in the gallery' – the more I observe politics, the more I perceive my own complete unsuitedness to the business. A writer and academic can devote him- or herself to the linear business of organising and communicating knowledge, with a reasonable expectation that an end-product will result. Not only is the politician's task much more glutted with unproductive routine – votes, committees, party meetings – his or her whole ambition might quite suddenly be shattered by a miscalculation or by sheer chance. I couldn't stand this, though I think my reaction has more than personal weight. My hunch is that this unproductive element has been aggravated by the long-running malfunctioning of the 'Westminster model', and this hunch may be something that strengthens the views here expressed.

My assistants, Paddy Bort and Helmut Schroder, must feel about Scottish politics as Lady Eden felt about the Suez Canal. It seems to flow through the office. It is, in fact, very easy to keep in touch from Southern Germany. The *Scotsman* usually gets here the day after publication, while the London papers take from four to ten days – an interesting and important example of the inefficiency of the metropolis. Tape cassettes, videos, PCU's and of course the phone expand the communications net. Hardly any of this would have been possible, financially or otherwise, ten years ago. If I feel less of an exile here than in London, new technology is almost certainly the reason why.

Yet, ultimately, the diary records an attempt to get back. Given a 25% revaluation of the Deutschmark against the pound sterling, why? Not sentiment or loneliness, certainly. More the sense that Scotland has huge economic, social and environmental problems and (though only prospectively) the means to solve them. If we can adapt our political structures to do so, we might again influence Europe as we did in the eighteenth century. If we don't try, or give up at the first obstacle, then our failure will measurably lessen the hope and commitment that Europe and the world need.

Tuesday 23 September

We drive to the Conservative Club at Airdrie, via Motherwell, where we suss out possible panoramic sites for a to camera piece by me. My original notion of Babylon Bridge, between Motherwell and Bellshill, won't work. This is a pity, for the name Babylon gives a link back to to Robert Owen's Orbiston Community and Scotland's first socialist experiments a hundred and fifty years ago. But the bridge scarcely apppears above the trees and industry appears nowhere. Above Cleland, however, the whole panorama of Motherwell and Ravenscraig opens out, the latter sending healthy jets of steam and smoke into unusually mild blue air. We agree to return here later to film. In contrast to the sheer expanse of Cathcart Labour Club, the Coatbridge and Airdrie Tories' place is a somewhat poky Victorian villa, done out in grubby vinyl wallpaper and yellowing paintwork. Lunch of ham and salad is set for about fifty by friendly elderly ladies (the average age of the whole gathering I'd place at over sixty – and that's including the youthful Secretary of State and his entourage). JM remarks how American many of the men look, and indeed they resemble so many Ian MacGregors. The prospective candidate, a Pickwickian lawyer in his fifties (just readopted for this hopeless seat) bustles industriously about.

I encounter the S of S in the lavatory, with no indication of recognition or memory of two less-than-enthusiastic articles. Aside from the Ian MacGregor Gathering, the men wear dark suits with the thin white stripes, darkening as they rise in political importance. The S of S wears – and carries off – a natty double-breasted grey number. He goes about pressing the flesh. The *porro unun necessarium* of any political meeting, a pretty girl to sit in the front row crossing her legs, is all but absent, the striking blonde who has been carting up loads of hot tatties staying downstairs in the kitchen.

The S of S begins his speech, which lasts for twenty minutes. Hard Thatcherite stuff – not even the most cryptic indication of dissent, or any notion that problems exist which may require cross-party collaboration. The £30 million allocated to Ravenscraig will end doubts about its future (although at least 50% of this cash is routine and Mrs T was notably unforthcoming about Ravenscraig's future in her STV interview on 4 September). Even the programme to renew Caterpillar's Uddingston plant is presented as some sort of triumph of market forces, rather than the 'triumph' of Rifkind throwing SDA money at Caterpillars (which would sound just like the Callaghan government and Chrysler at Linwood a decade earlier).

What I hadn't been prepared for is how frightening Rifkind is as a speaker. The voice is well-projected, but the face seems to have an independent life, with staring eyes which outBenn Benn and a visor-like smile whose effect is appalling. This may change on personal encounter.

The chairwoman reads out a list of pre-selected questions – on grants to business; were these going to incomers rather than old-established firms with cash-flow problems? On rates, council-house sales, immigration (here the S of S managed to be intriguingly liberal and conservative at the same time, praising the Asian community for its reverence for traditional values and defending their right to respect), fielding the hardy perennials of birching vandals and hanging drug-pushers. Nothing on devolution or specifically Scottish affairs. Response was polite but never really emphatic or attentive. One man, whose speech reminded me of my Tory grandfather, mourned the loss of members because of the closures of local steelworks and foundries, and I suspect, wasn't much reassured by Rifkind's defence of a profitable, rationalised British Steel. In general the atmosphere was polite and listless, closer to the Rotary than to a gathering of the party faithful.

'In fact there are a good few Rotarians here,' said a nice bustling lady in her early fifties who had been a candidate in the regionals, the wife of a man who runs a power-tool shop in Uddingston, 'The rest are local businessmen, a lot of their wives, and four or five doctors.' (GPs rather than from the local hospital, I'm later told: the hospital doctors are black). They come from up to four separate parties. The two ladies talk to the other – 'from *Bonkle* originally but I went to Hamilton Academy and my brothers went to Dalziel' – they strike me as SDP figures who are in the Tories because they could never ever be Labour and in places like Motherwell and Uddingston there just is no other non-Labour presence. The local youth seem to them apolitical. There is no functioning Young Conservative branch. 'Roddy was a Young Conservative wasn't he?' 'He was, but now he's in the Young Social Democrats.' Frankly I'm amazed to find there is such a thing, but not amazed to find ex-Young Conservatives joining it.

It's too easy to see Airdrie Conservative Club as hopelessly moribund. Its problem may stem from Lanarkshire peculiarities. Later on, John Smith says that in this area Conservatism is synonymous with Protestantism. So you wouldn't find Catholic Rotarians there, despite the fact that not a few Conservative MPs are Catholic – Gerry Malone, Michael Ancram, perhaps a greater proportion than those on the Labour benches like Canavan, White, Home-Robertson, Ernie Ross, Martin O'Neill. Despite the S of S's presence, I didn't see anyone else who was, or looked, Jewish, or any dusky Grunwick-type entrepreneurs. It was old-fashioned Scots Unionism, dying on its feet, and if Rifkind gets into his stride, he'll want to see quite a different ethos.

Wednesday 24 September

In the morning JM and I walk through the Botanic Gardens to interview Harry McShane, the last survivor of the Red Clyde. He lives a hundred yards along from Roy Jenkins in Baxter House, a Church of Scotland Old Folks Home – originally, I'd guess by Rowan Anderson around 1905 in a very Edinburgh style of architecture.

Harry is in a wee room in a modern extension at the rear. There has been an industrial dispute here about union recognition and rumour has it that Harry threatened to starve himself to death if the Kirk didn't recognise the union. A little man, pebble-lensed glasses, hair younger and darker than mine plastered down. He sits in a chair in a neat brown suit, a bookcase-full of dialectics behind him, and welcomes us. He is used to film crews, STV were up some months ago, filming him over two days. I mention Ian MacDougall, whom he knows, 'though I haven't seen him for a few years' and his book *No Mean Fighter*. Did I think it good? I say (honestly) yes. It was the best account of the Red Clyde. 'I didn't write it. Joan Smith took me down on the tape recorder and we edited it.' He says Pluto Press have just gone bust, but they paid him and Joan Smith a thousand each. The problems in interviewing him are a slight speech impediment, and his tendency to conjure up obscure parties and controversies, baffling to anyone but me (and only understandable because of my own specialised knowledge). He needs a lot of filming, and we can never be quite certain whether he thinks that matters – re working class consciousness and organisation – have got better or worse.

Worse: the rigour and grounding in dialectical materialism have disappeared. Better: there is more of a Scottish dimension; women are more involved, 'We never thought about women!' He has little time for the modern leaders of the Labour Party. He thinks Kinnock is a lightweight and Meacher 'goes on about exploitation, but can't explain about surplus value.' He sees a lot of Kay and Neil (Lord) Carmichael and is, thanks to them, better informed about me than other politicians a third his age. A member of the

SDP national executive, Jim Latta, comes to see him most weekends; and he treats him with sceptical respect. 'We were not nationalists. We thought they were mad. But now, I'm in favour of a Scottish Assembly, and the sooner we have it, the better.'

I stay on after the crew leaves. After the lights go and the tension drops, we talk on for another half hour or so. Harry is relaxed, curious, ironic. 'Manny Shinwell. Not a nice man. But he was the most intelligent. I knew him well. George McLeod, Lord McLeod, was here two years ago and he said I was going to become a Christian. Nonsense, I said, but he's a good man, I like him. In fact they're very nice here. I get about a lot, and I've lots of visitors, and trips out. Scotland 2000? – I won't see 2000. If the Queen sends me a telegram on my 100th – I'll send it back!'

Then we drive to Kippen to meet Lord Wilson of Langside (Lord Advocate 1967-70 in the Harold Wilson government and in 1979 a strong anti-devolutionist). This, I think, is a JM boo-boo. JM thinks that Lord W of L, having switched from Abominable No-Man in 1979 to SDP in 1981 must have changed his mind about Devolution. Lord W of L has not. He goes on at great length about how appalling the whole business is/will be. I say, well, what happens if Scotland ends up governed by people for whom only 17% of Scots vote? Surely you have to have consent. He seems to think that much more evil would seem to arise from Thatcher vs. Scottish Assembly than from Thatcher/ Younger vs. Scottish local authorities. JM seems desperate to prise out of Lord W of L that he's really changed and acquired an open mind by joining the SDP.

My own notion is Lord W of L has advanced not one sodding millimetre towards the SDP or anyone else. My impression is of a decent West of Scotland professional lawyer. Did a political stint for a bit, and was damned glad to get out of it and Edinburgh. The things that strike him as the arguments for continuing Unionism strike me as the obvious reasons for cutting the connection. But bashing holes in the Scotland Act is as much his hobby as his beautiful garden.

Thursday 25 September

We go doon the watter to film the Polaris depot-ship in the Holy Loch and the shipyards at the Tail of the Bank. The weather is dull and overcast all morning and hardly anything is visible when we go off in a 36' motor tug, the *Fencer*, from the almost-empty container depot at Greenock Princes Pier. Only one regular line now uses it. 'We're keeping our fingers crossed,' says the boatman, Mick, and the container park, from which (in its railway station days) hundreds of thousands left for Canada or America, is desolate.

I speak to camera about seeing the *Queen Elizabeth* refitting in the dry dock at Scott Lithgows' twenty-two years ago, about the importance of Sir James Lithgow in inter-war Scottish politics, and the subsequent decline of his yard. It has now only one order, a massive rig for Britoil (three years overdue on delivery date) and is owned by Trafalgar House, who also own the *QE2*. Will its slipways ever see another ship, let alone another rig?

There's a dry-dock, two subs and a freighter alongside the depot-ship. Yellow tarpaulins show where something hush-hush is being unloaded or stripped. We cannot enter the Loch without permission, and we can get no closer than 200 yards. I manage to get my piece off on cue after only one shot, and the freighter *Marchfield* obligingly sails out of the Loch. 'Word of command on her's Spanish,' says Mick. 'Crew are all Puerto Ricans.'

That evening, walking up from St Andrews Square, I was struck by all the smooth young men in suits, presumably out of the 80,000 Thatcher claims work in financial services in Edinburgh. Ties, let alone suits, are as rare in Castlemilk as among German Greens. Is Scotland thus breaking up into separate socio-economic regions each with its own character, class structure and problems? Finance in Edinburgh, new technology in the new towns, oil in the North East, Labour-administered depression in the West?

We then go off to Royal High, almost as difficult to get into as the Holy Loch. The first time that I've actually been there since it ceased to be a school. The Crown Office, the Lord Advocate's headquarters, is now there but otherwise it looks patently untenanted, something evident less in the Chamber itself than in the Lobby and common room (formerly Bill Bowie's music room) outside it. I show where I used to sit among the Celts, although comfortable (though sticky) simulated leather seats replace the old wooden benches. Before the clerks' chairs, where George Cubie (my university contemporary and a Commons clerk who would have gone North in 1979) would have sat, is a console which registers voting patterns with green lights activated by press buttons on the seats. Very like the *Bundestag*, but, oddly, without the latter's facilities for permanent TV coverage. These may not have been started on by 1979. Also no arms of any kind, which is strange given the symbolic eagle of the *Bundestag* or the House of Commons. No royal arms, no symbolic saltires or lions. This may be deliberate, an attempt to tone down potentially dangerous symbolism, but the effect, on me at least and taken in conjunction with the severe classicism of Hamilton's building, is republican. If elected politicians ever meet here, it won't be in a northern branch office of Westminster.

I am considering the feeling this place invokes – more rebellious than I've felt for some time when I notice a familiar figure limping up the playground. Lord Wilson of Langside on his way to see the Lord Advocate. He says he's just written to JM to say that he felt he didn't seem coherent enough when interviewed and would have liked to have more time. At which we're all rather stiffly polite, perhaps with the feelings of someone surprising a ghoul haunting the grave of his victim.

Tuesday 30 September

Then by car to interview Gordon Wilson at Broughty Ferry. Weather marvellous. GW friendly, plump, relaxed; his constituency assistant in attendance. Those ears which seemed to radiate national grievance have somehow retracted. We interview him next to Broughty Beach, which looks almost Mediterranean. Perhaps his confidence is stimulated by the fact that I sent him a donation for his 1983 campaign (I did the same for Gordon Brown and Archy

Kirkwood). He is deliberately vague (though not to camera) over SNP membership, but confident that his party and Plaid Cymru can call the shots at Westminster in the event of a hung parliament.

He has read at least some of *No Gods*, and his assistant seems to have read the lot and likes it. But what is really interesting is what he discloses after the interview, and how he states it. It appears that in 1977, on the defeat of the Scotland and Wales bill, the English Home Office expected riots in Scotland, and made contingency plans, including moving London police north by special train. 'That just shows, how much they misunderstood us,' he says, with a smile of pride. I'm not sure that a few blackened and roofless shooting lodges wouldn't have expedited the whole devolution business.

Thursday 2 October

JM picks me up early and we drive down to Albany Street to interview John McGrath at the 7:84 headquarters. Rooms packed with computers (like Tom Nairn's in Fife; the left is not slouching towards the new technology, but sprinting). McGrath sweeps up into an even more congested office. He also runs Freeway films. He is tall, prematurely white-haired, witty and energetic. He has read my books (Ken Alexander maintained that no-one had, so sod him!), both of 'em; and he says he based much of *Joe's Drum* on *Scotland and Nationalism*. Not sure I respond with mindless enthusiasm. *Joe's Drum* wasn't 7:84 at its best, always excepting John Bett's crazy imitation of Nicky Fairbairn at his most OTT.

But he is a fine, waspish interviewee, after taking disconcertingly copious notes about what he's being asked. He sees a much more democratic art in Scotland, reaching out to the working class, quite different from in England. 'In Scotland, we let the people speak, in England they try to fit people into frames.' He sees this as supported by the Scottish arts establishment. 'We don't scream about Marxists being like Fascists, like Rees-Mogg. In fact there are Marxists right at the centre of the Scots cultural bureaucracy.' And he says, 'Scotland sings.' Drama overflows into song and folklore, which is what he's trying to do in his latest show, Fionn MacColla's *The Albannach*. He sees the miners' strike as the real point of divergence between Scots and English politics.

My stuff on Scotland's lack of enthusiasm for the Falklands war is new to him. 'But the miners' strike, the sense that people who were only trying to protect their jobs and community, were savaged by the police and the press, this was something that really revolted ordinary people in Scotland!' He doesn't know about Ian MacGregor's estate on Loch Aweside.

After the crew has gone we talk about the *Centre of Things* (the book I'm writing on political fiction) and Joyce Cary and John Arden. I make my point about the relevance of the provincial, radical tradition to 'real' political fiction. He is obviously ambiguous about Arden. 'He sent me the first draft the first fifty pages of the *Non-stop Connolly Show* and it was marvellous. It made my cry. He started it with Queen Victoria as an Indian Goddess with lots of arms, and then with Connolly packing bibles in an Edinburgh bible factory. It was great.' But then Margaretta d'Arcy and nationalist dogma took over. He likes *Pearl,* though.

We then go along George Street to the Assembly Rooms where McGrath is rehearsing 7:84 in *The Albannach*, which they're taking on tour to Canada. This is the same hall where Angus Calder, Hamish Henderson and I were drinking after the Commonwealth Writer's Ceilidh two months ago, and I'm not certain it's the best place as the acoustics leave something to be desired, and frankly I find (admittedly after only half an hour) a certain obviousness in MacColla's contrast between amiable Celts and dour Freekirkers. I remember MacColla (or T Douglas MacDonald) as a frequent visitor to Morningside Public Library, one of these huge craggy men, all beard and eyebrows, with an air that suggested ethnic grievance fermenting away under his ancient raincoat. He was a convert to Catholicism and took the Muir, Mackay Brown, Compton Mackenzie line of a native jollity banjaxed by Calvinism. Not one I really share. Jansenist Catholicism would produce equal misery in Ireland and inflict itself on urban society as well. It would be interesting to know if MacDiarmid and Grassic Gibbon could be read in 1930s Ireland.

Our last interview is with Robin Cook at Old Mill House, Corstorphine. The mill is a hexagonal horse-mill, with a two-storey house adjoining, both so extensively converted as to appear new. Neat garden, neat children and loads of videos, books, pictures etc about horses. Also practically the complete works of Trollope – the really obscure novels, *An Old Man's Love*, etc. Is RC modelling himself on T, and is this, rather than Jeffrey Archer etc, his real reason for interest in political fiction?

Cook arrives from Blackpool via the Scottish Office. Manners even more ornate than usual. When I say he was in favour of devolution in the mid-'70s he can't remember this. I remind him of his article in the *Guardian*. He is saved by something going wrong with the camera from a nice bit of Orwellian double-think. He believes that the Manpower Services Commission will have to be devolved, and that in the long term fewer Scottish MPs will go south to Westminster – although it seems that he will be among them.

No, he's not prepared to speculate what will happen if Mrs Thatcher wins. Afterwards he gets JM and me a whisky and I ask him about his role as Kinnock's campaign manager. 'When Neil got the position. I felt myself unutterably smug.' 'Ah yes,' I can't refrain from replying, 'Just like 1963/4, but I don't mean that in congratulatory terms.' I can see all the old will to believe, as in Wilson's day, but with even less economic content and an eerie rephrasing, in Kinnock's speech, of the rhetoric of the right – 'moral majority' etc. And behind this I can't sense any deep, principled debate really going on about the nature of democracy and a replacement for our wretched and inequitable voting system which will give us some sense of fairness and involvement. Without this, Scottish devolution will simply be seen as a Labour ploy to tie up Scottish votes, the Alliance will shift again at what's on offer, and enough of the old centralist gang will vote against and ruin it. The answer to this, I think as I fly down on the last shuttle, may end up being some above-party grass roots movement in Scotland sufficiently powerful to pin the politicians down to their commitments.

Tübingen, November 1986

Whitehall has used the Referendum result to put the Jocks firmly in their place, their bluff having been well and truly called. This was something that ought to have been spelt out in words of one syllable to such as Robin Cook in 1977-78: we had been set up in such a way what we would lose both ways – lose devolution and lose the sort of bargaining position that the St Andrew's House system needed. Perhaps the lesson has been taken (I write to the presumably-now-contrite RC, licking his wounds after his expulsion from the Shadow Cabinet, urging him to explore positive economic policies for the sort of economic relationship that devolution will set up) but the costs may have been, politically, excessive. I have the general feeling that the sense of dual-nationality (John Mackintosh's phrase) has markedly diminished since 1979, even if it's only been replaced by a sort of embittered distancing.

Lord Home, according to JM, seems to have been about par for the course in coded language, evidently unhappy about the way the wind is blowing at present and eager to distance himself from the Thatcher government, while not going back to a Heathite devolution line. Still he signalled that, with PR and some sort of federal relationship, it might be on again, somewhere, sometime. A man as shrewd as Home must feel the ebbing of the Conservative tide in Scotland acutely, and it must leave him feeling exposed. When he was elected in 1935 there were only 21 Labour MPs in Scotland and all the rest were Tories or National Liberals. Now the position is precisely reversed and only likely to get worse.

13-14 December

Going back over the past few months, who, among those I've interviewed, really impressed? Campbell Christie, John McGrath, Neal Ascherson, the bankers. The politicians are a more difficult proposition, as they are obviously constrained by their position, and don't want to give hostages to fortune. This counts particularly with Rifkind. He, Gordon Wilson and David Steel performed averagely; Roy Jenkins, Jim Sillars and John Smith a bit above average. Donald Dewar could have done better, but this was partly my fault; Robin Cook was 'insufferably smug' and subsequently paid for it. The Tories were pretty dreadful. Would the caveat about politicians have worked with a real 'character' like the late John P Mackintosh? I doubt it, but his frankness didn't do him much good at Westminster.

But how much do all these people count? Do Scots voters recognise Scots politicians? This would seem to be a useful component of JM's opinion poll. Perhaps a multiple choice, like so: Is Donald Dewar Open Champion/ Shadow Secretary of State/ Secretary of State/ Actor in *East Enders* and so on? It would be interesting to know exactly who the Scots would in any case consider important, or an 'authority', in helping make their minds up over a constitutional issue like the Assembly – a Westminster politician, a councillor, newspapers, TV commentators, neighbours and family?

I came away from the whole business of interviews and filming with my faith in professional politicians not much enhanced. At least, that goes for the Westminster men (as for getting women on the programme, I tried, God knows I tried). Westminster's fascination seems so great to the politicos that the obverse – that their constituents may see the whole business as a waste of time, an ego-trip at their expense – doesn't seem to occur. I had the feeling in 1979 that the expectation of yet another crop of parliamentary professionals in the Assembly was something that ultimately stuck in people's throats: so that the worse Westminster behaved over devolution, the more the stock of the Assembly sank.

I can't help regarding the state of Britain with greater and greater pessimism each time I return. Even Virginia is worried about continuing to live in central London on the grounds that social polarisation is bound to lead to greater crime and there has been an increase of 29% in assaults on women this year alone. The creation of the British counterpart to the ghastliness of New York and Tokyo must at least be making its psychological presence felt. I've always felt uncomfortable there, except when I'm in the seclusion of libraries or the few islands of quiet left – along the canal or, oddly, in the City on a Sunday. I find the 'cosmopolitanism' of the place hard to take, not (I hope) because I'm a xenophobe or a racist (the Paki shops and West Indian guards on the underground have their legitimate place and, curiously, seem to preserve Victorian values of self-help and evangelical religion better than most whites) but because no-one seems at home there. The place is a supermarket which wins the loyalty we owe to supermarkets and no more. And increasingly it seems to be a place which, as Neal Ascherson suggests, can only survive by creating a sub-proletariat without status, rights or the possibility of any long-term life there. If this is the case then, by any decent democratic theory, the culture claimed for it will in due course rot.

Perhaps an attitude poll to the various regions of the UK would be useful here: to what regions do the Scots feel a particular empathy/antipathy and why? Again, there's a series of cultural questions we ought to ask:

(1) How many of those polled have heard of (to take a random sample) Hamish Henderson, Bill Forsyth, Jean Redpath, Alasdair Gray, Douglas Dunn, Sorley MacLean, *Cencrastus*?

(2) Assuming some such list is made up, how would certain key groups (such as secondary school pupils, teachers of history and social studies, local councillors, etc.) respond to the same slate of people?

(3) Are there differences in opinion within the main poll group and between it and the 'key groups' about whether Scottish culture is currently being strengthened/being weakened? And whether they think an Assembly would/could do anything about this?

(4) Are the punters pleased at having London as the cultural capital of the world (which I suppose it still thinks it is) or would

they rather see culture being encouraged at the grass roots? How would they react to the proposition that education should begin with Scottish culture and history and then broaden out into Britain, Europe and the world?

There's still a sense of horror in realising the nature of postwar Germany. We live in the country Hitler wanted, with the Jews eradicated. And it is as if Germany had succeeded in blowing part of its own brain away. The Jewish attempt to integrate produced, after all, the greatest triumphs of the post-industrial German intellect in Marx and Freud, and then in twelve short years (less than the period since Harold Wilson got back to power in 1974) a bunch of thugs and perverts who couldn't by themselves have run a Wolf Cub pack were allowed (and that is the indictment against the German people) to wipe it out.

What we have is the German people, now sufficiently chastened and contrite (this, as my colleague Walter Greiner pointed out, was the enduring legacy of 1968) to exercise self criticism, but still in a way wounded. Germany isn't simply a divided nation lacking the group which, more than any other, contributed to its idea of mission: the linkage of language and people with ideas. Hence the attempt by conservatives presently to sanitise German history isn't simply a menacing political gambit, it's an inherent absurdity. Which is, I suppose, why I as a Scot find it relatively easy to integrate. I am a sort of surrogate Jew, part of a radical, much more honest, attempt to reintegrate into a new Europe.

Now, when we shift to England, we see a similar nationalistic reassertion, in the rubble, so to speak, of empire, provoking another Jewish self communing. What has been realised by Thatcher, more than anything else, is an aggressive Englishness. The cosmopolitan liberal period of the Josephs, Brittans, etc., has actually been brief – the same thing could happen to Saatchi and Saatchi – but the precipitate will be, for Mrs Thatcher and the great number who think like her, a reversal to the simplicities of the 1930s Grantham.

February 2, 1987

Things that don't appear significant at the time suddenly become monstrous. Back in September, as we were running around the central belt, interviewing Jenkins, McGrath and company, mention was made of a programme series called *The Secret State*, also being filmed from Queen Margaret Drive. It seemed interesting, but as the arcana of defence planning seemed to have only a marginal – though symbolically important – role for *Scotland 2000*, it didn't impinge further on our activities. By the end of January it threatened to drive us all from the screens.

The series had been seen by Alastair Milne, the Director General, in January and one programme, on a £500m spy satellite called Zircon, was banned by him. Again, I'd heard of the Zircon programme around Queen Margaret Drive, tut-tutted about such a huge amount of public money being allocated (surely illegally) without parliamentary approval, and forgotten about it. But not only was the programme banned by Milne, a committee of Labour MPs – headed by Robin Cook were prevented by injunction from seeing it.

Margaret Thatcher, naturally, approved all this, grotesquely seconded by Neil Kinnock. But the *New Statesman* printed the story on Jan 23 and when I phoned its editor John Lloyd the next day about my modest piece on the German elections, the government had sent the Special Branch into their offices. By the end of the next week (Alastair Milne having resigned) they'd raided BBC Scotland as well. The behaviour of a second-rate police state was how Roy Jenkins described this last in parliament and indeed the whole episode suggests what it must have been like to be a British journalist observing German politics in the last days of the Weimar Republic, particularly as Mrs Thatcher took to the screen in the course of the week to demand that socialism be eradicated from British politics.

Now the interesting thing about all this is that Mrs T is sure as fate going to ride it out. The Zircon scandal will cancel out the Guinness scandal, as Westland cancelled out Ponting. This indicates something quite new in British politics – the complete failure of the mechanism to work whereby the polls pile up against the party in power, and a couple of governmental *faux pas* lead to the party grandees going to the leader to hand him the equivalent of a loaded revolver. The collapse of two party politics and the eclipse of a 'British political community' mean that the government never appears more than momentarily in trouble, while the sort of politics bred of the scandals (and the attempt of the parties to score off one another in exploiting them) mean that the long term criteria for assessing Britain's political management shift further and further into the shadows. I almost feel sorry for Malcolm Rifkind, picking up some cross-party support for his defence of the workers at the Caterpillar Tractor plant, only to appear either as the instigator of the raid on the BBC, or as someone powerless to do anything about it. It's like being called away from the bedside of a seriously-ill patient to someone in the last stages of hydrophobia, noisy, demanding, and doomed.

Yet Westminster was always like this. It's always been hopeless at economic management, and in its great days, right up to the 1930s, its main concerns were almost exclusively with foreign and imperial policy and defence questions. This agenda hasn't changed. Only it's become more destabilising as its irrelevance to boring bread-and-butter issues has increased.

April 25, 1987

Scotland 2000 runs until the end of April, to variable comment in the press. Effectively, however, we are more than lapped by BBC Scotland's other project – which accompanies us on Tuesday evenings but is (unlike us) networked: John Byrne's *Tutti-Frutti*. For those who can get on the wavelength of the dialogue (and the London literary men have their problems) this saga of a band of superannuated rock-musicians on a luckless, doomed anniversary Scottish tour, becomes hypnotic. It manages to be both funny and serious enough to bear its weight of heavy cultural interpretation.

Tutti-Frutti seems to have roots going back to Barrie. I wonder how much Byrne was influenced by the black Barrie of *Tommy and Grizel*, let alone *Peter Pan*? The whole Majestics business seems impregnated with their wish to remain eternally-young 'lost boys', until interrupted by Susie Kettles' Wendy and Robbie Coltrane's high-carbohydrate version of Peter Pan. It's both a fable of the sex-war, in which Susie comes out more or less victorious, and a tragedy when time and change catch up with the macho-rocker Vince Diver. The Majestics' minibus wanders aimlessly about post-industrial Scotland like the Tardis run amok, and one realises that when Vince and Co climbed into their time-capsule, in 1961, Scotland was still a he-man's steel-steam-and-ships country, and rock-and-roll the latest delivery from that Atlantic culture into which Scotland had been plugged for a century.

How do you assess this, or Jam Jar Films' *Brond*, adapted from Lindsay's very complex novel? The picture both project of Scotland is a place where broken glass crunches under your feet, of dereliction, inequality, disorientation – but both seem to have got rid of one monument blocking out the sun, homo Clydesidiensis. This rivet-chewing creature was still sighted alive and well in Bill Bryden's *The Holy City*, but with Brond bumping Primo off, and the self-immolation of Vince, he seems to have been buried – with any luck for good.

Tuesday 10 June

To Scotland by train, a relief after the longueurs of flying back from Germany via Frankfurt because of the air traffic controllers' strike. The weather, as bad here as in Germany, has left the land sodden and the sky grey, a gloom enhanced by the decrepitude around the railway – rusting rails, grubbed-up sidings, and beyond that dead trees, shabby farms and ruinous factories. In Germany great goods trains are always rumbling past; here I don't think we pass one in a hundred miles, partly because most goods go by road, partly because there just isn't the industrial production to fill them. Perhaps the Channel Tunnel will inject new life into this artery, but at the moment it looks as if its associated veins have atrophied, making it that much more difficult to push development beyond the South East. All over the continent the infrastructural preparations are being made for the next generation of industry. Not here. Nor are we in the least concerned about the destruction of the environment. What is collective is, almost by definition, a candidate for neglect and short-term exploitation.

It's because I think that, in Scotland, some general awareness of this exists, that self government seems to me to have benefits which go beyond any 'national' claims. An Assembly becomes the only possible means of coordinating the educational, environmental and industrial policies needed to regenerate the country. And I know I'm not alone in believing this. The Tories point out, with an aggrieved air, that Scotland is doing, in British terms, much better than was the case twenty years ago. Why therefore isn't it rewarding them? Then they say, 'Scotland votes Labour because it's trapped in a collectivist ghetto mentality.' What they aren't perceptive enough to see (if they're based in London) or aren't allowed to say they see (if they're in Scotland) is that the Scots are quite rational about what they want. And what they want is something which increases the place's capacity for enterprise and innovation in a way of which the British system is no longer capable. In this sense Scotland's politics are far closer to European social democracy than to the confusions and implausibilities of contemporary Britishness.

Friday 12 June

Election morning-after. On the *Good Morning Scotland* programme Jack Brand (who has been number-crunching for BBC Radio Scotland) and I agreed that there was a point about seven hours earlier when what was happening on UK network seemed to be taking place at a Belgian or Italian election – not much to do with us. Obviously, we might have overdosed on politics but we seemed to have been watching a small country voting fairly solidly on the left, trying to plan out its future, in a sensible, Scandinavian way, while down south everything was an animated hallucinatory frieze extolling bulldogs, nuclear bombs, Stock Exchange gambling and credit card affluence. It was a very strange and disorienting sensation, not much to do with devolution *per se* but with a slate of ideals being sanctioned by 'our' countrymen (who were also persuaded that they wanted to govern themselves). These might be rubbished somewhere else, by other people, but they were our ideals, and Thatcher, or anyone else, had no right to interfere with them. I found later on that JM had had much the same sensation up front on the telly, the tension making him physically ill. By lunch, we all sort ourselves out a bit, cheered by the sight of Rifkind looking defensive as hell at the Tories' press conference, and the last Tory seat falling to Ray Michie in Argyll. An eleven-seat loss is very bad news indeed.

Over breakfast, Joanna Hickson had said that Donald Dewar appeared sunk in misery on *Good Morning Scotland* and had to be reminded that Labour had won six Tory seats (Renfrew West, Cunningham North, Edinburgh South and Central, Strathkelvin, and Aberdeen South). This suggests problems for the future. Donald believes in devolution and has been advocating it since first elected to parliament in 1964. But he's alse a lawyer and right-winger, and prone to fathomless pessimism about the whole business. In this he'll probably be joined by Helen Liddell, who adds to it the traditional Glasgow Catholic suspicion of Scottish nationalism. (On the election night programme she was still denouncing the SNP as 'the right-wing successor to the Tories', which can no longer be true and is scarcely helpful).

Saturday 13 June

But the great problematic is the way the new Labour MPs will react – because over a third of Labour's Scottish parliamentary party is new. From first soundings I'd reckon the automatic contenders for prominence are going to be Galloway and Brian Wilson. The latter has always been strongly anti-devolution but seems to have shifted a lot of ground, and George Foulkes assures me he's now reliable. Galloway's was the most impressive victory of the whole campaign, and his record at War on Want must put him in a strong position. Notionally, the Foulkes-Home-Robertson-Canavan wing must have been strengthened and the antis silenced (Tam Dalyell told George Foulkes that he was still 'in his heart of hearts' hostile to devolution, but would abide by the collective decision of the party). But could this change if the party splits? According to Gordon Brown, this is what must at all costs be avoided. One can see – but only to a certain extent – why.

The reaction of the Labour leadership is of more than marginal importance here, and realising that Neil Kinnock would be at the Miners Gala at Holyrood, I trooped down to Hillside Crescent to watch them set off. Hillside Crescent, the HQ of the NUM in Scotland, and on the other side of Calton Hill from Royal High, is packed with bands, fourteen or fifteen of them, and droves of bairns done up in leotards and shakoes as drum-majorettes, lorries with floats, etc. Miners as such seem in a definite minority (there are now only four deep pits left in the Lothian/Fife area) and many of the village bands are half, and sometimes completely, made up of girls. To see one of the old-style pipe bands, Lochgelly I think, stepping out in their bearskins and Inverness capes, is like watching a steam locomotive arrive in Waverley. It's difficult to see an old man walking behind them, bearing the battle honours of the Scottish Company of the International Brigade in the Spanish Civil war, without a catch in the throat. What do those bastards in the City know about this, etc.? Yet the Spanish parallel seems appropriate, as MacNeice said,

> Spain would soon denote
> Our griefs, our aspirations;
> Not knowing that our blunt
> Ideals would find their whetstone,
> that our spirit
> Would find its frontier on the Spanish front,
> Its body in a rag-tag army.

I remember, almost thirty years ago, when the marching miners – and there were plenty then – seemed to us at Royal High an alien, hostile force as they passed our playground. Now this diminished, rag-tag army is 'ours'. We are in a sort of civil war, and here we've beaten them back, but we're going to have to fight to hold our land. Everyone I meet seems to come out directly with something along these lines: Roy McIvor, whom I run into in Marchmont, Chris MacWhirter of CND, my parents (on David Steel's committee in the Borders), Chris Fyfe, Reader in African History at the University, of the Duke of Edinburgh's Gordonstoun generation; Liz Peach, who was on the Labour candidates' list in the 1970s and now, like me, commutes between Edinburgh and the Continent. The whispered question – what are Scottish politicians going to do? – seems to drown out Neil Kinnock's plea for unity and the renewal of the Labour Party. The man of the day isn't Kinnock, but Mick McGahey, once the muckle black deil of the far left, now the embodiment of the decencies, the wit and tolerance of his people.

Kinnock's speech, well-delivered, is still void of content, overweight metaphors struggling into the air, circling slowly and then coming back to rest – in terms of policy or argument exactly where they started. Kinnock has the people on his side, but their sympathy is a donation – he needs us more than we need him.

20-21 June

I end this diary back in Germany, more or less on top of the Black Forest. I came here via Freiburg, like Tübingen a very Green university town, but also part of an intriguing international community in 'Dreieckland' – triangle country – where Canton Basle, Baden-Würtemberg and South Alsace abut on one another. They have their own multilingual radio, and soon they'll have an international suburban railway service. Whether this notion of an 'Allemanian' community will really ever take root is problematic, but it's a heartening example of how small-scale nationalism can coexist with *ad hoc* international cooperation, when a common problem – like pollution or *Waldsterben* – is encountered.

I find the British situation a rather disturbing contrast. After the election results were out, the term 'bloody English' was on a lot of lips in Scotland, and I found myself falling into this, probably to the concern of my English friends. Thatcher seemed to be hated so intensely north of the Border because she personified every quality we had always disliked in the English: snobbery, bossiness, selfishness, and by our lights, stupidity – and the English seemed to have applauded her precisely for these. I sensed an ill-temper and irritation which went beyond politics; not in itself violent but the sort of atmosphere in which recourse to violence could become tolerated. The Ulster Catholic who hates the IRA but, if he saw a boy from his community on the run from the police or army, wouldn't turn him in. This sort of thing, according to Franz Fanon, provides 'the water in which the fish swim'. Despite our deep structure of legalism, I can now see circumstances where this critical breakdown in law and order could become possible.

In his book on the political psychology of the English, the French political scientist Emil Boutmy wrote that even the success of the Empire couldn't mask the lack of affection between the component nationalities of the UK. If this was the case in 1900, how much more aggravated must the situation be today? Yet hatred still presupposes some sort of relationship, and I find that, in my own case, it's giving way to a cool distancing. Thatcher just doesn't represent me or my country. If the English want her, well and good. But to use her own words, she isn't 'one of us'.

I have visited two buildings in the last week. The first was at Melrose – Chiefswood House, which has just been put on the market by Lord Dacre (aka Hugh Trevor-Roper). This little house is a few hundred yards from my father's house. Outside it looks like a Border farm, but inside it's decorated in a strange French imperial style, just about as exotic as its mysterious owner seems to have decided that his days as an authority on Scotland are over. An odd place with more than a hint of some of the chill events of twentieth century Europe brooding over it.

The other building was a farm called Schniederlihof, on the Hofgrund plateau, some 3000 feet above Freiburg. This wooden building, dating from the 1680s, had been tenanted until 1964, and is now kept up as a museum. Everything in the house, itself ingeniously constructed, is of wood, or made by using wood to prepare local materials like glass-sand and iron. Smoke spreads from the oven throughout the house to cure the sausages and hams in the loft and pickle the wooden shingles on the roof. It's an example of a 'wood-culture' which, says the old man who looks after it, '*ist nun fast zu Ende*'.

Yet this culture managed to exist practically intact until seven years after the Treaty of Rome and four years before the 'revolutions' of 1968, At the foot of this hill, Engels and the Baden rebels retreated towards Switzerland in 1848; German troops invaded Alsace Lorraine in 1870; the Kaiser and Hitler rose and fell. This continuity seems something common enough in Europe, but almost totally absent from Britain, because of the early onset among us of forms of capitalist exploitation, like the commercial exploitation of timber which denuded the Scottish highlands and converted their economy into a sort of endemic banditry.

This seems both to suggest the scale of the sociological trauma enduced by the rapidity of German industrialisation in the nineteenth century, and the *anomie* which possessed the German society when that industrialisation broke down after 1918. But it may also mean that contemporary Germans, Greens or conservationist socialists, need only reach back into the immediate past to discover a functioning eco-system. This has been completely wiped out from the British memory, and replaced by a merely sentimental vision of the countryside as place into which to retreat, away from the tension of the town. Hence the British Conservatives can junk Baldwinian rural nostalgia for an ideology purely concerned to reckon value at point of sale, and the attachment of Labour to a class formation which appears more and more to have been a specific historical development of temporary, rather than revolutionary, significance.

Earlier in the week Tom Nairn and John Curran phoned to say I had been attacked on the TV by Malcolm Rifkind in response to part of my interview with Ian Ross for Channel 4 News. Harvie was 'a well known Labour militant' or words to that effect, 'who had been spouting this claptrap for years.' I'm not quite sure to what he was referring, but I could see the obvious comfort he derived from slotting me into part of the recognised political system. The point is that I'm not a Labour Party member, and I am unlikely to rejoin while they oppose a Scottish Constitutional Convention and electoral reform. Eight years in Europe have strengthened convictions which are socialist, but they have so diminished my faith in British parliamentarianism that I believe any form of humane and prescient reconstruction of British society requires decentralisation and a fair electoral system. On a British scale this means – can only mean – an electoral pact between Labour and the Liberals aimed at introducing PR after the next election. But, to be frank, in Britain the old fantasies – of the free market, or of class politics, or of parliamentary sovereignty – have put down roots too deep to grub up. Only in Scotland do we seem to have the chance to break out. Can we take it?

18
In the Shadow of the 'Craig
(1990)

Thematically a sequel to 'Steelopolis', this
Guardian article makes a case that without a
steel industry the economics of shipbuilding
and rail were at a disadvantage in Scotland.
Craigneuk, where many Ravenscraig workers
lived, is now one of Scotland's worst problem
schemes and prompts thoughts about the
utility of traditional industrial policy.

The news of the Ravenscraig closure came over the World Service
as I was making breakfast in my kitchen in Germany. In the
background was the noise, by now almost unnoticed, of cars roaring
through the Schlossberg tunnel en route to the morning shift at
Daimler Benz.

I had enough contacts in the know not to be surprised. 'Black
Bob' Scholey, a Sheffield man to his roots, had always had it in for
Ravenscraig, and now he had his chance. As for Nicholas Ridley,
the Flashman *de nos jours* had already made his intentions plain:
the Jocks had to be brought into line, and as painfully as possible.
But the news still had an arresting brutality. This was my town that
was being attacked.

I was born in Motherwell, and spent four years there, in a
pre-fab scheme beneath the 'Babylon Bridge' which carried the
West Coast main line over the River Calder. (The local clergy had
little time for Robert Owen's Orbiston Community, which in the
1830s stood on the other side of the ravine.) Then I moved to the
Borders, but the place still fascinated me – the noise and flares

from Dalzell steelworks, the tank engines clanking across the streets, the pervasive smells of coke and gas. Compared with the tranquillity of St Boswells, where the arrival of a bus was an event, this was life!

Later on, when I was completing my history degree and Ravenscraig was rising to the north of the town, these memories began to settle into an historical narrative, which I used for an undergraduate thesis. My family, rather like Motherwell itself, had resisted industrialisation until late on in the process. Motherwell was a little weaving-and-hunting hamlet, quite distinct from the ironstone fields of the Monklands to the north and the collieries of Hamilton to the south; they were tenant farmers in nearby Dalserf. Then after 1848 Motherwell became the most important railway junction in Scotland, the first ironworks were opened, and the Harvies, like thousands more, flocked into the new centre. About four thousand in the 1860s, over forty thousand by the century's end.

Motherwell was the first major Scottish heavy industrial area to depend completely on rail transport. This caused trouble, then and later. Its street pattern fitted between the railway lines, not the other way about. Moreover the colliers continued to tunnel their way under it, with the result that houses, the town hall, tramway lines, would suddenly subside, causing what would be, in our money, millions of pounds of damage.

In the 1880s and 1890s the place had a distinctly frontier-town atmosphere, with law and order problematic. Government was in the hands of a Commission, elected on a very narrow franchise, until the local government reforms of the 1890s. Massive sandstone churches, of all the usual Scottish denominations – and a few more exotic ones thrown in – fought it out with equally massive sandstone pubs for the souls of the new Motherwellites, recruited from Lanarkshire, the Highlands, Donegal, Lithuania.

It was a high-wage, high-risk sort of place. A skilled 'puddler' stirring molten iron in the 'Malleable' works, could make enough to qualify for the vote under the 1832 reform, but had to drink gallons to survive – beer usually; 'Irn-Bru' was the temperance alternative. By 1900 dozens of foundries, alloy works, rolling-stock builders, boiler works, structural engineers, clustered round the steel furnaces of Colvilles Limited. I found the photograph album of Hurst Nelsons in the Public Library: tramcars, light locomotives, carriages exported throughout the world. More photos showed Papa Russell, sales director of Anderson Boyes, with smiling Poles and Chinese. Anderson Boyes made most of the world's coal-cutters.

My experience of Motherwell was, oddly, closer to my grandfather's than to my father's. We knew it in prosperity, he had grown up in it during the Slump. The frontier was closed by World War I. Demand for steel and munitions soared but fell back once wartime losses had been made good. (Rightly) fearing inflation, shipowners bought into shipyards, who in turn took over steelworks, and steelworks took over collieries. When demand fell away, all toppled into recession. By the early 1930s Motherwell had 40% unemployment. When Edwin Muir began his *Scottish Journey* from there in 1935, he recorded that he had never seen a town in such despair, something only lightened – at least for him – by the piety of Catholic miners who built a replica of Lourdes at Carfin.

Motherwell experimented with politics. In 1923 it returned Britain's first Communist MP, a Manchester Quaker called Walton Newbold. He didn't last long, and ended up a Tory. Hughie Paterson didn't, because he was too proletarian and extreme, so he sat as an 'Independent Loyal Orange Protestant'. The Rev James Barr had been a Liberal but became a Labour man of strongly Scots nationalist sympathies, and in 1945 Motherwell elected the first, and for a long time, the last, Scottish National Party MP. My mother voted for Robert MacIntyre, and I must have been taken along to the poll in my pram, making it my first record of political involvement. It was what the Germans call a *'Denkzettel-Wahl'* – a sharp nudge to the establishment party, in this case Labour, not to let the preceding twenty years repeat themselves. Since then, it has been unwaveringly loyal.

To what effect? With over 80% of homes in Council hands, Motherwell seems to be an identikit of what the Thatcherites call 'dependency culture'. Closer up, the schemes and tower blocks can seem depressing beyond belief, the 'Cross' – even in Muir's day the centre of the place – tatty, the shopping centre a clutch of mediocre chain stores. With practically every decent building either knocked down or boarded up, Motherwell looks far more battered than its German twin, Schweinfurt, which the USAF 'took out' in 1943. Very often, with its steam and smoke coiling into the sky, Ravenscraig is more beautiful than anything supposed to serve the citizens of Motherwell.

And yet, this place has produced Sir Alexander Gibson the conductor, Liz Lochhead the poet, Ian St John, John Tuckwell who runs the publishers, John Donald, Tom Winning the Archbishop, Willie Barclay the theologian and Professor Tom Devine the historian. I can think of bigger and more prosperous towns in Britain and Germany, which haven't done anything on that scale.

The problem remains. How to account for the fact that Motherwell's children distinguished themselves anywhere but in the steel industry. Absentee ownership, poor technical training, an environment which would chase anyone of reasonable imagination away, Dalziel High school as effective an exporting business as any of the steelworks. Most of my German students expect to get a job near where they live. For how many Scottish students has this ever been true?

In the 1920s Colvilles commissioned the American consultants Brasserts to report on the future of the Scottish steel industry. Brasserts recommended a waterside steelworks on the Clyde, at Erskine. When recovery came (largely through rearmament in the 1930s) there wasn't enough time for so drastic a move, and Ravenscraig followed in the old pattern. Possibly Brasserts had the right idea. Apart from Ravenscraig and Bob Scholey's Sheffield, every major British steelworks is on the seacoast. Moreover, the steel-using industries which Ravenscraig was supposed to supply –

Linwood, Bathgate – have followed the North British Loco and Hurst Nelson's waggon works into oblivion.

No-one disputes that Ravenscraig is efficient, yet already one hears plausible voices suggesting that to resist closure is to be sentimental, that Scotland's future lies in electronics and the service industries. But look at it in this perspective. Throughout Britain, office blocks are going up which will have to be filled by an additional 1.6 million office workers. Current forecasts suggests that office workers will fall by 300,000 over the next decade. Compared with this sort of cock-up (brought to you by free enterprise), Ravenscraig's career has been practically exemplary.

The demand for steel may change but it won't go away, particularly with a new railway age looming up before us. The last body to take economic instruction from, by contrast, is the present British government. Motherwell's struggle is Scotland's struggle, but in no way should Ravenscraig's fate be taken as a useful political tactic for nationalists, a dead steelworks equalling a dead Tory party. If the 'Craig goes, much of Scotland's future goes with it.

19

With Salmond up the Danube
(1994)

The SNP was picking itself up
from the setback of 1992 and, under the
guidance of Allan Macartney, cultivating the
EU's new members. This report to the
Scotsman came from a country
that had lost an empire
and found a role.

Oh God, it's like that bit in *The Third Man* when Wilfred Hyde White puts poor Joseph Cotten, who has never written anything more literary than 'We're comin' to get you, Kincaid!' up to speak on the modern British novel. Salmond is clearing off to London for a vote and I have to address the Vienna Liberal Club on *'Schottland los von England und Unabhangig in Europa'*.

For two days I have been the intellectual bit – *'Herr Professor Harvie von der Uni Tübingen' 'Sehr angenehme, Herr Professor!'* – of the SNP's charm offensive, directed at the New Members. Alex is trotting around old Vienna in a green coat as thick as a wall and being educated on the hoof by Angus Robertson, who has worked for two years for Austrian broadcasting and is already alarmingly streetwise. 'Alex, when you meet any Austrian politician, call him or her Doktor. Nearly all of them are, and if they're not, they'll feel complimented.'

Otherwise it's taxis, coffee, studios and more studios. Men with designer stubble and pony-tails. No, the SNP is not personally led by Sean Connery. We have the man here. Alex being endlessly patient with journalists whose sympathy for Scotland is matched by their vagueness about it. Scotland hasn't a parliament, and it doesn't have internal federalism, as you have here. Yes we have regions. They are roughly the same size as your *Länder* but London is just about to abolish them. Are we in Scotland consulted about this? You must be joking.

On and off a gleaming 1960s tram on the Ringstrasse, past a milky way of trees festooned with tiny lights, and hundreds of red Japanese lanterns outside the City Hall. Parliament: like Royal High, but on a vast scale. Miles of pseudo-marble corridors, with daft modern sculptures. A state-of-the art Lower House, and then altogether elsewhere, the caryatids and six hundred empty wooden benches of the Imperial Chamber. In one high-ceilinged room the Liberals, in another the Greens, worried about the fizzing nuclear reactors of the East, and exclusionist ethnic nationalism. More coffee. We don't intend meeting the populist Jorg Haider, besides in no way can our mongrel Scotland be called an ethnic nation. We are out for a civic Europe. Nuclear power? Trident has trebled Scotland's killing power, if you see it that way. The UK could nuke Belgrade a hundred times over, but it can't logistically sustain proper policing operations. More corridors, a pillared atrium. Dr Fischer, the Speaker and a Social Democrat, had been to Edinburgh for John Smith's funeral, found the service strange but moving, the red stone church, the Gaelic singing . . .

The education ministry, somewhere in the lee of the vast Hofburg, behind Adolf Loos' *Vereinsbank*, 'that building without eyebrows' (but with more than a nod towards Rennie Mackintosh) which the old Kaiser disliked so much. We mount staircase after grand staircase. Habsburg civil servants, thoughtful aristos in frock coats, gloom down from cream and gold walls. Dr Busek, the conservative party's Vice-Chancellor welcomes us in his office. Yet more coffee. The Europe of the fifteen will be more of a small nations' Europe. Even the great powers, France and Germany, are moving in a direction of internal federalism. Why is Britain so reluctant to move in this way? There must be destruction of old outworn structures before there can be reconstruction . . . Scotland, we chirrup tactfully, was the only bit of the UK which the recent *Financial Times* poll found actually voting in favour of Europe.

OPEC and serious eating. The Deputy Secretary General and his aide. Two quiet, charming Arab diplomats, and Alex doing his ex-oil economist act. He has news for them about West of Shetland – higher quality than expected, and easier to work, the possibility of another seventy years' offshore production. OPEC has already read *Fool's Gold*, and I think we get plus points. General bafflement about why the UK government sold out so totally to the oil multinationals, and a stress on the common interests that an independent Scotland would have with OPEC in keeping the price of oil up. After a few choppy years, we'll be in a sellers' market again by the millenium.

Back to the Hotel Bristol, and Alex off by taxi to the airport. He will return tomorrow for a speech at the Industrial Society. An infinite capacity for taking planes. And now, for me, the Big One: an hour on Scotland and Europe *auf Deutsch*. Well, I didn't wave at the audience or fall over the scenery . . .

Questions. Why does John Major talk to the IRA but not to your Scottish MPs? I explain about slippery slopes, but suggest that in the city of Freud a bit more probing of the ex-imperial psyche is necessary. Wave another Salmond line about, 'The next election will be fought by Major on slogans which will be simultaneously anti-European and anti-Scottish.'

A final huge meal with the Defence Minister, waiters gliding about in their full soup and fish. In the background a small pianist with an alarming wig plunging into the *Blue Danube*. I get out before a huge trolley of brandy, schnapps, whisky, sways towards me. The six o'clock 'Max Reinhardt' to Tübingen, and my two o'clock lecture, has to be caught.

A success, I think. At least the Austrians now know we're not them from there, if you see what I mean. Although I have coffee coming out my ears, and must be two kilos heavier. As I slump towards sleep, crossing a watery Upper Austrian landscape, I think gratefully about hospitality, and about Defence Minister Malcolm Rifkind's 1993 entertainment budget, which came to £13. Come, Malcolm, let us discuss the problems of Scotland, and revive your democratic principles, over a bottle of Irn-Bru . . .

20
1997: At Last!
Reflections on the Devolution
(1998)

First published in
the German magazine *Hard Times*
and in the *Newsletter*
for Edinburgh history graduates

Those of us with St David's Day, 1979 carved on our hearts, didn't consider it an auspicious start. After a truncated and on the whole pretty negative campaign, slow polling ran through a dull day. The *Scotsman*'s London edition (I found out later) went to press with a turnout in the 50-55% range expected. Then, waking from a drowsiness induced by Theodor Fontane's *Der Stechlin* – a marvellous novel, but didn't life in rural Brandenburg make Jane Austen read like *Dallas*! – I found at 12.30am Clackmannan, a dwarf county resurrected in 1994 as a ploy to preserve a Tory majority for Michael Forsyth's Stirling, was about to declare. It voted 80-20% for a Scots Parliament and 69-31% for tax-raising powers.

Then came the realisation that the other counties were all going to be closer to this than to the miserable percentages of 2 March 1979. Some kids in Edinburgh burst out with 'Come all ye at ease wi' freedom' and just about got Hamish Henderson's words – our real national anthem – right. After 290 (or eighteen, depending on your perspective) years we were out of the tunnel, one of these epiphanies which (awkwardly) brought Siegfried Sassoon rather than MacDiarmid on cue: everyone had suddenly started singing, we *were* filled with such delight . . .

This was the sort of situation, like shipwreck in the mid-Atlantic, where past life flashes before you. I remembered Tam Dalyell, ludicrously overestimated (chiefly by the London press) as a controversialist, engaging Gordon Brown at close quarters in that hellish winter of 1979. Then he only throve because Labour was palpably divided, and after John Mackintosh's death no-one was around to stitch him up. Gordon was far too intellectual to derail 'Tam the Obsessive Engine' blasting along his narrow-gauge track. But in 1997 there were too many volunteers able and willing to do just that.

This was a Scottish, in great part an Edinburgh, government. Heavens, I was Robin Cook's referee for his first job – tutor-organiser for the WEA since you ask – but I still find it odd to think of them (remembered in libraries, pubs or parties) *qua* cabinet ministers.

The pictures have, of course, got smaller; the money's no longer in politics. I wonder what the differential is between Cookie's salary and that of his Royal High classmate John Kay – now (I think) at the City Business School? The evaporation of socialist ideology is more telling. *The Red Paper on Scotland* was sharply argued – I dissent less from it now than I did in 1975; but so dogmatic has the City establishment's madeover New Labour become it doesn't even bother to argue with those of us hidebound and conservative (such is the decay of political language) enough to suggest that market forces and enterprise, freed from any obligations of social justice, could be lethal.

But we've been given this way out. The Edinburgh Parliament – as power-house or, as Allan Massie put it, Britain's granny flat? Irritation at Massie, as excellent a novelist as he is misguided a politician, stems from envy of his marketing abilities. For every time I have said, 'Balance? You want a literate Unionist? Ah well, you'll have to try Massie', the man ought to pay me my ten per cent. Let him be punished by watching Lord Archer leading the keening in London.

For, behind the devolution majority there was I think a Diana factor – or, more properly, the absence of a Diana factor in Scotland. The story demonstrated the press at its most self-obsessed. Even the Scottish qualities didn't pick up the fact that 'public grief' was much more restrained outwith London. In Scotland the floral tributes weren't negligible, but they were tiny compared with those in Northants. From the limited newspaper coverage, only about 10,000 seemed to have attended commemoration services throughout Scotland. In two or three days irritation at what Angus Calder called the 'Evitafication' of the princess, and the populistic ritual, half-republican, half-deferential, which possessed south-eastern England, had become a barely-concealed editorial line. Perhaps the readership of the *Record* or the *Sun* were more moved. But were they moved more than tabloid readers elsewhere in Europe?

Emotional declarations were likely in Scotland to lead to comparisons with Piper Alpha, Lockerbie, Dunblane – or even the death of John Smith. Somehow the juxtaposition of the 'subject's revolt' in London – Chesterton's 'secret people' speaking at last, though in no straightforwardly rational way – and the civic republicanism on offer in Edinburgh, seems to have reacted in particular on the 'New Scotland' which polled so impressively on the 11th. This is roughly made up of the same social class of people who surged into London with their flowers, but with a quite different identification, which neither the monarchy nor the lyrics of Elton John – the 1990s answer to Ivor Novello, when you think about it – are likely to win back.

31 August to 12 September cut more deeply into the ligatures of the Union than Thatcher ever managed to do.

Though she did us proud, the daft old bat. The biggest comeback since wossername, Roderick Usher's sister, caused the House to fall apart. Edinburgh history had a role in this. Thatcher's political adviser Ferdinand Mount was actually quite enlightened about constitutional reform. Which is presumably why he cleared off to the *Times Literary Supplement* and revenged himself on his former employer from there. The governing dogma in the Tory party was thereafter tended by one Alastair B Cooke, whom I remember as a somewhat Wodehousian figure – immense, bovine, squirearchical – in Geoffrey Best's postgraduate seminar in 1966-68. Given to bellowing whispers in the reading room of the National Library, Cooke was researching on Liberal Unionism in Scotland – my own interest when I started as a postgrad. He went on to produce *The Governing Passion*, about how Gladstone didn't really believe in Home Rule in 1886, with that other Thatcherite oracle John Vincent. Cooke left Central Office last year, his high politics dogmas apparently intact. How much of this great, obsessive construct is left now?

A footnote. On 12 September I did a broadcast for Radio Wales and was walking back from the BBC when, without much in the way of warning, there was a sudden torrential downpour. Finding myself without an umbrella I took refuge in the Wheatsheaf in Charlotte Street, once the local of Robert Colquhoun and Robert MacBryde, Julian MacLaren Ross, WS Graham, Tambimuttu and episodically Dylan Thomas and Louis MacNeice. The place was long, dark and narrow, a plan I connected with the grimmer sort of Edinburgh bar, though incongruously decorated in Brewer's Tudor. Stained-glass roundels bore the arms of West of Scotland burghs: Rothesay, Dumbarton, Paisley . . . Anyhow, here, where the beautiful ideologies had burst, I downed a pint in honour of that Celtic diaspora. YOU DID NOT DRINK IN VAIN. After all these years, may my lot have the fun, and something to show for it as well.

Seeing the End of Our Own Actions

21
Mythos Mittelstand:
and can we have one too?
(1996)

While the self-satisfaction of market economists seems increasingly fatuous, great damage is being done to regions by overstressing inward investment, lowering production costs, 'downsizing', and exporting production. These policies create diseconomies which are toxic and divisive. The need is to integrate social policy and production.

'All progress is the realisation of utopias'

Oscar Wilde

'Depend upon it, sir, the prospect of being hanged in a week concentrates a man's mind wonderfully.'

Samuel Johnson

The Dark Woods Outside

To compare the management of modern industrial society in Scotland and Baden-Württemberg is to run straight into a paradox. Britain's New Labour, prospecting after 'stakeholder capitalism', eyed the Baden-Württemberg *Mittelstand* – for a few moments in 1996 – as a good example. The latter is far less confident about the future than it used to be. Scotland, Wales and Ba-Wü face a bundle of challenges composed of new industrial techniques, increased competition, and general European unsettlement. Are these the marginal frictions of a fundamentally sound system, or do they add up to a crisis of civil society? In the quest for the *Mittelstand*, is political economy retreating from an ominous present to its origins in rhetoric?

The eclipse of the nation state in the 1980s has thrown up the *Mittelstand* – the star performer of 'bourgeois regionalism' – as a compensating myth. A benign and Europe-friendly myth, but still a symbol rather than a strategy. This is being made to minister to a range of dislocations throughout our society. As an actual instrument, it may serve as a subject for diagnosis and possible improvement, but first we have to define its challengers, starting with the European 'unsettlement'. Since the 1970s economic progress via the market has knocked out state socialism. But although in theory unquestioned, markets are in practice running into a range of alarming counter-currents. These can be classed under six main heads:

Gross inequalities:
The old Iron Curtain now resembles a cliff, whose arid summits have Gross National Products per head between 25% and 10% of the fat lands of the European Union in the valley. Economic gravitation, through refugees, competition from low-wage countries, and relocation to the same, is a fact (Baden-Württemberg, whose population increased by 10% in the last decade, is affected by all three). Attempts to 'marketise' Eastern economies bring with them the threat of revolt against ruling élites regarded as predatory, and further emigration.

Unresolved conflicts:
Terrorist organisations pose a major threat to highly sophisticated financial service centres. The attacks of the IRA – the most recent early in 1996 – cost about £2 billion and nearly destroyed the future of the City of London.

Problematic economic activities:
These don't just involve financial risks, like the sagas of Nick Leeson,

Barings, Sumitomo and derivatives trading. Climate deterioration is making insurance more risky, as is terrorism. In 1988 the Lockerbie bomb knocked billions off British tourist income, while the Ariane disaster of 5 June 1996 cost DM 11.3 billion. None of its equipment or satellites were insured, as the premiums were literally astronomical.

Individuals alienated from society:
At both ends of politics, social pathology can cripple economic effort. On one side megacrooks such as Robert Maxwell or Jürgen Schneider brought huge losses to banks and pensions funds, while the *Rote Armee Fraktion*'s assassinations of Alfred Herrhausen and Detlev Rohwedder crippled the reconstruction programme for the former DDR. Overall, economic criminality and political violence is far more salient that ever before – crime costs South Africa, for example, £6 billion per annum, the same as the total of inward investment. And there is, within the 'realist' discipline of economics, no scientific analysis of the impact of tourism (the greatest transnational business) let alone prostitution, gambling, drugs or counterfeiting.

Social consequences of industrial productivity:
Gains to private firms through 'lean production' are recycled as social problems. Declining apprenticeships, redundancy and early retirement demand higher taxation income and expensive social repair work.

Lack of infrastructural planning:
causes wasteful competition. This has turned cross-Channel communications into a financial disaster. The same thing looks set to happen in Germany with the *Transrapid* between Hamburg and Berlin – an even bigger turkey than *Concorde*. Even these may be as nothing once we 'monetarise' the hidden costs of motoring and air transport, and find out the longer-term burdens of a mobility up by a factor of three since 1960.

The result of such malign concatenations is that when we try to construct the framework for a market, even in the short term, we can't restrict this to the supply-side but come up against concealed costs which involve massive social upheavals. Yet the social science professions seem either inadequate or reluctant to deal with them. In 1868 John Ruskin, art critic, writer of fairy stories like *The King of the Golden River*, dissenter, whose *Unto This Last* (1855) challenged – successfully, in the view of the proto-Keynesian JA Hobson – many of the definitions of classical economics, demanded of the businessmen of Bradford:

> 'If you will tell me what you ultimately intend
> Bradford to be, perhaps I can tell you what Bradford
> can ultimately produce.'

Our problem, in this post-industrial, post-historical world, is that we don't know what we want Bradford, or anywhere else, to be. Therefore we can't comprehend the proper scope and function of economics within society.

In this confusion *Mythos Mittelstand* becomes something out of the Brothers Grimm. The German South-West's apparent security and solidarity is admired by the Scots and Welsh, but its own folk see on TV the tales of the dark woods outside, and increasingly fear that these creatures might hammer at the door. While *inside* they sense uneasily that, instead of Granny Daimler in the big bed there's a high-technology future wolfing huge amounts of investment but yielding few jobs. In America the Wall Street darlings Microsoft and Intel have now a much greater capital than Ford, but together employ 48,000, against Ford's 325,000. What Edward Luttwak has called 'turbo-charged capitalism' is laying waste not just state socialism but the structure of the 'Fordist' firm itself.

Moreover, despite the resources of economics departments, our experts in this area find themselves producing pathological specialists – the MBA generation – within a profession in which the tools of the trade have become puzzling and unreliable. Our political vocabulary – liberal, conservative, radical – now seems meaningless, and thanks to environmental crisis, economic 'goods' such as low energy prices are no longer good.

The Vanishing Nation

This insecurity has been linked to the demise of communism, an opponent which, like Cafavy's barbarians, was 'a kind of solution'. But it's also connected with the dissolution of something taken as axiomatic by Adam Smith in *The Wealth of Nations*, the sovereign nation-state as the container of the market. In the mid-eighteenth century David Hume as well as Smith argued for the state as a minimal but still powerful force suppressing 'corruption' in the interests of a community on British lines within which all classes could derive their own benefits from the market. But what happens to the logic of *political* economy, the self-acting rules of getting and spending in the *polis*, when the bond between the economy and the nation-state snaps?

Adam Smith's Scotland was the sort of 'local or provincial government' he envisaged as the frame of wealth-creation, but its owners and rulers had to be visible and accountable, if wealth were to trickle down to the rest of society. Otherwise the dominance of wealth over the *polis* brought 'corruption'. Scotland, he and Hume believed, was simply too small to withstand this. The Edinburgh folk differed – 'We could aye peeble them wi' stanes when they were na gude bairns' was their lament when the Scots parliament went south in 1707. But Smith believed that a post-ethnic 'sympathy', a 'notion' of human solidarity and moral responsibility, could glue market society together. This was a learned drive and people had to be inducted into it; but if they were circumspect moral actors, they would shun a life of remote and irresponsible luxury. As his most famous – if unexpected – disciple, Robert Burns, paraphrased it in *To a Louse*, the lesson of the *Theory of Moral Sentiments* (1759) was:

O wad some Pow'r the giftie gie us

> Tae see oursels as others see us!
> It was frae monie a blunder free us
> > An' foolish notion:
> What airs in dress an' gait wad lea'e us,
> > An' ev'n Devotion!

Reflected in the mirror of history, the civic ideology of the Baden-Württemberg *Mittelstand* is like this, but far from flawless. The *Mittelstand* helped provoke populist opposition to modernisation, and allowed itself to be used by the Nazis in the 1920s and 1930s. Many of its members benefited by the expropriation of Jewish competitors. Nor, in its postwar evolution, was it even particularly Swabian, as much machine-tool expertise came from East Germany after 1945, along with up to half of the population of many local communities. The farmer-workers of Daimler-Benz's *Sindelfingen* were a highly-subsidised labour-force, major beneficiaries of the Common Agricultural Policy. The rules that the *Mittelstand* enforced and enforces are almost pre-capitalist – strict shop-opening hours, compulsory membership of Chambers of Commerce, absence of price competition in local markets – and defeat even death, forcing families to tend graves, to keep gardeners, sculptors and cemetery managers happy.

In recent years the *Mittelstand* has been coming to depend more on immigrant labour and less on an unenthusiastic younger generation. Yet as a group it retains Adam Smith's sense of a public presence. It's meant to be there, in the flat over the shop or the workshop, in the *Industrie- und-Handelskammer*, at the *Skat-runde* or the *Stammtisch*, doing various extraordinary things, like prancing around in drag, as part of a *Karneval Vereine*. . .

It's expected to wheel and deal, to pull off coups near the edge of legality. It's not expected to export its capital and, via offshore financial centres and tax manipulation, maximise its own income regardless of any trickling down. It's expected to keep a dialogue open with the unionised farmer-workers in the villages of the Schwarzwald and the Alb. Does the fall from grace of Lothar

Späth, the Land minister-president, after allegations of over-close relations with business, and the bankruptcy after a fraud of the Sudmilch dairy concern mean that its decadence is now beginning? Do the finances of the Land's favourite granddaughter, Steffi Graf, tangled up in international advertising and tax evasion, signify the onset of 'luxury and corruption'?

Presence emphasises the historical differences between Baden-Württemberg's capitalism and the 'imperial' version to be found in the old hyper-industrial 'Atlantic Arc', from Bristol to Glasgow. The *Mittelstand* is a legal and cultural as well as a manufacturing phenomenon: it involves technology through the *Tüftler* (widget-makers), solidarity through local politics and associations, strength in retailing, construction, and patrolling the functioning of the *Rechtstaat*. The grimness of the 'German weekend' – Sunday in Stuttgart makes Sunday in Stornoway look like Carnival in Rio – seems a continuing projection of Max Weber's 'ascetic capitalism', surviving beneath both the organisation of the factory and the *folie de grandeur* of the Wilhelmine and Nazi *Reich*.

But the sort of capitalism which evolved in the aggressive context of Imperial Britain and the Atlantic, climaxing between 1880 and 1914, was different. In coal, anthracite and slate, tinplate and steel, railways and shipping, docks and the service industries that these built up, it was large-scale, joint-stock, anonymous – and tied to that partly-Scots, partly-Welsh creation, the City of London. In place of the *Mittelstand* and the worker-peasant were the *Gwerin* and the *Folk*: a moralised proletariat and its intelligentsia, and between these and the bourgeoisie existed a hostility which predated the industrial upsurge.

The Welsh capitalists fled in the 1920s, when coal prices collapsed and the railways were taken over by London companies. Scots coalowners and shipowners retreated more slowly from their mansions, their gains trickling sideways into property speculation and foreign investment, indifferent to the dereliction they left behind. The mark of subsequent imaginative efforts to capture the Scots and Welsh predicament was not just the fiction of industrial confrontation, but the tragedies of a collapsing would-be *Mittelstand* , in novels such as Grassic Gibbon's *Cloud Howe* (1934), Lewis Jones's *We Live* (1937) and Emyr Humphreys' *Bonds of Attachment* sequence (1971-1989).

Yet the giantism of 'Atlantic' capitalism is no longer absolutely alien from Baden-Württemberg. Daimler Benz in 1994 is as dependent on world markets, and the *Mittelstand* on Daimler-Benz, as the Ocean Coal Company and its local suppliers were in 1914. The Scots or Welsh experiences seem precedents for a capital becoming so mobile that in post-historical 1991 the al-Sabah family of Kuwait could, in going into exile, form a state without a country. In this they followed the Lebanese, many Indians and Sri Lankans. *Neue Russen* will doubtless be joined in London and the South of France by Hong Kong Chinese. In the age of real-time communications 'serious' wealth – and remember that these two demon-kings Rupert Murdoch and Donald Trump are partly Scots – knows no international boundaries. Where, in this new situation, will the Baden-Württemberg *Mittelstand* find itself?

The European Playing Field

The Smith-Hume case is still relevant. Mobile capital requires a state with appropriate powers to contain it. This democratic argument for European unity draws on *Mittelstand*-like precedents – Kohl's Europe is a larger version of Adenauer's *Rheinische Bundesrepublik*. But a lot has changed since 1985, and unity, unless efficient, can't outweigh the traditional, comforting notions of national sovereignty.

Now, to Brussels' internal babel has been added the debate over East Europe. Is the future EU to be a compact federation, or a baggy free trade zone? With the transformation of the General Agreement on Tariffs and Trade (GATT) into the World Trade Organisation (WTO), and the end of Comecon, the latter tendency has been strengthened. But compromise offers the worst of both worlds, when frustrated federalists conflict with unappetising nationalists, and global capital slips past both.

In East Europe prudent American advisors like the Brookings

Institute pleaded for a 'planned' transition to a market economy; instead 'shock therapy' produced an *ex-nomenklatura* able either to dominate privatisation or to return to power at the head of 'democratised' former Communist parties. Some states bartered full sovereignty for association with the EU; others repeated the depressing histories of the 'succession states' of the Versailles treaty seventy years earlier – endemic economic problems, irresponsible élites, irridentism and racialism, with arms dealers and the superpowers waiting offstage. Worse still, the balance of investment into and out of the former Soviet Union, 1989-1993 showed $2.5 billions in and a suspected $40 billions out. The West's qualified boom was in part directly due to the East's collapse.

The effects of this upheaval have been to blur the moral and functional distinctions on which Smith and Hume insisted. Two examples illustrate the recurrence of the 'corruption' issue in Western politics. The former British foreign secretary, Douglas Hurd, increased his salary by a factor of three by becoming a part-time banker. Lothar Späth, leaving Baden-Württemberg under a cloud, worked himself back to respectability as head of the Saxon nationalised firm JenOptik: a civic destiny of a sort, but the result was to make him far more critical of the inertia of West German politics.

The problems of of a regional polity in Europe parallel the aimlessness and opportunism of the post-1989 period. The Cold War had its positive aspects, as the minor national players and organised labour could bid for support from one side or another. When it went, the competition of regions for multinationals' investment and the attentions of Brussels produced a diplomacy more Darwinian than Bismarckian.

In Germany, decentralisation ought to have created paradigms for the rest of Europe, but with the traumas of unification leading to political introversion, Germany replicated the tensions of the Euroopean 'home'. Internationality appeared to be evicted by the passivity of *Deutschmarkpatriotismus* – something that only worked *outside* the home country, and anyway stressed accumulation over manufacturing enterprise. The fact that *Deutschmarkpatriotismus* continued when the Kohl government devalued the DM by 20% to promote manufacturing says much for German economic organisation, and little for German political consciousness.

To this has been added monetary union, whose 'convergence criteria' have, paradoxically but not unexpectedly, strengthened national authority over currency and welfare. At the same time right-wing 'Little Englandism' has owed a lot to the gambling propensities of a City of London always on the *qui vive*, supported by an unashamedly exploitative international (mainly American) financial and media élite. All of these factors frustrated pacific 'bourgeois regionalism' of the Baden-Württemberg sort evolving into a European federalism, based on the 'civics' of cooperating regional élites, and backing up a UNO-guaranteed international order.

But could such common organisations be as efficient as Smith's nation-state? The precedents were unhelpful. International bodies, as much as multinational firms, had for years provided élites with a short cut to Western affluence, actually strengthening the ability of the wealthy – in Sri Lanka as much as Nigeria or Northern Ireland – to remain detached from the 'irrational' confrontations of the disadvantaged.

Capitalism, of course, provided a more dynamic and consistent motive – the accumulation of wealth. The sort of 'Atlantic capitalism' with which Scotland and Wales are all-too-familiar has (at least in fiction) evolved into a 'global solution' which legitimises the big players. Frederik Pohl and Cyril Kornbluth forecast this dystopia in their science-fiction novel *The Space Merchants* of 1953. This had multinationals replacing states, government and diplomacy taken over by advertising agencies, and a proletariat fuddled by narcotics. They got closer to the real *1984* than George Orwell in his anti-collectivist novel of 1948. The Space Merchants can cope with News International and McDonalds. Resistance to this neo-marketism, in Pohl and Kornbluth's book, comes from the 'Conservationists', though they could only retain their hope for human civilisation by quitting the chronically-polluted planet for Venus.

Pollution was the dragon in this fairy tale – surrealistic but not absurd. The interplanetary technology may not have arrived but the menace has. In West Germany every second tree is sick, in mountain areas four out of five. Real-existing socialism left atomic power stations, chemical works, uranium mines and factory farms as toxic timebombs from Sonneberg to Vladivostok. 56% of the waters round the British coasts in 1992 had an 'unacceptable' coliform bacteria content, the worst record in the EC, and we all know about British beef. Not to mention the greenhouse effect or the ozone layer. . .

There seems to be a corresponding pessimism about the human implications, picked out by the more morose German weeklies in the Techno-slogan of the young and post-literate: 'The world is past saving, let's have a party!'. In the early 1980s the New Right touted an individualised 'bourgeois' millenium, with sophisticated domestic technology facilitating home-based work for the Western élite, while a policeman state and minimal welfare kept the underclass in its place. Something like this was happening in Reaganite suburbia, and behind some of Thatcher's ideas, notably her hostility to public transport and local government, there lurked Kipling's notion of high technology plus a retreat to the family square.

The immediate result was the *Zweidrittelgesellschaft*. Wealth was transferred from the underclass to the 'consumers' of the middling ranks, while real incomes were maintained by retailing cheap imported goods in the new world of the shopping mall. Although Mrs Thatcher deprecated 'society' it remained unavoidable, and when sapped by the breakdown of law and order in urban England, and by the effects of de-skilling and de-classing on the upper working class, it reacted on the economy. 'Consumers' – another Pohl and Kornbluth coinage – were remote from the old solidarism of trade unions, but they were by definition not part of any manufacturing process, and derived most incomes from the

237

low-productivity service sector. With privatisation and commercial-
isation reaching them after 1989 – not least to pay for the costs of
the takeovers promoted by the City élite – the security of the middle-
class was undermined as the infrastructure which it took for granted
as a publicly beneficial service became sharply profit-oriented. By
1998 the Scottish Council Foundation was talking of a three-way
division into 'settled', 'insecure' and 'excluded' Scotlands.

Here, in the break-up of what Gramsci called Fordism, the
Western middle class, and one uses class advisedly, realised its
economic predicament. The self-examination of the Baden-
Württemberg *Mittelstand* is only one aspect of this. Its 'civic
Fordism' has provided a tougher armour, but this crisis is dividing
it into three sections, now more loosely linked. The manufacturing
Mittelstand, out to surf 'flexible specialisation', still requires high-
waged, high-skilled workers to install new technologies, yet realises
that IT is making the high-profit window shrink rapidly, and is
under pressure to export production and cut its labour force. The
service/retailing *Mittelstand* needs affluent customers, and in their
absence goes for cheap imports and automation or low-wage staff.
Ingenuity transfers itself to the business of cutting tax demands
through transnational accounting and tax havens, so taxes
increasingly hit labour costs rather than capital. Thus the public
sector *Mittelstand* concerned with socialisation – teachers, social
workers, municipal employees – has to tidy up after the foregoing
and cope with with budget cuts.

This growing crisis has hit the *Volksparteien* (the CDU and
SPD), encouraged radical or anti-system parties, or a retreat from
politics. Further pressures on traditional society – family breakdown,
the shrinking of educational and religious authority – threaten to
produce an an asocial individualism whose links are mechanical,
not humane.

Chernobyl: 'Tis Ten Years Since

This sense of crisis may be therapeutic. The decline of the defence-based nation-state and academic over-specialisation have produced dangerous 'closures'. Social disruptions are ignored by economists; politicians neglect economic realities. Researching my book on North Sea oil, I found that not only had little been written on the politics of the subject, but *three* biographies of Harold Wilson, the key political figure, didn't mention it at all!

Nor do universities emerge with much credit. In Germany there's a neglect of such interdisciplinary areas as the history of science and economic history while in Britain the teaching burden and rather mechanistic research assessment are together marginalising research into real social issues. The result is an intellectual sclerosis. Searching the archives of key economic periodicals – *Economica*, the *Economic Journal*, etc. – we find that huge areas of economic activity – tourism, drugs, crime, information technology, even financial services themselves – fall completely out of the calculations of the alleged experts.

A civic mode is – usually – more open to expanding the agenda. Environmental issues, scarcely considered in 1970, compel this. On 6 May 1986 the Chernobyl reactor blew up. Radioactive caesium was deposited in huge quantities over South Germany, an experience which eliminated conventional borders and changed economic priorities. Chernobyl lodged itself in our political subconscious, grimly contradicting the glossy surfaces of post-Fordism, but it was also, ironically, obscured by the political revolution of 1989-91 which it caused.

People can live without democracy and the market. They revolt when a régime – of whatever sort – starts to kill them through sheer incompetence. At issue was not the decadence of Communism *per se* but that of any economic system which becomes incapable of detecting and dealing with malfunctions. The disaster of the 'little tigers' suggests that a capitalism which has also lost touch with its social environment could be approaching a cognate moment of hubris.

239

In this context the *Mittelstand* myth has become part of an 'emergency reappraisal' of civic and community values sweeping the West. This has been advertised by the likes of Amitai Etzioni, and although his references are restricted to the contemporary USA, and loaded with tautology, his popularity shows the need for an interdisciplinary agenda. If inter-regional partnerships, of which the Four Motors (Baden-Württemberg, Rhone-Alpes, Lombardy and Cataluna) is a powerful precedent, are to be effective, they must expand into two more dimensions by 'monetarising' social and environmental factors (crime, social breakdown, pollution), and 'historicising' the dynamic evolution from manufacturing into services.

This model has to be coupled with educational reform and conscious political (and consequently ethical) priorities. It assumes (1) that information and education become the prime resources of social and economic organisation, and (2) that pragmatic forms of organisation extend this into inter-regional and international fields, expert without being bureaucratic, and free of interest-group pressure.

This involves making two sideways redefinitions, their rationale derived from everyday existence. One, that computers, chips, etc, are better regarded as raw material rather than as manufactured goods (can you, reader, tell me how a semi-conductor is actually made?). Like coal or land, they are there to be worked with, to facilitate and cheapen conventional industrial processes. Two, that in our problematic international economy more money is to be made by the 'flexible specialisation' of adapting, repairing and maintaining what exists – for example, in fully comprehending and shaping that fuzzy monster the 'service sector' – than by concentration on further mass production of consumer goods.

The information revolution presents an unreassuring, unequal world. Measured in US dollars, Scottish per capita income rose from about $6,000 in 1982 to $16,000 in 1995, about 30% under West Germany ($9600 to $23,000). In India GNP per capita was $245 in 1982 – and $310 in 1995. Scotland's money income rose by 166%, Germany's by 140%, while India's rose by only 26% – in real terms an actual decline.

Is this the result of a 'third world' increase in population? Yes, but a recent project found that Indian villagers reckoned their quality of life, in terms of the things that mattered – cooperation, care of the young and the old, hope for the future, better than that of people in a dead-end Scottish housing estate, with its long-term unemployment, ill health, vandalism and drugs. Does this sentimentalise poverty? But the Scottish estate is what the Indian village is evolving into – the world's dysfunctional megacities – while global warming and the destruction of the ozone layer are 85% due to 'us' – mainly through excess energy production.

Scotland and Baden-Württemberg view such challenges of adaptation with exhaustion as well as apprehension. In Britain the 'market utopia' may have wrecked state socialism, but it has failed to evolve self-regulation and apparently eluded legal regulation; the City of London and the British microstates – Jersey, Guernsey, Gibraltar, the Caymans – are complicit in the sort of plunder observed in Russia. Baden-Württemberg's *Mittelstand* may contribute some of the institutions of civics, but Scotland has also learned – we hope – from imperial capitalism and Fordism. Can a 'synergic' outcome ensure that manoeuvrable political communities emerge as conscious actors in a new strategy, able to take on multinationals and European bureaucracy?

The Enlightenment and the Network

Phil Cooke, in examining Baden-Württemberg's *Mittelstand*, stresses the importance of developing exporting industries. But this raises the question of who controls them. The *Mittelstand* has always prided itself on re-investing its profits locally, but the memory of the export-dominated Welsh and Scottish past, and its limited contribution to national well-being, is sobering. And some attempts by inward investment bodies like Locate in Scotland to woo firms are worrying. Computer technicians at £9,000 per annum may attract some manufacturers, but what are the longer-term social costs of a salariat without the resources to get married, let alone set up their own businesses? Absence of prospects brings its own appalling costs. Glasgow has a drug problem that the Scottish Select Committee estimates at £633 million annually, and this is *after* selling itself successfully as the Merchant City.

Scotland has in whisky and woollens exemplary types of *Mittelstand* goods. (Who wants a Singapore malt or a Czech twinset?) Marketing these develops symbiotically with high-value-added tourism. But Scotland *qua* conference centre has its Mr Hyde side, that *demi-monde* where the conference business and organised vice meet up. European politicians see the trade in people, of which prostitution (involving perhaps 500,000 women in the EU) is only a part, as an even greater menace than drugs, a supply-side economics which neglects factors that, collectively, outweigh its developmental impact.

The Glasgow drug bill is over £150 million bigger than the 1995 budget of Scottish Enterprise. The New Economics Foundation has suggested that if such total-cost accounting were applied to the UK economy since 1950, our index of Sustainable Economic Welfare, after roughly doubling between 1950 and 1975, has gone back to where it was.

In *Cultural Weapons* (1992) I argued that Scotland should invert traditional industrial policy, enhancing solidarism and limiting the waste of resources and energy – the 'Gross National Destruct' – in order to developing a healthy, highly-educated and participatory society. This would enable a fusion of market and planning to produce the high-value-added expertise which the 'repair and maintenance' of the planet demands. It would also require new *Mittelstand*s to tap resources in environmental and energy-conservation policy, educational innovation, and third-world contacts, to re-create a critical civic culture. The enlightenment inheritance of Ferguson and Smith was common to Scotland, Wales, and Germany. It stressed the negative impacts of individualism and the division of labour – in 'corruption' and alienation. Current technological and financial organisation simply projects such

242

inequities worldwide, at the expense of Smith's 'sympathy' or Ferguson's 'social bands'.

The narrow ideology of a privileged finance-driven minority dominates public bodies, from the Nobel Prize for Economics committee to the World Bank, powerfully backed up by the media. At the edge of Europe, Scotland and Wales seem poor relations of that minority. Will their futures be as collaborators or as rebels?

Most manufacturing in Scotland and Wales is English or foreign-owned. This doesn't rule out innovations, apparent in 1994 when Phil Cooke and I visited the Staedtler pen and pencil plant in Bridgend. But these resulted in a fall in the workforce. Better a slimmed-down firm than no firm at all? Maybe. But the arithmetic of increased productivity can be negative for the region in other ways. A firm's profits (and hence taxation) are accounted to head office, usually London, while the costs of unemployment and other disruptions remain with the region, as statistics of dependency.

Have privatised utilities enhanced local capitalism, as they claim? The interplay of banks and bus and power companies in Scotland in the 1990s has been dynamic. But one takeover could end them. Or is privatisation more about enabling American capital to colonise overseas service industries? Thatcherian 'people's capitalism' boiled down to one-off speculation – most punters took their profit, went back to the building societies, and now gamble on the National Lottery.

So far Adam Smith's 'tax on all the fools in creation' has attracted no macro-economic analysis – so what's new? It may have done wonders for many local shops (as well as for the directors of Camelot) but it has sapped voluntary activity, as charities and arts groups have to lobby for the funds which they formerly raised directly.

The need to create (and in Germany to renew) Smith's 'local or provincial state' has now convinced even shellbacked marketeers like the Institute of Economic Affairs, which argues that takeover policy be biased in favour of regional development. Here we have to recognise that the power of *Commune* and *Kreis* authorities is as much a part of *Mittelstand* culture as decentralised banking, with cooperation enforced through proportional representation and (particularly in Baden-Württemberg) the division of powers between mayor and council. Is this compatible with a globalised, inward-investment model? Or might it be inhibited by it, with incoming executives being short-term and mindful of head office, or liable to be 'delayered' out of existence?

To retreat from certain sorts of manufacturing is positive, lessening energy demand and pollution and conserving natural resources. If Wales hasn't got Scotland's whisky and woollens, as William Hague (while Welsh Secretary of State) pointed out to the Welsh Select Committee, a 'Wales the Brand' strategy of stressing high value-added services may relieve richer regions of some of their surplus value in exchange for access to information, comfort, a clean environment and security. Both Scotland and Wales have elements of a 'Swiss' economy based on luxury goods and eco-tourism. If bodies at central and local levels can control it, and plan development options which meet European and world needs, drawing on the training and export of a high-grade labour force, this network might be superior to a manufacturing sector dominated by foreign-owned assembly-plants.

Manufacturing is now far more 'portable'. It can also be disaggregated; with networks of research, development, systems-creation existing remote from the point of production. A skilled and adaptable labour force remains necessary to 'lock' foreign investment, and to enable breakthroughs in innovation to be translated into volume production at the most profitable moment, but can this be left to market forces? Encouraging blanket growth of multinational manufacturing in a specific area – Scotland's 'Silicon Glen' for example – hoping that this will reach 'critical mass' and suck in high-value-added Research and Development and managerial sectors, has rung false. Compaq (for example) may produce computers in Scotland, but its high-value-added functions are in the US and Munich. Ireland's success, by contrast, has depended on the supposedly discredited *dirigiste* strategy of 'picking winners' in pharmaceuticals and computer software.

In this sense Baden-Württemberg isn't an example for Scotland and Wales but a cause of past defeats. The massing of the headquarters of international firms in the *Land* took place while between 1945 and 1980 industry in Scotland and Wales was marked by stagnation, branch plants, de-skilling and capital outflow. In the 1980s Britain was the largest foreign investor in Germany and in Baden-Württemberg. This has now changed, with large-scale capital being presented with investment conditions – low wages, 'flexible' labour, limited worker protection – aimed at reversing this tendency. But are Scotland and Wales foreseen as 'headquarters' players in the international cartelisation of high-technology industry represented by the Four Motors? Or are they simply a couple of possible low-wage assembly points among many?

Our advantages depend on the direction we expect future developments to take. With an ageing population in the richer European countries, health care and labour itself will appreciate in value. Congestion and environmental costs will force some high-value-added industries to disperse from the 'golden triangle' (can they afford the lassitude of an ozone-laden atmosphere?) to the 'Celtic fridge'. The information revolution will push them in the direction of universities and libraries.

The 1990 slump hit the 'over-heated' British south, and stayed, because of London's planlessness, decaying infrastructure and congestion. Scotland and Wales have in contrast rich natural resources, well-developed agriculture, a broad manufacturing sector, good road and rail links with the continent and ferry links to Ireland. A Celtic *Mythos Mittelstand* is essentially to do with networking these advantages through the density of internal and international contacts, and a conscious strategy of selective, flexibly-planned re-industrialisation centred on high-value-added services, stressing education, planning, design, and control. But since much high-value-added service-industry work may be carried on away from home, attitudes to migration – in and out – have also to change.

Challenges

'It has been seen that these injuries to individuals and
groups of individuals, and through them to society,
arise naturally and necessarily from the unfettered
operation of the enlightened self-interest of individuals
and groups of individuals employed in obtaining for
themselves, by the freest use of industrial means
available, the largest quantity of money.

'So far as these evils are in form or magnitude the
peculiar products of the last two centuries, they are in
large measure traceable to the means of production
controlled by machinery, and to the social estimate of
the machine-products which gives machinery this
controlling power.

'If this is so, such progress as shall abate these evils and
secure for humanity the uses of machinery without the
abuses will lie in two directions, each of which
deserves consideration:

1. An adequate social control over machine
production.

2. An education in the arts of consumption such as
may assign proper limits to the sphere of machinme
production.'

JA Hobson, whose *Imperialism: a Study* (1902) was cribbed by
Lenin to justify the Bolshevik seizure of power in Russia – and
hence helped create the 'barbarians' who made Western capitalism
conduct itself circumspectly until 1990 – has renewed relevance
when the money-obsessed are again unfettered. Adam Smith
approved of entrepreneurs, but he mistrusted them and invoked
the state against their cartels. His successors praise the
Existenzgrunder, the small-scale firm-founder, but back the
advertising agency, the hypermarket chain and the profit-driven
bank which will, sure as fate, put him or her out of business.

Their notion of individuality dwindles to consumers' predictable responses to crude economic or emotional stimuli. Their argument that planning will be defeated by lack of precise information can't be squared with their interest in the *distortion* of information: advertising campaigns, the fetishising of brand names, the targetting of children. Their favoured 'supply-side' policies, the 'Keynesianism for the rich' of Reagan and Thatcher, threatened middle-class incomes, yet are now backed by most employers' organisations. These are deserting 'social partnership' for 'Anglo-American' competition, where unemployment is reduced through McJobs with poor conditions and social security, and (at 13% of workers) minimal union protection.

Turbo-capitalism has now set thousands of white-collar jobs on the line, with consequences in social breakdown, crime and demagogic politics. Its controllers, the 'masters of the universe' are remote, for they don't like looking their victims in the eye. This sort of market is metropolitan, not *Mittelstandisch*.

Market-government relationships, as Will Hutton has pointed out, are so varied that there is as much difference between capitalist systems as between *Communismo alla Toscana* and *real-existierende Sozialismus*. The Germans, Japanese or Swiss have always protected their industrial structures. The gulling of the EU into subsidising Daimler-Benz's Rastatt works in the mid-1980s is a case in point! Anglo-American capitalism withdrew headquarters from Scotland and Wales, despite a good social and transport infrastructure. But Ireland has moved from an industrial development régime based on tax concessions, which failed to create a lasting base, to using its autonomy and EU status as a full member, to move from a GNP per capita of around 55% of the UK in 1975 to 87% in 1994. Thus European economic union makes the case for the regional state; or at least for the institutions which can manage it.

The issues that such a state will have to deal with are severe, but also interlinked:

'There are few trades now that a youth can be put to

with a certainty that they will furnish employment to
him for life. In ten years time they may be
revolutionised, or almost cease.'

Relax. This is the Chartist Robert Lowery writing in 1857. Job
insecurity has been around as long as machinery. But there has
been a qualitative change, both in technology and in our evaluation
of it. Export-oriented manufacturing was always too dependent
on over-specialised workers and unstable international markets, with
price the only determinant. Competition plus Information
Technology meant that in the 1970s machines edged ahead of men
and productivity gains inevitably meant unemployment. (In the
North Sea nearly £100 billion was invested for fewer than 100,000
jobs, and technological advances are whittling more and more of
these down.) The Japanese even envisage fully-automated factories
eliminating such labour-associated costs as heating, lighting, toilets,
canteens and car parks.

The man from the assembly-line told Henry Ford, when the
latter was muttering about such prospects, 'Who's going to buy
your cars?' Fordist firms worried about this; hyper-marketism no
longer believes in the firm. But how is the dividend from such
activity to be distributed? Shareholders are less invisible than the
dwindling workforce, but ex-workers land on the taxpayers. Can
you have collective bargaining when there's no-one there?

On the other hand there were many invisible folk in the old
unionised order. Work conveyed status, but this disregarded
housewives, carers for the elderly or handicapped, voluntary workers
whose 'calling' was more important to them than the way they
earned their wage? Nor did work automatically bring well-being.
Scotland and Wales didn't boom in the 1950s as in the 1900s, but
Aneurin Bevan's people had better social benefits, better health
and housing, more sex equality, more facilities for recreation than
the Edwardians. If the 'market' has receded, and a civic society had
advanced, then it has to negotiate on behalf of the community, and
acquire the appropriate institutions and powers.

EF Schumacher's *Small is Beautiful* had considerable impact
when published in 1973. Despite its 'green' reputation, it stood in
the ethical socialist tradition of Hobson, Tawney and Bevan. The
centralisation and waste of resources it warned against has
continued, although in Wales, where intermediate technology and
small-scale organisation are more deeply embedded than in
Scotland, the limits that the environment puts on our freedom of
action are explicit. Studies which 'monetarise' the external costs of
profit-driven enterprise – motoring, gambling, fast food – show
huge concealed deficits, and subvert that triumphalist marketism
which assumed that its arrival meant the end of the historical
dialectic. The disruptions already catalogued have seen to that, with
civil society involved in unending and expensive confrontations
over road schemes or animal welfare, generating such external costs
as the £15 million to police the Newbury by-pass, or the upheaval
of the Castor nuclear transport.

The Welsh meteorologist Sir John Houghton, Chair of the
Intergovernmental Panel on Climate Change, is one who believes
mobility should meet its global costs. As an active Christian, he
could be claimed for the *Mittelstand* , by definition rich in
individuals and voluntary groups apt to question why markets are
cheap, where concealed costs lurk, who actually benefits from
globalisation. They discover that the WTO, the IMF and World
Bank aggravate monocrop economies, inequality and dysfunctional
urbanisation; that lean production produces fat social costs. They
are, in short, citizens, not consumers.

Rather than court a turbo-capitalist future which will turn
out both dangerous and obsolete, is it not better to define a revived
Mittelstand as starting with our evaluation of society and what holds
it together? Here that other branch of the enlightenment – social
science – seems more fruitful than straight economics. Patrick
Geddes and Lewis Mumford would have called our present situation
neo-technic – the resources for fulfilled human lives are now
available within our current technology. Only with a social division
of its proceeds will people get secure, useful and dignified jobs. In

this sense, what the Norwegians did with their oil gains – increasing the 'density' of civil society – is exemplary. It also paid off by securing for the country three times the oil revenue that came the way of 'privatised' Britain!

Resources

This inquiry started off with the problems of 'secondary' manufacturing industry. Yet these really implicate the primary and tertiary sectors. Regional planning issues in Baden-Württemberg, Scotland and Wales have much to do with agricultural change; the environmental consequences of energy production are already serious. If, as Phil Cooke argues, networking is a learning process, then it belongs in the tertiary sector. The topography of 'services' – notoriously ranging from hamburger-flipping to computer programming – is little understood, or even quantified, yet contains the key to reforming the manufacturing sector. Education and training are central to the processes of socialisation which provide the civic fabric, while the environmental crisis demands change from Baden-Württemberg's major employer, the car industry.

Conservation and agricultural development requires the region to control its natural resources, such as land ownership, the production of energy and the maintenance of health. These are social goods which need well-researched policies, involving the universities and the communities – long-term options which cannot be justified in immediate economic terms. This form of subsidiarity is essential, and involves encouraging local organisation over the alleged 'economies of scale' of international operators (how can a hospital be more efficient by being run from the Cayman Islands?), while transportation change and heat insulation programmes can both reduce energy demand and create jobs. A comprehensive strategy for health and housing – assaulting unhealthy eating patterns and *compelling* exercise, for example reconstructing mis-planned communities – can increase the commitment to the locality which the *Mittelstand* has traditionally exemplified.

Education falls into the tertiary sector: but adequate manpower is a primary resource. Robert Owen, the theorist of the work-based community, believed that education should be about enjoyment as well as enquiry, and that teachers had to challenge and stimulate what Friedrich Schiller called *Spieltrieb*, the compulsive enjoyment of the job. The Germans, with their individual research- and bureaucracy-determined system, are good at training and planning, but less good at the spontaneous collaboration of the team, the quality which carried the British Open University past the rather earlier *Fernuniversität Hagen*.

Again, this places on regional government the business of humanising an educational experience affected by technology. 'Feedback' – essentially operational research – can be used to match demands for skill with the sort of jobs people find satisfying at the various stages of their careers – when they require a high income, when they want to spend more time on other activities or want to retrain. It's quite likely that someone may hold three or four jobs in the course of their working life, so the means must exist of giving them the chance to reflect on, choose, and train for the sequence of activities they want.

This also applies to a media which is about providing information and encouraging self-expression and citizenship. Here the German local daily press is exemplary, while the less said about the papers which (alas) 80% of the British read, the better. The tabloids are no longer a disgrace, good only for a giggle. In their mindless sub-literacy they are a social danger, and the rot is seeping up into the broadsheets. Honours are more equal in broadcasting, and Wales has through S4C a lot of innovation to its credit. But in Germany, as in the USA, the impact of private satellite channels has been disastrous, particularly on children. This is now visible, alas, in the retardation of students' capabilities in reading, organising and expressing knowledge – something for which no number of nets and webs can compensate.

Networking is about intelligent manufacture, which means appraising criteria other than immediate profit. To take one case which bridges manufacturing, networking and services: the Eritrean railway. Eritrea requires $30 million to restore its railway on its own; the World Bank costs a western-style reconstruction at $700 million, most of which would go to Western banks and manufacturers. Which scheme should be aided?

A narrow economistic/industrial answer would be the World Bank's, but no network would result, while judicious aid, aimed at stimulating the local economy, would not only spare resources for further investment, but create a relationship of trust. The West usually regards aid recipients as markets for equipment which builds up exports and creates an élite that it can 'do business with'. Baden-Württemberg's supply of Mercedes to the *bisnesmeni* who have looted Russia raises only qualified sympathy when the region is threatened by top-of-the-market Japanese cars.

This shows how at variance supposedly 'neutral' market forces and consistent economic development can be. Yet networking can include programmes of distance learning in East Europe, decommissioning nuclear plants, neutralising industrial pollution. One part of the future of Scotland, Wales or Baden-Württemberg will almost certainly involve working abroad again, and the links to be built up, if they are to last, will have to be those of mutual trust and respect.

Against the 'global market' envisaged by the WTO and the World Bank, this suggests an alternative approach whereby economies develop within a relatively closed system, with direct partnerships involving a sophisticated social and educational programme, for example, exchanging the capital goods and technical expertise of Baden-Württemberg or Scotland, for local raw materials and manufactures, cutting out middlemen and international speculators. Just as, before World War I, much of Scotland's world dominance in coal, steel and shipping was secured by 'men on the spot', now educational capital is crucial to the third industrial revolution. New information networks give the chance to detect such opportunities and provide equitable solutions. Instead of a region being the victim of multinational-determined markets, regional governments can use IT systems to model a range of responses to particular situations, and shift resources appropriately. Properly handled, the computer is the steering-wheel of the mixed economy.

One major source of investment in alternative industry and social development is the present wasteful and self-destructive transport system, which consumes about 25% of energy production. Presently cars, lorries and aircraft meet only a third of their global costs. Alternatives to them, from computer conferencing to walking, can reduce car dependency by up to 70% in a country where 80% of the population have potentially easy access to public transport. Adequate resources can be transferred to new types of 'eco-hi-tech' industry which cope with such other transforming factors as power generation, insulation, energy-recycling and waste disposal. Ironically *Mittelstand* Germany is both more dependent on the car industry, and more worried about it. Only about 15% of the world's population has a European or level of access to the motor-car, and even to double this would be environmentally lethal. But the car industry is no longer like the cotton factory a necessary first stage of industrialisation; while it aggravates the international ramifications of supplying raw materials and petrol. IT on the other hand encourages the rational planning of localised reindustrialisation.

Institutions

There is a calvinist temptation to end with a sermon. Given our predicament, this can lead to the Private Fraser mode – 'We're aa' doomed, I tell ye!', etc. I hope to avoid it. Confronted with the apathy and insecurity of a younger generation baffled rather than sustained by new technology, approaches of the 'pull yourselves together and face up to impending horrors' sort merely induce a further 'Generation X' paralysis. The PR-guided triumphalism, the absence of self-criticism of our marketeers, has brought this on themselves – as Adam Smith said it would.

In tackling a globalised capitalism, which promises so much but is in fact so destructive to the very idea of systems, we are driven back to the social institutions that we have to hand. Can we use these to develop an autonomous intelligence – a steerable economy – of their own? And through this can we give confidence to the new generation through enabling them to experiment and learn by practice and feedback at a regional level?

Hyper-marketism creates not individual freedom but, in replacing the firm by speculation and the multinationals, an alternative and far less responsible sort of state. While 'fordism' had some notion of community, it reduces its subjects to 'human resources' and 'consumers'. If entrepreneurialism is to revive it has to be part of an all-round sort of culture, which can encourage microcapitalism (or for that matter 'market socialism') to function intelligently and adaptably at a local level. As in Adam Smith's day, markets will only operate equitably within 'strong' civil society and responsive governmental structures.

This involves new appraisals. Manufacturing is regarded as a straightforward 'good' and has been the biggest bit of the *Mittelstand* success story. It's about picking technological winners, maximising profits and ploughing these back, and extending research and development. But these historic strengths are unlikely to promote job creation. Our ageing society is seen, by contrast, as a problem; yet the elderly have capital and they have a need for the sort of self-development activities – distance-education, gardening, voluntary civic organisation – which can create not just a thriving, labour-intensive, high-value-added microcapitalism, but the sort of civil society which can minimise our 'Gross National Destruct'.

The problem is to adapt the institutions of the *Mittelstand* to reassure worried people that they have a future which is theirs to control. So consent to a high-technology economy can only be gained if the results of this growth accrue to society as a whole. State action, mainly in a decentralised and flexible form, has to be responsible both for setting the frame for a socially-acceptable market.

The European Level:
Tolerable economic development requires the supervision of an European body – I don't baulk at the term 'superstate' – to see that

markets work to goals compatible with ecological sustainability. The result will be, in deference to Reutlingen's son, a neo-Listian economy, with an executive speaking softly, but carrying a very big stick. This goes against the current enthusiasm for global markets – these are capricious, prone to promote the 'luxury and corruption' of which Adam Smith complained and incapable of creating the institutions or *mentalités* necessary for making the transition to a high-intelligence, low-energy-use economy. A common currency will strike a blow against financial speculation, and in favour of measures of value which accurately reflect human and natural resources.

The other function of a European authority is to build up a common, efficient infrastructure, and to promote civic bodies as a counterweight to multinational capital. Here, if the indispensable building-block is the region, we must rationalise the competencies of these bodies – four at the last count – which represent the regions in Europe. The Committee of the Regions could become the second chamber of the European Parliament. Indeed in any federal arrangement something more functional is required than national structures which put one small region – Luxembourg – on all fours with Germany, but disenfranchises others.

The Transport Factor:
Transportation must be the propellant of European nation-making, as it was in the nineteenth century, and the means don't radically differ. A rail-based system will logically divide itself into 'European' arteries and 'regional' feeders. I stress this not just because a largely pointless investment in cars and roads can be diverted to manufacturing and high-value-added services, but because of the remarkable success of the public-sector *Mittelstand* in Baden-Württemberg in creating a technology-based 'cluster' in urban and suburban public transport in the 'Karlruhe model' of sophisticated long-distance electric trams which can drastically lower infrastructural costs.

This is a classic example of the 'lessons' that a region with previous industrial experience can convey: how to control the relationship of technology, politics and society so that these serve the expectations of most of the people involved.

The Regional level:
How are the necessary synergies to be applied to productive industry, particularly shifting it to functions which repair a damaged environment? Networking is a learning process, and you can't legislate for your partners, but regions can advance synergically, creating 'mezzanine' organisations, like the Four Motors, which make the EU more flexible and better suited to international cooperation.

Such autonomy requires conscious economic intervention. Baden-Württemberg had this in the nineteenth century in its 'Central Office for Industry and Trade' under Ferdinand Steinbeis, which financed the experiments of Gottlieb Daimler. The STUC suggested in the 1980s a Scottish Economic Council, with an Economic Planning Office in support, with subsidiaries responsible for research, takeovers, economic development and investment. As a committee of parliament, with external back-up, this seems a necessary first step. It's here that there's a need for sophisticated economic modelling, which can locate the implications of investment programmes, and for the co-ordination of subordinate bodies, whether local authorities or voluntary organisations. But it's also important that such bodies should be as unbureaucratic and informal as possible.

Non-governmental organisations:
By using the single criterion of price, hyper-marketism has sapped not only the firm but mutual organisations: the building society, the cooperative, the trade union. British studies of the Mittelstand say a lot about 'relationship-banking' but little about the huge Baden-Württemberg agricultural cooperative movement, which follows in the Robert Owen tradition. In Scotland and Wales retailing co-ops, once in eclipse, are still hanging on, while

cooperatively-owned companies like the John Lewis partnership, trade successfully while diffusing their profits among their workforce. From the local credit unions, which have proved effective in mitigating the impact of unemployment, to these remarkably successful co-ops, the Great Little Trains, the Welsh mutual tradition may even be more innovative than the Scots.

Such bodies need a banking system analogous to the *Volksbanken* and *Kreissparkassen* (and creating such regional institutions throughout the regions should be an EU priority) but such a system can build on strong foundations.

Fordism approved of trade unionism; turbo-capitalism regards unions as outmoded. Their conservatism and male bias made them almost fatally slow in adapting to technological change, yet the argument for independent worker representation remains. The Welsh TUC is less experienced in community activity than its Scottish counterpart, but both seem better rooted than the TUC in England. The pattern of the *Deutsche Gewerkschaftsbund* (DGB) suggests the value of a federation of 'industrial' unions; yet the Scottish tradition of Trades Councils representing the local labour profile has also much to offer. The labour movement can coordinate its strengths in research and publicity, not just to match the employers' organisations, but to see that working people are protected in decision-making and retain union assistance whatever their working (or non-working) circumstances, and that training is subject to mutual control (STUC, 1983). Again, this can involve the parliament setting up a type of semi-autonomous body which can use IT within an integrative society to offer better education and a range of satisfying and community-sustaining activities that have the status of 'work'.

Social ownership:
The communications revolution can be built on to provide new forms of social ownership, which genuinely diffuse economic power, such as Robert Bosch in Baden-Württemberg, which is run by a charitable trust which promotes technical education and research.

The German union movement uses *Mitbestimmung* – social partnership – to provide at factory level and' within the policy-making structure of firms over a certain size, policy councils with 50% employee representation and an independent convener acceptable to both sides. But the variety of mutualism in society can be increased by taxation systems which encourage firms to set up socially-beneficial trusts. 10% of US GDP goes into these, compared with only 1% in the UK.

Such organisations make up an internal network, vital for the reconstruction of regional industry. In certain important areas, Baden-Württemberg, Scotland and Wales have complementary skills. The latter's position (presently threatened) as a world centre of agricultural research is one bargaining counter. The experience derived from coping with industrial dereliction and reclamation is exportable, particularly to East Europe. There is a lot that Baden-Württemberg could learn about tourism from Scotland and Wales – something very important both in absorbing manpower from manufacturing and inducing Germans to holiday at home.

The general principle here is that of the creation of synergy (a Geddesian coinage, made much of by the Japanese) by the exchange of expertise. It is possible to see an inter-regional diplomacy build itself up in this way, while a competition for inward investment may only offer unending and wasteful competition between regions.

One argument against alternative technology used to be that it would isolate communities, but this no longer works in the age of the Internet. With knowledge-based industries which have become far less metropolitan, utilising a resource like our National Libraries – for example by preparing marketable data-corpuses for social, educational and industrial use – will be more positive in its consequences for the local economy than discovering more oilfields.

Tackling the multinationals:
Going out from a strengthened society, European regional alliances should play hard politics with multinational firms. These *are*

sensitive to the pressure that communities can exert; witness Brent Spar. If such federalised consortia invest strategically in firms, they can get information about policy decisions, linkages to other firms, to banks, investment companies, and other governments. They can then build their own control networks. This ought to be a priority for the Committee of the Regions – enforcing access to firms' papers; enabling regional governments, through their pensions funds, to oversee these firms' policies, through liaison with EU bodies covering this area.

Where multinationals set up branch-plants, such a body can make assistance contingent on access to policy formation. Multinationals have not always the whip-hand, and the stronger Scotland and Wales are as centres of economic initiative and purchasing power, and the stronger their European links, the greater their power of manoeuvre.

Community development:
But the notion of the *Mittelstand* is about much more than expertise or even socialisation. Some aspects of it are irrational and archaic, but emphasise its roots in local solidarity. The Churches, community and political groups, which constitute part of it have a competence beyond the local. These have often questioned the economic self-interest of European countries and companies. It's possible to question how relevant church taxes are in a secular Europe, but also to work out ways in which this principle can be adapted to finance community service and cultural activities.

Just as the 'alternative service' offered to conscripts in Germany could be made the basis of training for running community enterprises. In Scotland and Wales income from the lottery could be precepted for the parliament and assembly to dispense for community and cultural purposes.

This book started with a long essay on the position of Scotland and Wales in the evolution of a predatory economic order obsessively concerned, as it seemed, with exploiting carbon resources. The twentieth century has been in part the American century – its history lacked the terrible breakdowns which afflicted Europe, and its record signified hope for most of the world's people, something apparently confirmed by the events of 1989-91; but the depredations continued. America remained and remains, in Geddes's terms *paleotechnic*. Euro-Europe offers cognate statistics, but seems to have moved consciously towards the necessary *geotechnic* transition. Regionalism, the *Mittelstand*, and a conscious cultural policy, for civic republicanism can't be anything other than cultural, are the necessary outcomes.

Mythos Mittelstand 's ultimate argument against its global aggressors is the exploitation, political impotence, and mindless tedium of the cultural future they offer. If man was made for something better than disturbing dirt, he was also made for something better than slumping in front of the television, paying Rupert Murdoch to watch a football match. Reviewing a great novel, about one of Europe's most tragic regions, EM Forster wrote of Lampedusa's *The Leopard* (1957), 'it shows us how many ways there are of being alive'. But we can only stay alive, and hope that our children and grandchildren see out the twenty-first century, by thinking and planning.

22
Mythos Mittelstand 2
– (i) rethinking tourism
(1998)

This two-part essay, parts of which appeared
in the *Times Higher Education Supplement*
and *Scotland on Sunday*, suggests ways
in which tourism (about 5% of Scottish GNP)
can be used to pump-prime extensive civic
education projects. If a healthy high value-
added services industrialisation is about the
dissemination of wisdom, then does it matter if
we quarry history rather than coal or ironstone
as the raw material?

Whilst some would nominate the drug trade or criminality in
general, at the end of the century demand tourism is likely to be
the largest international trading activity. If tourism as an economic
enterprise is amorphous, the other two are literally unknowable to
legitimate economics.

Yet there are obvious links – sex tourism, tax evasion tourism,
illegal immigrant-powered tourism. The capacity to smuggle and
exploit has been radically increased by the expansion in international
communications and the freeing of markets and has its consequences
for government. Such a huge element of international trade should
have attracted a similar weight of academic analysis, a literature
which would show how its fluctuations influence the usual
economic relationships of firms, entrepreneurs, wages, welfare and
exchange rates. Not so. There is practically no coverage of tourism
in the central periodicals of economics and economic theory. If it

is dealt with at all it's on the low-status fringe of the subject, in regional studies or economic geography.

Treatments of tourism practice and policy have developed as an outgrowth of hotel and restaurant management, transport studies, cultural management and regional geography. As part of the service-industry economy, they have evolved to supply and sustain promotional activity, connected with infrastructural development, conservation, and job creation, without much grounding in economic policy, or tendency towards self-analysis. Tourist journalism is – even in 'serious' papers – almost exclusively promotional. Travel journalists are notoriously reliant on 'freebies' – travel brochures mutating hey presto into editorial copy – and proportionately uncritical. Although the situation is not as bad in Germany, and alternatives exist, such as *Holiday Which?,* it is not analysed in such a way as to integrate it with other aspects of the regional or national economy.

Again, this dearth of information also applies to other aspects of the 'new economy' such as currency speculation, information technology and self-evidently to crime itself. The result is that statistics, the necessary bedrock of research, are hypothetical and vary so widely as to be largely useless. Yet 'global cost accounting' economists tell us that changes are impending, and inevitable, which will have radical effects on touristic income and infrastructural investment. If the air and road transport facilities on which much tourism depends only cover their environmental costs by a third through fares and vehicle taxation, then policies which recover these costs will mean a drastic decline in cheap mobility. The knock-on effects of this can be imagined.

Another area of opaque economics is the transition from 'hedonistic', largely seaside, tourism to (very loosely defined) cultural/urban tourism, currently underway, for various reasons – declining family size, cancer threats, pollution and ageing hotel stock. Mass tourism, with its fairly obvious economic, ecological and social implications is in retreat. Danger from pollution and from malignant melanoma has been threatening the traditional beach holiday. 'Quality packages' are already diminishing the low-cost Mediterranean mass market. But we know very little about the dimensions or direction of such changes.

'Ecological', 'green' or 'cultural' tourism is increasingly popular, encouraging walking, cycling and the use of public transport, and involving education-based activities, crafts, history, and environmental work, along with a greater involvement of the traveller in the host community.

But even such a benign shift raises questions of economic and community sustainability, when it's on the scale envisaged. Can transport and museum systems sustain the weight of mass use, without diminishing their cultural integrity? Can anyone derive a worthwhile aesthetic education – or even experience - from being herded briskly round the Uffizi Gallery in Florence after queuing two hours? How much is the collapse of the London Underground the result of overuse and undercharging of tourists? Can Edinburgh expand the Festival and Fringe any more and remain tolerable? Is any cultural interchange involved at all when mass-tourist hotels are internationally owned, serve 'international cuisine' and are staffed by low-wage imported labour?

Supply

Two of the 'supply-side' factors are of immediate significance, in Scotland, Wales and Baden-Württemberg: underused accommodation in traditional holiday areas, and academic and cultural investment used for only a limited period. We have plenty examples of the former. The drift of holidaymakers away from Victorian holiday resorts has meant that they have either had to diversify – often into academic activities – or become refuges for the socially underprivileged, though Scotland isn't yet like the North Wales Coast, where the homeless in bed-and-breakfast in former guesthouses have already made their mark. In Baden-Württemberg the cutting of subsidies for cure-holidays and convalescence threatened in 1996-7 to cut the income of *Kurorte* by up to 25%

and some of these places have already begun to accommodate refugees and *Aussiedlers* (Germans from the former Soviet block). Both groups bring problems along with them, made worse by unemployment and the availability of drugs, which accelerate a vicious circle.

The situation is not one where developing high value-added forms of tourism is a 'useful option'; a problem exists which has to be tackled before deterioration sets in. On the other hand, the sensitive development of a tourist/ culture/ tertiary education sector offers the opportunity of creating a whole range of mittelstand activities, and jobs for problem social groups.

Resources

In Britain the opening of 'new' universities in the 1960s and the expansion to university status of former polytechnics and colleges of education and technology has helped mitigate the holiday resort problem, by supplying tenants for former boarding houses, though this is qualified by declining student incomes, forcing many students to remain home-based, and the poor state of much of the property. Nevertheless the use of the universities for summer schools – most notably those of the Open University from 1970 on – helped ensure utilisation for over three-quarters of the year, and opened up university experience to new client groups.

In Baden-Württemberg the problem is somewhat different, with regional universities being attended by students who prefer to spend their weekends at home, meaning that the university week tends to last only from Monday afternoon to Thursday evening, and many university buildings and libraries are completely closed at the weekends. There are some summer schools, but no uptake of accommodation on the scale of the Open University. In this way expensive, heated, purpose-designed buildings can be fully used for only 120 days of the year.

In the last few years most British and German universities have been equipped with new information technology, without (so far) much assessment of its actual utility. Impressionistic surveys suggest that so far the costs of the new equipment, especially those of software and repairs, may impose heavier financial burdens than those of the pre-electronic period of typewriters and phones. One would have to research into varying academic productivity and output, but my own judgement would be rather pessimistic. Internetting and e-mail may have reduced available secreterial and research jobs within the university area without producing a qualitative growth in academic output big enough to compensate for this. Nevertheless, this equipment is, like the buildings, a potentially valuable utility.

Personnel

Here the situation is quite different in Britain and in Germany. In Britain the university careers service is well-developed, and through alumni organisations records exist of the subsequent employment of a large number of graduates. In Germany much stress has recently been placed, particularly by the *Land* authorities, on promoting self-employment among university graduates. (The figure of 10,000 *Habilitierte* who lack long-term university employment has been quoted). Unemployment is certainly lower among graduates than non-graduates, but there's little accurate information as to what graduates are actually doing, and how or whether their university courses have fitted them either for corporate life or for self-employment. If an inquiry into this is set up, finding out later careers, interviewing samples and assessing the usefulness or otherwise of education and training from the university, this merely brings Germany upsides with Britain. Yet German graduates are much more mature than their British counterparts – many of them doing part-time jobs as editors, booksellers, computer programmers and librarians – so that in terms of an orthodox academic education, the resources exist in Germany to create a parallel part-time system, using the above spare capacity, which could supplement Open University-type instruction by interactive communication by internet and CD, as in the case of the recently-founded Catalan Open University. The existence of 'libraries' of courses makes it possible for Open University-type institutions to function in a fully student-responsive way, with teaching material, audio-visual material and set books, being accessed by computer. There are dangers, of course – a 'bank' of student essays might also come into existence – but this means that examination and assessment would still require dedicated academic manpower, perhaps more than previously. Though this is less likely to apply to non-vocational courses, where the student's motivation will make him or her more 'altruistic'.

So the option exists of making education up to and including university level 'portable', something that gives culture-based studies a new potential. Brian Jones of University College Bangor has suggested using the internet as an information reservoir which would enable the potential non-vocational student to access information about courses, library facilities, cultural institutions, festivals and summer schools as part of a European cultural network. This still implies, however, that culture-students will require assistance. They may lack internet access, or may not be fully confident in using a computer, something more likely the older you are. They are also likely to need advice on the 'mix' of courses proper to their interests.

Two areas of organisation, probably by part-timers, are necessary: counselling of students through personnel located say in *Volkshochschule* or in Scotland through the WEA and university extension organisations; and packaging of the sort of cultural options cited above by local universities, using existing resources channeled through their external affairs departments, in co-ordination with local and regional development bodies (such as Local Enterprise Companies in Scotland or *Industrie und Handelskammer* in Germany). The imminence of devolution also suggests the involvement of the Scottish administration, in the organisation and co-ordination of information-gathering, personnel training, etc. This could be the responsibility of a staff-member of the Scottish education department.

The Market

Within the 'culture tourist' landscape it makes economic sense to divert resources from overloaded tourist areas to places where 'green' and 'culture-tourism' can effectively deploy local investment. This could be achieved by a combination of a conscious European tourist policy, and tourist taxes levied on a regional or national basis in heavily touristed areas. These could both direct tourists to out of season holidays, and build up alternatives.

There is surely a case for granting assistance which enables a continual access to education and cultural development for mature and senior citizens (perhaps in return for a proportion of pension income?) Likewise vouchers for expenditure on further education and training could be made available to workers at periods of their working life, for both vocational and non-vocational purposes. This involves liberating the resources already identified as being 'embodied' in the elderly.

Reviewing the future of the EU, the historian Tony Judt wrote:

> At the moment the underemployed elderly are merely an expensive burden. But once the baby-boomers begin to retire (around 2010 A.D.) the presence of a huge, frustrated, bored, unproductive and ultimately unhealthy population of old people could become a major social crisis.

A demoralised elderly population, requiring institutionalisation, is an expensive and daunting proposition. Yet the longer retired people remain independent, the more they remain social contributors, paying tax on their pensions, rates on their houses, etc. And programmes of cultural education can both help to keep them self-sufficient and, through this, provide job opportunities for younger people.

So an important task is that of estimating the likely returns from a microcapitalism based on further education (very broadly defined) for the retraining and the retired. Early retirement in the service and teaching professions, coupled with the funds accumulated by the generation presently 50-60 - in the case of a middling professional perhaps from £150,000 (DM 500.000) to £300,000 (DM one million) in buildings and moveables – provides (taking a move into smaller living accomodation into account) a disposable annual income of perhaps £12,000 (DM 36.000) in addition to pension. Such individuals are likely to continue active for at least a further twenty years. Moreover they are likely to be, in this project, as important as voluntary providers as they are as customers.

Pilot Schemes

Having established that there is a market for the culture/ academic/ tourism product, appropriate technology and personnel, it's now necessary to see how it would work out in specific areas. One aspect of research and policy, which will involve economic, cultural and historical specialisms, will therefore be to quantify the evolution of the tourist business profile in specific regions, the way it has changed over the recent past, and the expectation of future changes, in relation to the European economy as a whole, both with and without the sort of programmes foreseen. This would be gained by quantifying the input/ output factors of tourism in its various types in the existing local economy, assessing the relative roles of traditional family holidays, day trips, farmhouse holidays, second homes, educational holidays, both over time (using local authority, tourist bureau records, etc.). Such areas would then be matched against their potential for forms of culture/ academic tourism. The third aspect would be to assess the implications of this for important client groups both as resources and markets – people in higher education, those wanting retraining, and the retired.

But the essential thing is to present purposes which are stimulating and absorbing, which can literally captivate communities and give them both a pride in themselves and the ability to communicate. Such a chance, almost fortuitously, awaits Scotland.

Mythos Mittelstand 2
– (ii) Geotech Scotland
– a Scottish project for the Millenium
(1997)

In the United Kingdom the Millenium has been used, quite cynically, as yet another means of stuffing large amounts of public sector investment into Middle (or rather South-Eastern England) by building a superior sort of shopping mall on a derelict property in Greenwich, to the delight of estate agents throughout the region.

But in Scotland we will have in 2002 an anniverary to celebrate, and we can do it in an imaginative and generous way. In 1802 the Forth and Clyde canal was the birthplace of steam navigation, with William Symington's *Charlotte Dundas* of 1802. What Sir Patrick Geddes called the paleotechnic epoch began, with the application of new forms of energy to transport.

It's therefore timely to commemorate Scotland's contribution to the modern world in applied science and engineering. The 1800s was the age of, besides Symington, Thomas Telford, James Nasmyth, John Rennie and Robert Stevenson. In 1807 the Scots-Irish Robert Fulton (who invented a submarine for revolutionary France) put the first revenue-earning steamer, the *Clermont* on the Hudson, and in 1812 Henry Bell's *Comet*, on the Clyde, was the first commercial steamship in Europe, the first of thousands which bound the trade of the world together.

This is history, but it can still teach lessons, particularly when the UK parties have evicted science PhDs in favour of spin-doctors. A Great Working Academy was what Telford christened his Caledonian Canal – not just a utility in itself, but training for a new generation of engineers. An enduring project for the Millenium

269

would be the creation of a technology and emvironment linear park, from Forth to Clyde. Geotech Scotland would be based on the practical project – already part-funded by the Millenium Commission – of reopening the Forth and Clyde Canal, from Bowling to Grangemouth, whose abandonment in 1962 can be seen as a disaster for the Scottish tourist industry.

But it wouldn't be just another inert slab of heritage. This would be an centre – actual and a virtual – for science and engineering history, recreation and training. The virtual element would, through computer access, interactive CD instruction, databases, etc. communicate with all Scottish primary and secondary schools. Partly built by them, the actual theme centres would give youngsters practical engineering and construction capability, and help preserve and make economically useful one of Scotland's greatest industrial monuments.

The historical element would explain a Scottish contribution to world development which was triumph and tragedy. Steam at sea was pioneered by the Napier brothers in Glasgow and the Fairbairns in Manchester, and the freight steamer was made possible by John Randolph's compound engine in the 1860s in conjunction with Lord Kelvin's surface condenser. In the twentieth century the Clyde steamer *King Edward VII* was the first to be fitted with turbines, and in the 1950s the Denny-Brown stabiliser banished (or almost banished) seasickness and radically improved ferry transport, and fibreglass, another Scottish invention, revolutionised yacht-building. The winning of oil from the North Sea promoted such breakthroughs in marine engineering as 'positioning' rigs to within centimetres by satellite and computer and developing robot undersea vehicles.

Marine engineering was the core of Scottish achievement in transport and communication – from Bell and the telephone to Logie Baird and television – and of theory about technology and society, chiefly in the work of Geddes (1854-1932) as sociologist and town planner, the adviser and friend of Nehru, Gandhi and Weizmann. Geddes also recognised the part that women played in science, design and education, from designing ship and house interiors to astronomical study, and playing a vital role in tourism and education.

The ultimate product of this process was people. The Clyde shipyards and engineering works, almost as much as the universities, were still 'a great working academy' into the 1960s, something which has still left its mark on the media, business and entertainment. These 'graduates' are as important a resource as the coming generation.

Geotech Scotland takes its name from Geddes' concept of the 'Geotechnic' age, when mankind controlled its industry and environment in a way which created a new ecology of technology, welfare and the natural environment. The scheme isn't for a grand-slam 'heritage theme park' museum like Beamish or Ironbridge, but for a series of locally-originated and locally-constructed schemes within the linear park – usually based on an historic site, a boatyard, foundry, old church or school – planned to develop the skills which are at hand while being able to share expertise.

The funds involved would be basic pump-priming, co-ordinating and accelerating local initiatives, oriented around 'learning by doing', but also using modern communications networks to enable the various parts of Geotech to keep in touch with, and learn from, one another.

The Theme Centres

Symington-Fulton: marine technology.
In recent years replicas of the Patrick Miller's Dalswinton trimaran of 1786 (the predecessor of the world's first experimental steamboat, his catamaran of 1788), the *Comet*, and the *Vulcan*, the first iron boat put on the Monkland Canal in 1828 have been created by apprentices. Together with a replica of the *Charlotte Dundas* these would provide a profile of the birth of modern sea transport, to be housed at Grangemouth. Youngsters would also design and construct their own boats, from kayaks and sailing dinghies through to water-buses for the canal system.

271

Bell-Baird: communications.
This will be both a historical display of the role of the Scots in communications technology, and a centre for broadcasting, video, where kids can experiment with and record their own efforts and prepare their own teaching material for colleagues at other schools and colleges.

Clark-Maxwell-Johnston: power.
Named after the physicist and the pioneer of Scottish hydro-electric development, this site will introduce kids to the principles and practicalities of power generation and conservation: involving windmills and turbines, combined-cycle stations, recycling waste into insulation.

Somerville: theoretical science.
Named after the Scottish woman astronomer, this will be a key resource-base using new technology to teach physics and chemistry, supplementing practical involvement with theoretical instruction.

Cranston: cooking, catering, tourism.
Named after the famous Glasgow tearoom-owner and patron of Rennie Mackintosh, this will be a crusade to wean the Scots from Europe's most perilous diet. The kids would also run a restaurant, hostel, etc.

Slessor-Livingstone:
This will concentrate on development of alternative technologies for third-world countries, training through practical 'know-how' experience in irrigation, drainage, navigation and marketing. It will be tied into student exchanges of a VSO type and scholarships.

The UK millenium project is about shopping. Geotech Scotland is about our future, as a country and as part of a world ecology. Overall, It will provide both practical instruction for schoolkids and students of all ages in engineering and technology, with theory being transmitted by instruction and information through interactive programmes and databases, and linked up to education institutions of all levels throughout Central Scotland. These would both be twinned with specific centres and send kids to all of them depending on their own interests.

Geotech Scotland will take on the downside of life in Central Scotland – alienation stemming from unemployment, multiple social deprivation, being hit by decisions taken without any consultation and hundreds of miles away. Result: petty crime, vandalism and a drug problem which in Glasgow alone has been costed at £500 million per annum. Geotech Scotland's industrial tradition would provide the launching-pad for a project to provide pupils and students with a practical and theoretical entry into the science and engineering of the future.

And it would pay. The restoration of navigation between Forth and Clyde will open up the west coast of Scotland to yachts and tourists from Scandinavia and the North Sea countries, who have currently to sail north to the Moray Firth to gain access to the Clyde. The Shannon and Loch Erne navigation systems in Ireland – a joint Northern Ireland-Eire and European Union project – has been a great success in an economically disadvantaged area. The Forth and Clyde, a small ship canal (with 74' by 20' locks and swing bridges) can take large yachts and fishing boats, creating in itself a major 'high-value-added' tourist attraction, with huge spin-offs in job creation in hotels, boat-building and repairing, marinas, provisioning and chandlery, besides providing the core of a Central Scottish Nature-and-Technology Park easily accessible to two-thirds of the population. The Canal would be the basis of a transport spine with cycleways, public transport, water-buses encouraging people to get out of their cars and take exercise.

Tourist enterprise tends to develop under external ownership – and the London Millenium site is a classic example – producing only low-wage, low-value-added employment. Geotech would use tourism and educational development as a means of creating new skills and local enterprise, by an open experimental structure and mixed public-private investment. The London Millenium project will make the rich richer and go the way of the Glasgow Garden Festival. Geotech will be there for keeps.

Bibliography

This is more of a guide to further reading than a list of source material, and is inserted in order that readers who have found their curiosity roused can explore issues in greater detail. Hence a number of references to longer 'academic' papers and articles.

Section One

'Timberlands' relies most on personal impressions, but also owes much to a piece 'The Celts and the Atlantic' published in *Literature of Nation and Region* by St John University, New Brunswick in 1998. This project was also stimulated by the work of two Welsh historians, Gwyn Alf Williams, particularly in a unit he contributed to an Open University course A 202 *The Age of Revolutions* in 1971, and Dai Smith's *Aneurin Bevan and the Culture of South Wales* (Cardiff: University of Wales Press, 1992). This vision of the Atlantic as the 'great connector' has shadowed me for years, since 'The Sons of Martha: Technology, Transport and Rudyard Kipling' in *Victorian Studies*, 1977. It was much encouraged by reading in the work of Fernand Braudel, and turn-of-the century imperial and national ideology. Some of the results of this can be found in 'The Folk and the Gwerin: Popular Political Culture in Scotland and Wales, 1815-1930' (London: British Academy, 1992).

Section Two

Any work on modern Scots parliamentary politics must be indebted to Iain Hutchison's *Political History of Scotland* (Edinburgh: John Donald, 1985) and Michael Fry's *Patronage and Principle* (Aberdeen UP, 1987). 'The Scots and the Law' originated at Allan Macartney's symposium on Self-Determination and Self-Expression in Commonwealth Countries in July 1986 (proceedongs bublished by Aberdeen UP, 1987) and in *Cencrastus*, in 1987. Various political fiction themes are treated *in extenso* in *The Centre of Things* (London: Unwin Hyman 1991), among them the case for Carlyle as the Victorian political conscience, also developed in 'Thomas Carlyle and the Scottish Mission' in *Scotlands*, 1996 (see also the long biography by Fred Kaplan and the continuing Edinburgh/Duke publication of the correspondence). Pending David Daniell's forthcoming critical study, Janet Adam Smith's biography (1965, Oxford UP, 1985) remains the best thing on Buchan. Oxford University Press commissioned a long 'Introduction' to John Buchan's *The Thirty-Nine Steps*, in 1993. Colin Coote's *A Companion of Honour* (London: Collins, 1965) remains the only accessible source on Elliot. On journalism, my longer study 'Nationalism, Journalism and Cultural Politics' appeared in Tom Gallagher, ed., *Nationalism in the Nineties* (Edinburgh: Polygon, 1991). The Johnston article was linked to 'Scottish Labour and World War II' in *The Historical Journal*, 1983, and led to a 60 minute BBC radio biography with Fenner Brockway, Naomi Mitchison, Willie Ross, etc.; see also the biography by Graham Walker (Manchester UP 1990) and Bill Knox's *Scottish Labour Biographies* (Edinburgh: Mainstream, 1988).

Section Three

'Scotland in 1946', an introductory essay for *The People's Story*. BBC Network, 1987 drew a lot on my mother's *Patchwork Books* of family history (pp. Galashiels, 1982-3) and Jean Stirling's decade-by-decade surveys of Motherwell life (*Motherwell Times*, 1990 ff.). 'The Labour Campaign in Lothian' appeared in J Bochel, D Denver and A Macartney, eds., *The Referendum Experience*, (Aberdeen University Press, 1981), reviving memories of Gordon Brown and Christopher Harvie, *The Scottish Assembly* (Edinburgh: Mainstream, 1979), which has a certain piquant historical value. The politics of 1979-98 have been recorded in the third editions of *Scotland and Nationalism* (London: Routledge, 1998) and *No Gods and Precious Few Heroes* (Edinburgh UP, 1998).An essay based on 'Grasping the Thistle' was published in Ken Cargill, ed., *Scotland 2000* (Glasgow: BBC, 1987). The context of this juncture in Scottish political history is provided by James Mitchell, *Strategies for Self-Government* (Edinburgh UP, 1996) and Kenyon Wright, *The People say Yes* (Glendaruel: Argyll, 1997).

Section Four

Some of the ideas in 'Mythos Mittelstand' appeared in an earlier book *Cultural Weapons* (Edinburgh: Polygon, 1992). This essay was originally drafted for the Baden-Württemberg-Wales colloquium in 1995, and owed much to Will Hutton's *The State We're In* (London: Cape, 1994) and David Marquand's *The Unprincipled Society* (London: Collins, 1986). Some of it appeared in a contribution I made to Hutton's *False Economy* series on Channel Four in 1996. Many of its ideas were the result of discussions at the Freudenstadt Colloquia on regionalism and socialism, recorded in Eberhard Bort and Neil Evans, ed., *Networking Europe* (Liverpool UP, 1999).

Index

This isn't a comprehensive index, which would be formidably biographical and not suited to a collection of essays. Instead it locates where ideas and themes, featured in some essays, outcrop in other places.

Other books from Argyll Publishing

For details, availability, trade orders and credit card sales contact Argyll Publishing on 01369 8200229

The People Say Yes – the making of Scotland's parliament

Kenyon Wright 256pp 216 x 138mm pbk 1 874640 92 0
£7.99, June 1997

The People Say Yes is the story of how in the notoriously factional world of Scottish politics, those of differing persuasions were able to work together to enable the people to finally say Yes to self-government.

"remarkable" Life & Work Book of the Month

"should be mandatory reading" The Tablet

"the clerical Braveheart who guided and bullied Scotland's leaders along the road to self-determination" The Herald

Our Scots Noble Families

Tom Johnston with preface by J. Ramsay Macdonald and a new introduction by Brian D Osborne 208pp 196x130mm 1 902831 00 4 hbk £12.99, Feb 1999

Tom Johnston, son of a Kirkintilloch grocer, rose to become one of the most influential men to occupy the position of Secretary of State for Scotland.

His publishing in 1909 of *Our Scots Noble Families* on the thorny question of land ownership caused a sensation. This seminal text on its subject has been out of print for many years. Now with a full context-setting introduction by Brian Osborne.

Braxfield – the hanging judge?

Brian D Osborne 240pp photos 234x153mm hbk
1 874640 03 3 £15.99, October 1997
Recreated by Stevenson as Weir of Hermiston, Lord
Braxfield's (1722–1799) taste for bullying views and
reactionary judgements was a less than palatable aspect of the
Scots judiciary. At work at the end of the century that had
seen the Union of the Parliaments and the final inglorious
demise of Jacobism, the author assesses the man in his times.
"thoroughly readable" Journal of the Law Society of Scotland
"hits the nail right on the head" The Herald
*"closer to describing the real Braxfield than anyone else in the last
200 years."* Scottish Law Gazette

The Ingenious Mr Bell

Brian D Osborne 288pp photos 234x153mm hbk
1 874640 31 9 £15.99, June 1995
*"not only an authoritative biography . . . but a major
contribution to the early history of steam navigation"* Lloyd's List
"scholarly and readable" Ships Monthly
"an absorbing story that reads in places like a film script"
The Herald
Henry Bell (1767–1830) was the pioneer of steamship
navigation. This is the first proper biography of the man who
introduced the steamship into practical commercial service.

Imagine a City – Glasgow in fiction

Moira Burgess 352pp 216x138mm hbk 1 874640 78 5
£12.99, February 1998
This comprehensive account of how Glasgow has been
presented in fiction over the last two centuries enlarges
the discussion about the essence of Scotland's literature.
"clear, critical, historically balanced, immensely readable"
Douglas Gifford
"a considerable achievement" The Scotsman

The Lady of Claremont House – Isabella Elder, pioneer and philanthropist

> C Joan McAlpine 240pp photos 234x153mm hbk
> 1 874640 97 1 £15.99, September 1997
> Until her early widowhood, Isabella Elder was the archetypical Victorian woman – largely operating in the domestic shadows. At a time when women could not take advantage of higher education Isabella Elder bought Northpark House (now BBC Scotland's headquarters) and gave it as a home to the newly formed Queen Margaret College in 1884. She was especially sympathetic to the notion, not acceptable at the time, of women training as doctors. She set up a Medical School in the College and fought for parity of status with the men students. As a result the first woman graduated in medicine at Glasgow in 1894. Dr Joan McAlpine has thoroughly researched the life of this neglected heroine of women's equality.

Walking in all of the Squares – a biography of Alexander Thom, Engineer and Archaeoastronomer

> Archie Thom 384pp photos 234 x 153mm hbk
> 1 874640 66 1 £16.99, October 1995
> "... *an amazing intellectual adventure as well as an historical detective story ... an incredibly exciting book.*" Colin Wilson
> Industrial engineer, aerodynamics pioneer, Oxford professor – Alexander Thom (1894–1985) achieved much. But not enough for this inquiring mind and restless imagination! Through his study and surveys of the relics left by megalithic man, Thom continued to reach for the stars.

Guilty by Suspicion – a life and Labour

> Jimmy Allison 256pp photos 234x153mm hbk
> 1 874640 36 X £14.99, March 1995
> Written by "The most formidable and powerful manager Labour has had in Scotland."